INTERROGATING the NEW ECONOMY

INTERROGATING the
NEW ECONOMY
Restructuring Work in the 21st Century

edited by
Norene J. Pupo and Mark P. Thomas

A Garamond Book

University of Toronto Press

LIBRARY AND ARCHIVES CANADA CATALOGUING IN PUBLICATION

Interrogating the new economy : restructuring work in the 21st century / edited by Norene J. Pupo and Mark P. Thomas.

"A Garamond book"
Includes bibliographical references and index.
ISBN 978-1-4426-0055-3 (pbk.).—ISBN 978-1-4426-0057-7 (bound)

1. Labor—Canada—Textbooks. I. Pupo, Norene, 1952– II. Thomas, Mark P. (Mark Preston), 1969–

HD8106.5.I58 2009   331'.0971   C2009-906182-1

We welcome comments and suggestions regarding any aspect of our publications —please feel free to contact us at news@utphighereducation.com or visit our internet site at www.utphighereducation.com.

North America
5201 Dufferin Street
Toronto, Ontario, Canada, M3H 5T8

2250 Military Road
Tonawanda, New York, USA, 14150

ORDERS PHONE: 1-800-565-9523
ORDERS FAX: 1-800-221-9985
ORDERS EMAIL: utpbooks@utpress.utoronto.ca

UK, Ireland, and continental Europe
NBN International
Estover Road, Plymouth, PL6 7PY, UK

TEL: 44 (0) 1752 202301
FAX ORDER LINE: 44 (0) 1752 202333
enquiries@nbninternational.com

The University of Toronto Press acknowledges the financial support for its publishing activities of the Government of Canada through the Book Publishing Industry Development Program (BPIDP).

Cover and typesetting by Em Dash Design.

Printed in Canada

Contents

Acknowledgements

We would like to acknowledge the generous support of the Social Sciences and Humanities Research Council of Canada through the Initiatives on the New Economy (INE) Program. All of the contributors to this collection of essays were members of the Research Alliance, *Restructuring Work and Labour in the New Economy*, under Principal Investigator Norene Pupo. The INE funds not only allowed us to engage in individual and collaborative original research projects, but also enabled team members to meet with one another and their communities through conferences, workshops, and a variety of interactive community forums.

Over the four years of funding, *Restructuring Work and Labour in the New Economy* was housed at the Centre for Research on Work and Society, York University. We would like to thank Robin Smith, the Centre Administrator, for her ongoing support, her superb administrative and budget-management skills, and her expertise in planning events and interfacing with the community. Over the lifetime of the project, three project managers, Russell Janzen, Reuben Roth, and Daphne Paszterko, in turn were instrumental in supporting the research program, generating knowledge transfer, and managing the details of a large and complex project. We owe our success in this project in large part to Robin, Russell, Reuben, and Daphne, who all kept the project running smoothly, allowing the research team to focus on developing new understandings of work in the new economy. Finally, we would like to thank the many researchers, community members, graduate students, educators, and policy makers who participated in and provided assistance for the various research projects and who generally showed interest in our work.

Throughout the process of putting this collection together, Anne Brackenbury has been unwavering in her support. Anne has not only been tremendously helpful in guiding us through the various stages of this project, but she has also been very patient and understanding of the particular "time clocks" by which academics work. It has been our pleasure to work with you, Anne.

Introduction: Work in the New Economy
Critical Reflections

NORENE PUPO AND MARK THOMAS

For more than a decade, social analysts have written about the "new economy"[1] and the crisis in the realm of work in Canada. What is the new economy and how does it affect workplace relations, family life, and citizenship? These questions are made all the more pressing in the context of the crisis in financial markets that shook the global economy beginning in late 2008. In Canada, the fallout from the crisis has been dramatic in many sectors of the labour market. Rising unemployment rates in both manufacturing and financial services are the most visible indications, but workers across the labour market are caught in a climate of dramatically heightened insecurity brought on by recessionary economic patterns. As unemployment has risen, so too has the number of part-time jobs, as full-time employment continues to be eroded. Moreover, the climate of insecurity further threatens the ability of unions to defend workers' interests, as employers, particularly in manufacturing, seek dramatic concessions from even the traditionally most powerful of Canada's trade unions. While the sharp escalation of these conditions points to the immediacy of the crisis, the authors who have contributed to this text point out that these patterns—whether it be the decline in manufacturing, the growth in "precarious" (i.e., casual or contractual) employment, or the heightened pressure on unions—reflect many of the long-standing trends of the so-called new economy. Thus, the chapters of *Interrogating the New Economy* help us understand the ways in which the impacts of the crisis were built through social relations rooted in transformations that began long before 2008.

Understanding the new economy and recent changes in the organization of social and economic life entails a complex and detailed consideration of shifts in the structure of labour markets and workplaces, as well as the ways in which workers are responding to new economic conditions. Clearly there is ample evidence of the transformative condition of work both in the traditional strongholds of manufacturing and health care, as well as in the burgeoning service sector. Yet, while many recent studies have considered patterns of change within contemporary workplaces, there is no consensus on the complex factors that may contribute to these transformations, or on the personal, cultural, and social significance of these changes.

Interrogating the New Economy: Restructuring Work in the 21st Century is a collection of essays based on a multi-year research project undertaken between 2002 and 2006. Under the directorship of Norene Pupo as Principal Investigator, the research was conducted by an alliance of academic researchers and trade-union partners funded by the Social Sciences and Humanities Research Council of Canada's Initiatives on the New Economy Program. The project, *Restructuring Work and Labour in the New Economy*, was coordinated through the Centre for Research on Work and Society at York University. Emerging from the research conducted through this project, *Interrogating the New Economy* examines the social, political, and economic transformations often associated with the new economy, the organizational responses to these changes, and the impact of these responses on the social and cultural experiences of work within Canada. The essays in this collection build upon the assumption that recent changes in the new economy include a series of transformations in the ways in which work is organized, in individuals' expectations regarding access to work, in the ways in which work is managed and defined, and in the institutional and state support provided for workers and their families. This includes changes in labour-market structures, compensation and employment relations, workplace technologies, labour-market policies, and forms of collective organizing and bargaining.

The "New Economy"

For a number of years, social scientists who study the workplace and labour markets have argued that there is indeed a "New Economy," concluding that the upward swing in potential output levels or productivity is indicative of a new economic profile. Others suggest that major technological innovations, new forms of knowledge production, and changing communications technologies have redefined capitalism and the global economy, ultimately affecting the ways in which work and business are conducted (Castells 2000; Huws 2003, 2006). Definitions of the new economy also commonly focus on networked relationships between organizations and on flexible workplace practices (Adkins 2005). Within the new economy paradigm, although a variety of perspectives prevail, consensus is emerging that workplace relations are being transformed in a myriad of ways and on multiple levels—personal, community, national, and global—and, in turn, affect relationships within families and households.

Within Canada, transformations in the global economy have had profound implications for the structure of the labour market, as well as for the institutions that support workers' well-being, shape labour-market training, and ensure general social welfare. Together, the rate and scope of these changes are unprecedented. Huge innovations in technology and the reorganization of public- and private-sector workplaces have given rise to new economic and occupational opportunities and, at the same time, have shifted attention away from traditional centres of prime economic activity and ways of working, while pushing the focus toward alternative structures of work and patterns of employment.

The restructuring of workplaces and labour processes is intertwined with processes of economic globalization and advancements in communication and information technologies. A characteristic feature of economic globalization is the notion of mobility. Movements of work and workers have taken a variety of forms, each of which raises questions about regulatory practices; rights and protections; environmental, health, safety, and security issues; and impacts on local communities. Work has been moved around the globe as transnational enterprises search for the ideal (i.e., the cheapest available and often captive) labour force. In turn, the global economy has entailed the development of a transnational labour force and has swelled the number of migrant workers searching for a means of survival and, in some cases, an escape from politically unstable conditions. Workers in communications industries, who interact through information age processes, may be located in familiar surroundings within their homeland but may find themselves adapting and connecting to "another world" during their workday. Still others experience movement of the products of their labour within transnational commodity chains involving workers in various capacities and skill levels. These workers may receive vastly different levels of remuneration, social benefits, and legal protections, but they are connected by their contractual obligations to transnational corporations and their subcontractors. They are usually governed by a just-in-time practice designed to maintain a smooth flow within the chain's numerous links.

A popular image of the new economy workplace is of a highly wired, sparsely populated space where workers are engaged in knowledge-intensive work and use new information and communications technologies to connect to customers and clients around the globe. This work is often associated with "creative" industries (Hartley 2004). However, the term "new economy" is also commonly used in government, media, and business accounts of a wide variety of contemporary workplaces. Such accounts typically claim that new forms of workplace "flexibility" create the capacity not only to improve productivity, but also to eliminate the hierarchical social relationships that define wage labour under capitalism (Adkins 2005). In this contemporary context, "flexibility" is presented as an ideal for employees, achieved through management strategies that promote "multi-skilling," training and re-training, performance-based pay, and employee adaptability to rapidly changing economic conditions (Rubin 2005). Proponents of the new structures suggest that the practices of the new "flexible" workplace replace hierarchical management structures of traditional workplaces, creating greater possibilities for creativity and input within the work force. Overall, the new economy paradigm defines a "third industrial revolution," suggesting a boost in economic performance and efficiency through the use of advanced technologies, the employment of new business practices, and the coordination of national and international economic policy (Harms and Knapp 2003: 414).

The new economy has an impact, it is claimed, not only on traditional class-based hierarchies but also on gender inequality in the workplace. The technologically advanced workplaces of the new economy purportedly provide women workers with "new opportunities and outlets" that are not shaped by traditional, gendered hierarchies (Wajcman 2007: 291). In conjunction with new technologies, flexible employment practices such as "flextime," part-time work, and teleworking are thought to enable both male and female workers to strike a better balance between time in the workplace and time in the household, thereby reducing work–life conflict and leading to a more equitable gender division of reproductive labour (Perrons et al. 2005).

Flexibility in these accounts of the new economy also extends to labour-market policies, where governments have redefined the regulatory frameworks of the Keynesian era through neoliberal approaches, opening free-market reign over public services and industries (Jessop 1993; Peck 2001). Where Keynesian labour-market policies sought to protect workers from the full effects of market forces, neoliberal policies of the new economy seek to promote flexibility by removing or altering policies and legislation that defined labour rights and access to social benefits for a generation of workers and their families. The neoliberal perspective maintains that Keynesian-era policies are rigid and "inflexible" and thereby hamper economic growth. Flexibility initiatives, including revised labour-market policies, labour-rights legislation, and health and social-welfare policies, along with practices such as privatization and outsourcing, are expected to eliminate regulatory barriers to economic growth.

Yet not all accept the optimism of the new economy paradigm. In the face of these numerous recent transformations in labour markets, labour processes, and working conditions, there are many who question the assumptions of the new economy paradigm and who suggest that the so-called "new" economy maintains many of the long-standing inequalities characteristic of capitalism. The optimism of the new economy paradigm generally, and neoliberalism specifically, has been challenged by critical studies suggesting that the "flexible" workplace of the new economy has increased employer control over work and heightened conditions of employment insecurity for workers. Rather than empowerment through multi-skilling and teamworking, critics argue that what is described and presented as flexibility by advocates of neoliberalism is most likely experienced by workers as work intensification due to lean production practices, and as insecure employment due to the proliferation of non-standard work arrangements (Rubin 2005). Workers in retail and other new economy service environments are held close to the minimum-wage point and are expected to get by with less, even when working at multiple jobs. Rather than being characterized by economic growth benefiting all, the new economy reflects the normalization of precariousness and the proliferation of poorly compensated jobs characterized by working conditions, shared by both blue- and white-collar workforces (Beck 2000; McBrier and Wilson 2004; Scott 2004; Sennett 1998). These changes in turn have altered the capacity of a growing number of workers to achieve satisfaction in their work, to enjoy relative security and permanent employment status, and ultimately to achieve the elusive "freedom 55" (or even "freedom 65") and retire with an adequate pension. Overall, critics of the New Economy paradigm argue that (1) industrial restructuring and technological advancements have given rise to new levels of insecurity with the introduction of new forms of employment relationships; (2) new occupational identities are often associated with greater disadvantages for workers; and (3) the proliferation of nonstandard forms of employment with the increased emphasis on time efficiencies, including flexibility initiatives, have effectively cut working life short or altered the course of working life, most often decreasing job security in the labour market (Doogan 2005: 67; Huws 2006).

Furthermore, many workers' experiences of work within a globalized economic context have involved intensified labour processes, "leaner and meaner" workplaces, and the unrelenting threat of unemployment and other forms of insecurity. The mounting intensity of work is regarded as a small sacrifice to be paid for the elimination of drudgery and monotony by means of technological breakthroughs. At the same time, technological advances have contributed to a homogenizing of work, placing workers on a trajectory of deskilling and degradation. Call-centre work, for example—perhaps the form of work most stereotypical of the globalized knowledge economy—is highly scripted, with workers' labour processes tightly controlled by both management practices and technological constraints.

Opponents of the new economy framework also argue that, just as class-based inequalities are intensified under the conditions of the new paradigm, so too are race- and gender-based inequalities. Critical studies of gender relations within the new economy question claims about the capacity of workplaces to be free from gender hierarchies and to promote greater gender equity in the redistribution of working time and reproductive labour (Diamond and Whitehouse 2007; Perrons 2005). It is further claimed that racialized segmentation has increased as well, in particular with growing numbers of migrant and undocumented workers holding a disproportionate number of the most insecure and lowest-wage jobs (Hudson 2007). The social relations of the new economy are seen to exacerbate, rather than alleviate, inequality. Hence, critics suggest it is more accurate to understand the new economy as an extension of the "old" economy rather than as an entirely new condition, particularly with respect to conditions of labour exploitation (Gall 2005).

The calls for flexible labour-market policies within the new economy can be seen to support the reorganization of capitalism in ways that enhance the power of employers over employees. While the flexible labour policies of the new economy purport to promote economic growth through less government intervention, critics argue that such policies support a resistance by employers to unionization, a lowering of labour standards, and a reduction in access to social benefits (Boyer

1988; Dennis 2007; Kalleberg 2001; Ladipo and Wilkinson 2002; Thomas 2009). In this view, the new economy is itself an ideological construction emerging from the free-market discourse of neoliberalism: it is a social context defined by increased corporate power and supported by neoliberal state policies, where relatively few benefit from new economic practices and arrangements (Harms and Knapp 2003; Miller 2004). In practice, the structure of the new economy, the processes of downsizing and work restructuring, and the elimination of a social safety net all have an impact upon workers' sense of security within the labour market as well as upon their personal lives, families, communities, and broader social networks (Koeber 2002). Increasingly, workers are expected to carry the burden of insecurity themselves, thereby internalizing a neoliberal work ethic and absorbing the costs of capital. This new work regime has set the labour movement back by forcing unions to negotiate for health and social benefits formerly guaranteed by social legislation. With unions having to revert to basic negotiations around bread-and-butter issues (wages, benefits, etc.) or work harder even to maintain past achievements, more progressive campaigns on the domestic front may be stalled. The movement of work and workers necessitated by shifts in global production processes forces the labour movement to enter new territory and to rethink questions of cross-border organizing, sectoral and pattern bargaining, and engagement in workers' rights and social justice movements. On a positive note, however, drives to develop global unions and campaigns for workers' rights and justice on a transnational scale may help to bridge progressive movements between the north and south and, on a local level, contribute to real improvements in the working and living conditions within communities.

The Structure of the Book

These debates frame the studies discussed in this text. How do the workplaces of the early twenty-first century differ from those of previous eras? Do new technologies produce new work relationships? Have the so-called "old" or traditional industries been replaced as key economic drivers or have they been transformed by new employment relationships? Further, how do we understand and characterize changes within the Canadian context and how do we place them within discussions of global economic shifts? Under what conditions have the recent economic transformations provided advantages or disadvantages for Canadian workers? *Interrogating the New Economy* engages with these questions in order to explain how the contemporary workplace has been transformed, but also to examine the extent to which the influence of older forms of work organization is still present. While conventional accounts of the new economy focus primarily on the impacts of information and communications technologies and their connections to other forms of change within workplaces and labour markets, *Interrogating the New Economy* is unique in that it takes a much broader approach, focusing on a wide range of new economy sectors (e.g., cultural production and tourism), occupational identities (e.g., young workers and migrant workers), and strategies of resistance (e.g., labour militancy and new forms of union organizing).

A fundamental component of these questions about the new economy is an evaluation of its impact on workers' lives. For at least a decade, social analysts have asked whether these economic transformations have contributed to greater opportunities for a greater number of Canadians, or whether they have led to an increase in the number of peripheral, insecure jobs and the demise of secure, well-compensated, and respected positions. The chapters in this book move beyond the "good jobs/bad jobs" debate by uncovering the ambiguities embedded within workplace transformations and by examining the conditions under which changes positively or negatively affect family dynamics and well-being, equity gains, collective bargaining, social citizenship, employment opportunities, and economic security.

Further, the reconstruction of work processes and the establishment of new economic relationships and patterns have affected the ways in which labour relations and labour regulation are played out within the workplace. Such changes, in turn, have had an impact on the organizational structure and power of trade unions, on the effectiveness of health and social welfare programs and policies, and on overall conditions of social and economic security. A primary purpose of this book, therefore, is to examine institutional responses or adjustments—within trade unions and in labour-market policies—to the changes within the Canadian labour market and economy.

The essays in this book discuss the ways in which a diverse set of factors—including technological innovations, new communication techniques, and the power of transnational corporations—has transformed the Canadian economy and workplace. While giving rise to new economic relationships and occupational opportunities, these same processes have simultaneously produced new forms of workplace-based inequalities and intensified long-standing power differentials between workers and employers. Thus, *Interrogating the New Economy* constructs a critical analysis of the new economy in order to identify both the potential for quality work experiences *and* the ways in which the organization of work remains a profound social problem.

The goal of this volume is twofold: first, to present new scholarship on labour-market change; and second, to direct new knowledge toward changes in work structures and policy making in order to improve the quality and conditions of work and community life. The essays construct a social analysis of the new economy that integrates broad-based, national labour-market studies with workplace-level case studies in order to examine the impact of change on workers, workplaces, unions, and communities in different contexts. The case studies clearly illustrate the dynamics of workplace change at both the national and local levels. This method of presentation presents a critical analysis of the character and implications of contemporary forms of social and economic change through theoretically informed, empirically grounded examples in a wide range of social settings.

The book is divided into three interrelated sections, each of which investigates the changing social organization of the workplace under new economic conditions. *Part I: Changing Structures and Processes in the New Economy* provides an overview of key social and economic transformations that define the new economy. The essays profile patterns of labour-market and workforce change, and also introduce key theoretical debates regarding the social organization of work in contemporary capitalism. Gregory Albo's chapter aptly sets the stage for the analyses that follow. He points out that capitalism is an economic system that is constantly undergoing transformation: through the development of new systems of production, the adoption of new management strategies, and the integration of new technologies into the workplace. Despite these transformations, the long-standing social relations of exploitation and capital accumulation characteristic of capitalism continue to shape the social organization of work in contemporary times. In other words, today's new economy, despite its apparent uniqueness, must be understood as the latest phase in the centuries-old system of capitalism.

Focusing on social policy and the neoliberal state, Dave Broad and Garson Hunter suggest that neoliberal policies have supported the restructuring of workplaces and labour markets of the new economy, prompting shifts from "welfare to workfare" and the re-commodification of labour. Neoliberal policies have enhanced the power of capital over workers, thereby increasing social polarization in contemporary capitalism. The so-called flexibility of new economy workplaces translates into economic insecurity for workers, with a weakened social safety net due to several decades of neoliberal policy reforms.

In asking what constitutes the new economy, Wallace Clement, Sophie Mathieu, Steven Prus, and Emre Uckardesler argue that four processes are key to the transformations of contemporary labour markets:

significant growth in the size of the service sector; the effects of new technologies, specifically computerization; an emphasis on knowledge-based employment; and growth in what they call "precarious" employment. Combined, these processes are indicative of structural changes in the social organization of contemporary labour markets, though they may take different forms in different national contexts. These four processes may also produce new configurations of long-standing inequalities based on class, gender, and race/ethnicity.

With a focus on workers in new economy workplaces—particularly those involving new information and communications technologies, and integrated into global value chains—Ursula Huws and Simone Dahlmann study the ways in which the restructuring of work has had an impact upon workers' occupational identities, class positions, and class consciousness. They find that declining job security and the routinization of work resulting from workplace restructuring has had significant, though varied, impacts on occupational identities, and that these changes may also be contributing to a deterioration of job satisfaction.

Part II: Transformations in Work and Labour Processes focuses on a range of transformations in labour markets and employment relationships within private- and public-sector workplaces. The deflation of public-service jobs is the central theme of papers by Jane Stinson, and Norene Pupo and Andrea Noack. Stinson focuses on labour casualization in the public sector, arguing that it differs significantly from the parallel process within the private sector. She establishes a strong case for the role of public-sector unions in protecting the good job characteristics of public-sector work and in influencing the extent and forms of processes of casualization. Similarly, Pupo and Noack examine new employment relationships within the public sector, as formerly "good jobs" are transformed into proverbial "McJobs." Their study of the transfer of work within the federal public service from face-to-face operations serving the Canadian public to a call-centre format raises questions about the future of work for educated white-collar workers and about the demise of service within the public sphere.

Steven Tufts and John Holmes draw attention to the experiences of young, upwardly mobile workers in the labour force in their study of the role of students within the new economy in two mid-size university cities in Ontario, Peterborough and Kingston. While it is clear that universities have been commercialized and certainly play an important role in the commercialization of knowledge production and its connection to new forms of consumption (Nelsen 2002; 2007), Tufts and Holmes expose not only the ways in which universities are involved in the production of the "new knowledge workers," but also the increasingly important economic role they play in integrating communities into the knowledge-based economy.

Starting with the processes of globalization, Mark Thomas focuses on patterns of international labour migration as another key dimension of the new economy. With many industrialized nation-states adopting foreign worker programs that rely on temporary foreign labour as a strategy to meet short-term demands within the labour market, the rights of migrant workers are often compromised. Using several examples of foreign worker programs in Canada, Thomas argues that these programs often contribute to patterns of labour-market segmentation, with migrant workers confined to low-wage, low-security employment by immigration polices that prevent both labour mobility and permanent settlement.

Chapters by Luis Aguiar and Tina Marten, and Larry Haiven, focus on the ways in which new economic activities are emerging in local economies where traditional industries are in decline. In their study of the development of wine tourism in the Okanagan Valley, an industry that has emerged in the context of the region's declining agricultural and manufacturing sectors, Aguiar and Marten consider the process of economic transformation bringing with it a decline in stable employment and growth in precarious jobs in the service sector. Taking the analysis one step further, their chapter also examines the role of "interactive" service work, as workers in the industry are subjected to a form of labour control through the scripting of their "emotional labour," a practice common in many service jobs of the new economy. In an analysis that contributes theoretically to our understanding of the role of creativity in community change and substantively to the agency of workers and communities in taking hold of the direction of change, Haiven studies two communities—Cape Breton in Canada and County Durham in the United Kingdom—that have been deindustrialized. With a focus on the role of creativity and cultural capital as these communities adjust to their new economic status, Haiven points to cases in which communities may re-invent themselves with creative industries as rallying points, rather than being doomed to accept a service-dominated economy.

The final part of the book, *Unions and Forms of Resistance*, examines the ways in which unions have responded to both the restructuring of work and the emergence of new workplaces and new employment relationships. Drawing on the case of increasing militancy among nurses, Linda Briskin provides an in-depth analysis of trends in the new economy with regard to workers' actions (strikes, militancy) and employers' agendas and unrelenting attacks on workers' previously won rights. Interestingly, Briskin exposes the new militancy as increasingly feminized, as women witness the erosion of their working conditions and attacks on their access to union protections. Finally, Dale Clark and Rosemary Warskett study transformations within unions attempting to adapt to the new economy through new organizing strategies. Clark and Warskett examine structural divisions and fragmentation within the service sector to demonstrate the challenges faced by unions in attempting to organize the burgeoning service sector. The authors point out the importance of mending the rifts within the labour movement in order to rise to the challenge of confronting powerful service-sector corporations.

As a collection, the essays in the volume explore the intersections of class, gender, race, and other social relationships that shape the dynamics and experiences of work in contemporary workplaces. Overall, the book develops a profile of social, political, and economic transformations in the new economy, examines institutional responses to these shifts, and explores the impact of these adjustments on the social and cultural experiences of work. The collection also points to the profound need for strategies to address the current crisis of work. In this climate of insecurity, workers are once again faced with the argument that "there is no alternative" to the current workplace realities. The essays in this volume, however, argue forcefully for the need to develop alternatives to the neoliberal model that produced the crisis, thus raising key questions about possible directions for social change. Will the contradictions of neoliberalism lead to a twenty-first-century version of the welfare state that counters the most extreme forms of insecurity present in the new economy? Will new forms of social citizenship emerge that are less market driven? Will social pressure build for more fundamental forms of social transformation? In raising these questions, this collection aims both to contribute to an analysis of contemporary capitalism *and* to promote debate regarding the need to chart an alternative course.

Note

1   In the articles in this book, this phrase will be presented in lower-case form for ease of reading. It appears throughout the literature in upper-case form (New Economy) and also in quotation marks to draw attention to the fact that it refers to a specific use of the term.

References

Adkins, Lisa. 2005. "The New Economy, Property, and Personhood." *Theory, Culture and Society* 22 (1): 111–30.

Beck, Ulrich. 2000. *The Brave New World of Work*. Trans. P. Camiller. Cambridge: Polity.

Boyer, Robert (ed.). 1988. *The Search for Labour Market Flexibility: The European Countries in Transition*. Oxford: Clarendon Press.

Castells, Manuel. 2000. *The Rise of the Network Society.* 2nd ed. Malden, MA: Blackwell.

Dennis, Michael. 2007. "Labor Against the Law: Unions Confront the Courts in the New Economy South." *Labor History* 48 (4): 403–27.

Diamond, Chris, and Gillian Whitehouse. 2007. "Gender, Computing and the Organization of Working Time: Public/Private Comparisons in the Australian Context." *Information, Communication & Society* 10 (3): 320–37.

Doogan, Kevin. 2005. "Long-Term Employment and the Restructuring of the Labour Market in Europe." *Time & Society* 14 (1): 65–87.

Gall, Gregor. 2005. "Organizing Non-Union Workers as Trade Unionists in the 'New Economy' in Britain." *Economic and Industrial Democracy* 26 (1): 41–63.

Harms, John B., and Tim Knapp. 2003. "The New Economy: What's New, What's Not." *Review of Radical Political Economics* 35 (4): 413–36.

Hartley, John. 2004. "The New Economy, Creativity and Consumption." *International Journal of Cultural Studies* 7 (1): 5–7.

Hudson, Kenneth. 2007. "The New Labor Market Segmentation: Labor Market Dualism in the New Economy." *Social Science Research* 36 (1): 286–312.

Huws, Ursula. 2003. *The Making of a Cybertariat: Virtual Work in a Real World.* New York: Monthly Review Press.

—— (ed.). 2006. *The Transformation of Work in a Global Knowledge Economy: Towards a Conceptual Framework.* Leuven: Hooger Institute Voor der Arbeid.

Jessop, Bob. 1993. "Towards a Schumpeterian Workfare State? Preliminary Remarks on Post-Fordist Political Economy." *Studies in Political Economy* 40: 7–39.

Kalleberg, Arne L. 2001. "Organizing Flexibility: The Flexible Firm in a New Century." *British Journal of Industrial Relations* 39 (4): 479–504.

Koeber, Charles. 2002. "Corporate Restructuring, Downsizing, and the Middle Class: The Process and Meaning of Worker Displacement in the 'New' Economy." *Qualitative Sociology* 25 (2): 217–46.

Ladipo, David, and Frank Wilkinson. 2002. "More Pressure, Less Protection." In B. Burchell, D. Ladipo, and F. Wilkinson (eds.), *Job Insecurity and Work Intensification.* London and New York: Routledge. 8–38.

McBrier, Debra Branch, and George Wilson. 2004. "Going Down? Race and Downward Occupational Mobility." *Work and Occupations* 31 (3): 283–322.

Miller, Toby. 2004. "A View from a Fossil: The New Economy, Creativity and Consumption—Two or Three Things I Don't Believe in." *International Journal of Cultural Studies* 7 (1): 55–65.

Nelsen, Randle W. 2002. *Schooling as Entertainment: Corporate Education Meets Popular Culture.* Kingston, ON: Cedarcreek Publications.

——. 2007. *Fun and Games and Higher Education: The Lonely Crowd Revisited.* Toronto: Between the Lines.

Peck, Jamie. 2001. *Workfare States.* New York and London: The Guilford Press.

Perrons, Diane. 2005. "Gender Mainstreaming and Gender Equality in the New (Market) Economy: An Analysis of Contradictions." *Social Politics* 12 (3): 389–411.

Perrons, Diane, Colette Fagan, Linda McDowell, Kath Ray, and Kevin Ward. 2005. "Work, Life and Time in the New Economy: An Introduction." *Time & Society* 14 (1): 51–64.

Rubin, Beth. 2005. "Contradictions of Commitment in the New Economy: Insecurity, Time, and Technology." *Social Science Research* 34 (4): 843–61.

Scott, Heather. 2004. "Reconceptualizing the Nature and Health Consequences of Work-Related Insecurity for the New Economy: The Decline of Workers' Power in the Flexibility Regime." *International Journal of Health Services* 34 (1): 143–53.

Sennett, Richard. 1998. *The Corrosion of Character: The Personal Consequences of Work in the New Capitalism*. New York: Norton.

Thomas, Mark. 2009. *Regulating Flexibility: The Political Economy of Employment Standards*. Montreal & Kingston: McGill-Queen's University Press.

Wajcman, Judy. 2007. "From Women and Technology to Gendered Technoscience." *Information, Communication & Society* 10 (3): 287–98.

Part I.   Changing Structures and
            Processes in the New Economy

1. The "New Economy" and Capitalism Today

GREGORY ALBO

Discussion of a "new economy" has been a characteristic of debates about capitalism since its first appearance as a socio-economic system in the eighteenth century. Adam Smith, for example, discussed the new exchange economy that emerged after the end of mercantilism in his *Wealth of Nations* (1776). Karl Marx, writing in 1867 as the modern factory system was forming in Europe, saw the continual transformation of social relations and economies—"all that is solid melts into air"—as one of the central features of capitalism. The development of monopolistic firms, mass production, and automated factories at different periods throughout the twentieth century drew similar claims of a new economic system coming into being. In an abstract yet very real sense, capitalism requires interpretation as a social order that is constantly producing a new economy.

There is also a need, however, to demarcate different phases of capitalism and define some of the features of the new economy in the capitalism of today. The economic developments of the last twenty years or so, for example, are often contrasted with the three decades after World War II. It was common to describe the postwar period with a variety of terms such as Keynesianism, Fordism, welfare-state capitalism, Pax Americana, and others. A large number of concepts have also been used to describe the current period: post-Fordism, cyber-capitalism, neoliberalism, globalization, and many others. Whatever the utility of these individual terms, there is a common analytical point: after a period of transition in the 1970s and 1980s, the social relations of work, the structures of power, and the functioning of capitalism took on new features that occupy our attention at present (Dicken 1998).

The transition to a new economy does not mean that the class divisions between workers and capitalists, or the dynamics of capital accumulation, have been transcended. Indeed, there is continuity across different phases of capitalism in the division between workers and owners and managers in the labour process, the cyclical movements in wages and unemployment as labour-market conditions change, the continual efforts by workers to organize in order to offset inequalities in power with employers, the organization of household and familial relations according to changing employment opportunities, and the competitive imperatives imposed on firms, workers, and families by capitalist markets. But it is my contention here that a new historical phase of capitalism has formed over the last two decades with several important features: first, the new way in which products and value are being produced in labour processes with the adoption of flexible manufacturing systems and then distributed via new information and communication technologies (ICTs); second, the pressures on unionization and wages as more precarious forms of employment spread, especially in the service sector; third, the new linkages of dispersed labour processes through international production networks organized by multinational firms; and fourth, the new ways in which flows of financial and commodity capital are circulating in national and world markets, forming what is commonly termed globalization.

These features of the new economy also raise questions about the "extra-market" institutional and policy configurations of capitalism today. Neoliberalism has come to dominate socio-economic policy thinking, power structures, and institutions in the current phase of capitalism. Neoliberalism can be defined as the set of policies that seek to reinforce a "free" market, private property, and capitalist social relations through privatization, deregulation, flexibilization (the increasing of management abilities to deploy labour freely), free trade, de-unionization, and financialization. Neoliberalism has become the social form of rule—the particular institutional and regulatory patterns in which political domination is secured—in this phase of capitalism. It is a fifth key feature framing the conditions of work and employment in today's new economy.

In exploring these issues I will first expand on some of the conceptual characteristics of capitalist economies. In the second section I will elaborate on the key features of capitalism today. Finally, I will discuss several ideas for alternative policy agendas in today's political context. The struggle for these alternatives is very important, since all phases of capitalism come to an end. The economic and financial turbulence that the world market has been plunged into since 2008 could very well signal a transition from the new economy of today. Capitalist firms and political elites are likely to attempt to reconstruct neoliberalism and existing institutions; therefore, it will be important to chart alternative political directions and policy.

Phases of Capitalism

How might we understand the different phases of capitalism? To answer this, it is necessary to begin with a discussion of capitalism itself. Capitalism is a system of generalized commodity production: haircuts, housing, money, labour-power, books, and most other goods and services all take the form of commodities (Saad-Filho 2003). These commodities are produced for sale in a market; the workers who produce them do not do so for their own consumption. While being use-values in the sense of meeting some need, they are produced only on condition that they can be exchanged for money (at an exchange-value or price that will allow a profit to be earned).

Money serves as a means to make commodities equivalent: the different concrete labours that make use-values in the labour process are represented as "socially necessary abstract labour-time" in the form of money in the marketplace. Money therefore has a number of important functions in commodity economies: as a means of exchange, as a measure of value, as a link between labour processes and markets, and as a form that capital takes in the production process. Money is one form of expressing the social relations of capitalism: it mediates between the private, concrete, heterogeneous labour of the labour process and the social, abstract, homogeneous form of labour in the sphere of circulation. In other words, money links the discipline produced by capitalist market competition with work and production.

The dual nature of commodities (use-values and exchange-values), labour (concrete labour and abstract labour), and money (value and means of exchange) allows capitalism as a social order to be specified more precisely. First, capitalism is a historically specific system of general commodity production. Typically, workers, households, and firms all purchase their inputs and sell their outputs as commodities. Second, commodities are produced for the purpose of making a profit; such profit regulates output, employment, and incomes. Third, money itself takes the form of—as well as being generally equivalent to—a commodity, and pervades all social relations. Fourth, markets are the dominant institutional mechanism, or system of provision, bringing buyers and sellers together, for the purpose of meeting needs and competing over the realization of profits. Finally, work is undertaken by a class of producers in the form of free wage-labour. Workers "freely" sell their labour-power to capitalists in order to earn their means of subsistence. Workers are just as dependent on the market for their reproduction as are capitalists.

It is self-evident that if workers do not labour, nothing gets produced. Workers sell their labour-power as a commodity to the capitalists: its use-value is the capacity to produce new value (or new commodities). Actually expended labour-time is the concrete use that capitalists seek to deploy in the labour process: they want to extract as much labour out of labour-power within the time purchased. The reason is simple enough: the harder the worker works in a given time, the more value that is produced over and above the wage that is paid for the labour-power purchased. This constitutes surplus-value for the capitalists, and it provides the basis for profits, rent, and interest, as well as covering investments in fixed capital. Capitalist firms organize the labour processes of their offices, factories, or retail stores in a way that maximizes their profits, either through coercion over their workers or by consensus with them.

There exist, then, inherent conflicts between workers and employers over the labour process, work-time, employment security, wages, and social issues such as health care. Employers seek to optimize flexibility in pay and employment and retain control over the labour process. Workers pursue appropriate income levels and employment stability and, in turn, attempt to exercise their own controls in the labour process. They organize collectively—mainly in unions but also in other forms—to establish the ability to struggle effectively against the concentrated economic and political power of capitalists. But the combination of market-dependence and antagonistic interests makes the relationship between workers and employers quite contradictory. It follows, then, that the organizational capacity, form, and ideological orientation of unions and workers will vary quite substantially across places and different phases of capitalism.

Capitalists organize their labour processes in a number of ways to increase the surplus-value produced. Workers can be pushed to work more intensely, for longer hours or with greater skills for the same amount of pay; concessions might be forced in wages and benefits but the hours of work stay the same; or provisions provided by the firm might be offloaded onto the household. These are all forms of absolute surplus-value: more labour for a given wage.

Alternatively, new technologies and capital goods might be introduced to increase the amount of output produced for a given level of labour input. If wages increase less than the increase in labour productivity from the new technologies, then total value-added (the amount of new goods and services produced) will increase as well as the share of surplus-value. This is relative surplus-value, and it drives the continual technological change that is characteristic of capitalism: innovating firms earn a surplus profit and therefore use that profit to reinvest in new techniques and plants. Indeed, capitalist competition and the tendency to profit-equalization—i.e., compete or go out of business—generalizes the tendency to adopt new techniques, if unevenly, across all firms. This is why capitalism continually forms a new economy.

The ongoing transformation of commodities and social relations characteristic of capitalism takes place through time and space. These processes of continual change and internal transformation are not simply the chaotic interaction of autonomous individuals. In fact, there are periods of economic and social stability in which social relations are institutionalized or regulated such that economic agents (such as capitalist firms and even unions) act to reproduce expanded accumulation. These periods of institutionalization are attempts to contain both the contradiction between the appropriators and the producers of surplus labour and the competition between capitalist firms. Nevertheless, periods of rapid accumulation of capital inevitably give way to extended phases of disorder and transition.

It is helpful to draw some distinctions among the forms that accumulation takes. First, the labour process must be linked to forms of accumulation. *Intensive* accumulation is essentially the application of science and technology to production, embodied in skills and machines, so that productivity advances rapidly (although growth may be slow if demand is weak). *Extensive* accumulation, in contrast, operates on the basis of extending the scale of production, with given production techniques, by drawing upon new sectors, workers, or land, a larger portion of the day, or more intensity during the existing workday. All phases of capitalism have some mixture of these forms of accumulation. It is quite possible, for example, for new technologies to be introduced in a way that increases labour productivity but also intensifies work-time.

Second, during different phases of capitalism, the wider institutions of the wage-relation, such as systems of industrial relations, processes of skilling, and welfare support, cohere into "regimes of accumulation" (Lipietz 1987). This means that particular patterns of employment

and allocation of social production between consumption and accumulation will recur in a way that for a period contains the contradictions and conflicts between workers and employers and allow extended
accumulation.

Third, lead capitalist firms assume distinctive characteristics in different periods in terms of how they organize the skill levels of labour processes and link their different operations spatially, within single plants and
between them. Also distinctive are the forms of legal ownership of firms
among different shareholder groupings, as well as the ways in which top
managers exercise their power to make decisions to invest and fund the
expansion of the firm. More highly institutionalized distributional relations associated with large bureaucratic firms might thus be contrasted
with more flexible distributional agreements and "networked" firms (i.e.,
a cluster of firms separated in ownership but linked in the final assembly of a commodity).

Fourth, capital has always accumulated in a world market, and individual capitalists are always compelled by competition to pursue new
markets and, consequently, internationalization. Capital alters its "spatial
fix" across time, shifting production processes and using new transportation and communication techniques to "shrink" distances (Harvey
1982). The internationalization of commodity, productive, and financial capital takes on varying features and relations in different phases
of capitalism. National models of development are thus defined by both
their labour processes and corporate firms, but also by the socio-spatial
matrix of production, consumption and distribution and the manner of
incorporation of these circuits of capital into the world economy.

Finally, even capitalist economic activity requires extra-market institutions and political relations to attempt to secure the conditions necessary for accumulation. States have been the key actor to play this role
and provide political legitimacy. They provide a common currency, legal
structure, and social institutions and are also a key locus for class formation. The discourses and policy configurations that state actors adopt
are a key aspect of different phases of capitalism.

The Current Phase of Capitalism

The features of capitalism today need to be located initially with respect
to recent history. Since the earliest days of industrialization in the nineteenth century, a revolutionary mode of work organization had been
evolving. By the 1940s, its principles had consolidated and spread. First,
the labour process was broken down into its component parts, each
worker performing simplified routine tasks. This was termed Taylorism

(named for American engineer F.W. Taylor) and the principle of separating conception from execution. Second, Taylorism was coupled with flow-line assembly, the product passing continually from one stationary worker to another. This "model of industrialization" had two additional principles: if work tasks were simplified, they could be directly incorporated into special-purpose machines; in turn, these machines could make mass-produced goods. The result of combining Taylorism and dedicated machines was large economies of scale and vastly enhanced productivity.

The logic of dividing mental and manual labour also expanded the number of semi-skilled assembly-line workers and technical and administrative workers. Previously, craft unions organizing workers on the basis of skill were common. Industrial unions, in contrast, gathered workers together by industry irrespective of skill level. And "white-collar" workers tended to be unionized mainly in the public sector. This division of labour also had a particular way of maintaining workers' dependence on capitalists. With highly skilled workers in high demand and semi-skilled workers easily able to move between production jobs, firms developed strong internal labour markets for promotion and wage improvements in order to bind workers more tightly to the firm.

The contractual core of the new unionism involved trading wage gains against management control of production. Implicitly, the nominal wages gained in collective bargaining were linked to the growth in productivity and the rate of inflation. Workers' demands often originated in a key firm and then spread to the entire branch of industry before influencing the economy as a whole. As a result, wage security was developed as unions removed the competitive process of bidding wages down and pushed instead in the direction of product and process innovations. This revealed an underlying contradiction, however: the increasing capital intensity undermined profitability and displaced workers in such a way that unemployment could be contained only by rapid rates of growth.

The postwar period is often referred to as the period of Fordism, so called for both the underlying production paradigm and the dominance of large hierarchically organized firms concentrated in a few major urban centres. This dominant paradigm also underlay postwar growth and social structures. Mass production with rising wages meant mass consumption by workers. Although international trade increased in importance, the expansion of production depended most on the deepening of national markets. Buoyant growth—in the order of 5 per cent a year, with unemployment falling below 5 per cent everywhere and to 1 per cent in many of the advanced capitalist countries—boosted government revenues and expanded the welfare state and public goods, such as parks, libraries, and universities. This sustained a virtuous circle of capital investment, productivity increases, and new markets across capitalist countries. Yet it also added a second contradiction: high rates of growth and employment encouraged workers to challenge their subordinate positions in workplaces.

The postwar boom came to an end in the mid-1970s, with growth rates in the advanced capitalist countries falling by half, and continuing to stagnate through much of the 1980s and 1990s (Glyn 2007). As the Fordist production systems reached their inevitable end, capitalist countries witnessed combined declines in profits, productivity, and investment. Moreover, the slowdown intensified class conflicts over wages and the distribution of the economic burden of the slowdown. Unemployment rates typically doubled, and often tripled, compared to what they had once been, contributing to the defeat of the efforts of workers and unions to resolve the economic impasse on more egalitarian and democratic terms. The fall in growth rates and the increase in labour reserves were even greater outside the core zones of North America and Western Europe, which led to a stifling of the efforts of many movements and countries of the global South to establish a new international economic order.

After 1990, however, growth rates in the US picked up during the "boom" period of 1993–2000, although across the business cycle a modest slowdown in US accumulation rates was apparent. The US upturn was a result not only of internal demand stimulus but also of enormous inflows of foreign capital and burgeoning immigration. The emergence of China as an economic player, reflecting the continued growth in the economic power of East Asia beyond Japan, also had a favourable impact. Indeed, the accumulation in these zones, and the gradual integration of the European Union nations, consolidated the new phase of capitalism (and gave rise to the popular usage of the term "new economy," particularly in North America). The more general economic slowdown, financial crises, and international payments asymmetries in world markets since 2001, and particularly in the core capitalist countries since 2008, have well illustrated many of the limits of this new phase of capitalism. And any light at the end of this dark tunnel has yet to appear.

A number of features of this new economy can be highlighted in terms of the labour process, forms of accumulation and wage-relation, the organization of firms, the internationalization of capital, and the policy regime. First, new forms of work organization and technologies have emerged within the labour process. These new production concepts stem from two key developments: the transformations of fixed capital in the labour process through new technologies and "robotization," and the adoption of lean production forms of work organization (Huws

2003). They can initially be contrasted with various aspects of Fordist labour processes: there has been a relative increase in both more highly skilled and low-skilled workers as opposed to semi-skilled mass production workers; an intensification of Taylorism to match the rhythms of new technologies for production and service workers, and multi-skilling among technicians and production support workers; a recomposition of the form in which work is conceived by designers and developers and executed by production workers; a relative decline in individualized piece-work and an increase in team-work; and a shift from dedicated machinery to flexible manufacturing systems.

The new economy, therefore, has involved both intensive and extensive forms of accumulation: the new technologies have allowed a large increase in the capacity for a given amount of labour input to produce increased output in any given labour process, but they have also intensified and increased the extraction of labour-time for the amount of labour-power purchased. This can be seen in the labour processes of any variety of occupations: in manufacturing work, robots limit any "downtime" for workers; personal computers have extended and intensified the work expectations and hours of lawyers and professors; and new technologies are used to monitor the work performance of all kinds of service-sector workers—for example, tracking the keystrokes of call-centre employees, videotaping the work of hotel workers, and so on.

Indeed, computer programmers are often imagined as the epitome of "immaterial labour" (i.e., labour that does not produce a material use-value but only ideas, although these ideas often get embedded in concrete use-values). But even these new knowledge workers are increasingly employed in software development "sweatshops," cranking out the code for new applications that get embedded in concrete products such as computers and the associated arsenal of hardware. Knowledge work in the new economy has proven to be just as subject to the real subordination of labour into industrial production and "proletarianization" as were earlier forms of work. The real paradox of the labour processes of the new economy is how they have greatly expanded the human capacity to produce, but also, in this phase of capitalism, given workers even less control over their work processes, how long and hard they work, and what they produce (Gorz 1999).

Second, in the period of transition after Fordism, it was often suggested that the new labour processes offered a bright—even utopian—future. Computer technologies would allow a major reduction in working hours, more leisure, higher incomes, better work as drudge work was eliminated, more democratic workplaces, and improved welfare states. Instead, the accumulation regime of the new economy has been quite different.

Labour reserves have been increasing in a number of ways: the levels of unemployment and the number of employees getting fewer hours of work than they want have been rising; as a consequence, the amount of "precarious" work in the form of involuntary part-time, contract, and temporary work has expanded; and the rate of job turnover has been growing as well. Occupational trends show a decline in stable, high-income, industrial-sector jobs and a large growth in service-sector jobs in both producer services (computer support, lawyers, etc.) and retail and personal services (with these jobs growing the most and paying below average salary levels). The new types of employment are often more individualizing, decentralized across many workplaces, and insecure. Thus they are often less easily unionized than the more concentrated industrial jobs and are more susceptible to the pressures of capitalist competition between firms and in the labour market (Hermann 2006). Instead of attempting to gain the loyalty of workers through strong internal labour markets, firms are doing so by offering individualized bonus and incentive structures, on the one hand, and by instilling fears that employees' already precarious work situations will become even worse or not exist at all, on the other.

These employment and occupational trends have given certain characteristics to the dynamics of income distribution in the new economy. Rather than being steadily reduced, working hours have been generally increasing for workers, often breaching the standard 40-hour workweek. However, while longer hours have become an endemic problem, an increasing number of workers are also having difficulty getting enough working hours at decent pay. Similar pressures can be seen in the area of income: annual wage increases for workers are being kept below the combined rates of inflation and productivity, thereby shifting an increased share of net income to profits; welfare and other social transfers to the dependent population are consequently being kept below the nominal rate of wage increases, thus adding to poverty levels; and with the racialization and gender discrimination of labour market access and pay, further inequalities are emerging amongst workers, as part-time insecure work in the service sector is increasingly dominated by women and workers of colour.

These labour market trends have commonly been referred to as "social polarisation": the rise in profit incomes and salaries of professional employees in corporate bureaucracies, the erosion of high-paying blue-collar jobs, and the steady growth of low-paid and unstable service sector jobs. The history of struggle over work and democratic control suggests that the new labour processes and wage-setting of the new economy were introduced as a way of weakening workers and unions. But now the distributional dynamic of the labour market is being reinforced, as weaker unions support the current occupational and wage trends; this, in turn, puts unions and workers further on the defensive and undermines their political capacity to address social polarization. As a consequence, individual workers (and unions) have increasingly come to incorporate the logic of competitiveness into their own strategies for coping with their dependence on the market for their individual livelihoods (and organizational stability) (Moody 1997).

Third, the new labour processes, coupled with ICTs, have allowed capitalist firms to reorganize themselves. Historically, the increasing intensification of the scale of labour processes caused an increasing concentration of capital in sectors, and also enabled capital to become increasingly centralized by joining different production phases into a single firm. These tendencies of capitalist development continue to exist, but firms are now able to disperse their labour processes and organizational components spatially. Production can now flow between firms, and value can be realized in sales in the world market, in new ways. Labour processes, for example, can be more directly linked to production flows. This allows for "just-in-time" production of, say, seats or wheels for assembly in cars. These distinct labour processes can also be coordinated through international production networks. Production in the auto industry (or the aerospace or shoe industry, for that matter) can then be organized along continental lines, or into global networks linking many labour processes to produce a final output. This production flexibility—with workers carrying a huge burden for this through increased precarious working hours and pay—allows firms greater economies of scope to produce for specialized markets within a common production platform.

This "network" logic has also influenced how firms have reorganized their ownership structures and relationship to financial markets. They have become more financially leveraged, linked by more complex corporate ownership structures to new financial entities such as private equity and hedge funds, and driven by the pursuit of "stockholder value" (share prices) in the new economy (Henwood 2003). In contrast to fanciful notions of "virtual companies" and "networks" escaping the imperatives of capitalist competition, firms have been driven to explore new means to increase long-standing forms of capitalist exploitation.

Fourth, the most powerful of these firms operate as multinationals, reflecting the increasing internationalization of value flows in the world market that has been central to the new economy (ILO 2001). The total amount of foreign direct investment, for example, is now in the area of several trillion dollars worldwide. This export of productive capital reflects the internationalization of production—linking both labour processes and work—in the form of both new investments and takeovers of existing firms. These investments have propelled the increasing circulation of commodity capital as intra-firm trade expands from international production networks and inputs are sourced from lower-wage zones. The share of traded goods in total output is more than double what it was in the postwar period and at a historical high point.

The internationalization of production and growing trade, particularly with the current account imbalances between different trading zones, encouraged the development of international currency and credit markets. The end of the postwar controls over capital mobility and exchange rates contributed to the growth of global money markets where debt instruments, stocks, and speculative funds like derivatives could all be sold and purchased. Indeed, international financial markets have grown exponentially, and financial transactions daily now exceed global trade yearly. New international economic institutions, like the North American Free Trade Agreement or the World Trade Organization, reinforce the processes of capital internationalization within their political frameworks and the competitive market imperatives brought to bear on workplaces.

Finally, the neoliberal policy regime that is central to the new economy is often portrayed as being anti-state and pro-market (Albo 2008). But this image confuses the way that the state has been transformed in relation to the market and social classes. The state still concentrates the legitimate exercise of power and the extra-market institutions necessary for capitalist markets to exist. The central issue is how neoliberalism has redeployed state power and restructured state institutions. In the framework of economic policies, for example, this has meant re-orienting fiscal and monetary policies to increase labour discipline and shift tax burdens away from capital and high-income brackets toward workers, via an increase in consumption and other taxes. This has been coupled with changing industrial policies on deregulation, privatization, and internationalization, while still maintaining subsidy structures and tax incentives for business investment. Similarly, trade agreements have favoured not just freer trade but "constitutionalizing" legal protections for private property and access of foreign capital to national markets.

None of these policy measures implies less state power, but rather the mobilization of that power in new ways. They are indicative of the state's increasing monopoly of the exercise of power in favour of business interests and over democratic actors such as unions, civil society organizations, and ordinary citizens. The state as an avenue for workers as citizens to pursue redistributional policies to reduce dependence on the market has been curtailed. But a state that is strong enough to enforce this neoliberal policy regime has been integral to this phase of capitalism. Indeed, the state has become even stronger in attempting to cope with the economic crisis resulting from the current chaos in the financial markets.

Challenging the New Economy

In the analysis above I have contended that capitalism has undergone a vast process of economic restructuring over the last two decades. Workplaces have been dramatically transformed, setting in motion intense pressures on unions and wages. Financial globalization and asymmetries in the world trading system have also increased competitive imperatives, while neoliberal policies have favoured de-unionization and labour-market flexibility. For collective bargaining, the new economy has often entailed extensive efforts to overhaul union agreements to give management increased prerogatives in determining employment, work rules, and wages. The dominant direction of restructuring within the new economy has often been toward work intensification, contracting-out, modest or no wage improvements, long-term contracts, and two-tier wage systems.

The task of outlining an alternative economic policy to the new economy of neoliberalism is thus as daunting as it is necessary. Two key contradictions have been integral to this period of capitalism: the enormous expansion of productive capacities through new technologies, while wages and employment have become increasingly insecure and market-dependent; and the growing openness of national economies in terms of trade and capital mobility as the world market expands and intensifies, while both economic instabilities and competitive imperatives increase.

An economic alternative will have to establish general principles to address these contradictions (Albo 1997). The notion that prevails today is that work must become ever more market-dependent and insecure in terms of wages and employment. This idea needs to be rejected. Such thinking divides workers into those who have paid work in core jobs and those who are excluded from either work or stable employment. An economic alternative must advance the principle that democratic citizenship begins with the rights to work, leisure, and a living income. Another principle is that political agreements at the international level must be built around the principle of maximizing the capacity of different national and local collectivities to democratically choose alternative development paths (socialist or capitalist) that do not impose externalities (such as environmental damage) on other countries and regions, without suffering isolation and coercive sanction from the world economy. These two general principles suggest the need to expand the scale and areas for democratic control, while constraining the scale of the market. They can be elaborated in terms of structural reforms that work both in and against some of the features of the new economy that have been highlighted.

First, new technologies and production systems have been consistently introduced into labour processes in a way that has intensified and fragmented working conditions for many employees. This raises a challenge to find alternatives to address the need for the re-qualification of work and to alter the overall structure of the growth model by raising skill levels for all workers and shifting production toward quality-intensive goods. Such an alternative would require altering the balance of class relations in the workplace and in society to avoid being driven by the requirements of competitiveness and would involve exploiting the capacity of the new technologies to involve workers in production and in the planned elimination of boring, repetitive jobs. A re-qualification of work would also mean forming long-term, broad skills rather than short-term, specific ones; transferable skills over firm-specific skills; theoretical as well as practical knowledge; and skills that extend worker autonomy over the labour process.

Rebuilding workers' skills also provides a foundation for workers and communities to pursue alternative production plans, collectively controlled technology networks, and socially useful products and services. In the transportation sector, for example, it would be possible to envision public-transit workers collaborating with riders, ecology groups, and builders of transportation equipment to develop innovative campaigns for the expansion of public transit. This is a vision of an alternative labour process that could expand workers' skills and capacities, embrace ecological and durable production techniques, lead to more free time for employees, and provide collective services such as daycare, parks, and museums, and quality products.

Second, the new economy has placed severe strain on unions and their bargaining capacity. A number of new strategies will have to be explored. Industrial relations reforms might, for instance, include sectoral bargaining or facilitate organizing in the service sector to boost union density. Sectoral bargaining would allow workers in sectors characterized by small workplaces (such as in retail outlets or coffee shops) to negotiate *en masse* with employers, giving them greater protection against competitive pressures. Community-wide union organizing and labour centres might also be developed.

In the area of collective bargaining, new ways to expand the parameters of negotiations beyond wage improvements and employment expansion need to be attempted in order to address both ecological and distributional issues. Policies that radically redistribute work through work-time reduction, overtime caps, and sabbatical and parental leaves must be vigorously pursued. Collective bargaining needs to put an annual work-time reduction factor alongside an annual wage improvement factor so that productivity gains can be shared more equitably. Such an approach has been debated at times in the auto sector as part of collective bargaining, and the postwar collective bargaining system in fact included both annual real wage increases and a steady decrease in working hours. Work-time reduction could also be redirected toward education and skills that expand the capacity for self-management at work and leadership in the community.

Third, the command over employment, resources, and production that has fallen to the international networks of multinational corporations is a daunting obstacle for alternatives. These organizational forms have endlessly expanded the scale of production while decreasing the control of individual workers in all sectors of their enterprise. Therefore, alternatives will have to address both the scale of production and the democratic control of enterprises. It is possible to insist that the new technologies provide a capacity to more adequately address social and ecological needs, for example, if deployed in new ways. Changing production strategies are necessary to move agricultural production, for instance, away from monoculture crops toward biodiversity, reduce the energy-usage and carbon-emission consequences of the geographical scale of trade, and adopt labour-intensive techniques when capital-intensive ones, like clear-cut foresting or factory fish trawlers, have such colossal environmental impacts. It is also entirely feasible to expand the democratic capacities of self-management through right-to-know laws of company finances and investment and production plans, controls over plant closures and capital movements, an expansion of unionization rights, and works and community councils.

Fourth, this period of capitalism has seen an upsurge in the internationalization of production and finance. It is difficult to envision either stable macroeconomic conditions or alternative development paths while these export-orientated processes and the competitive austerity they have engendered remain dominant. They will have to be replaced by more inward-oriented economic strategies, i.e., those that focus on domestic rather than international concerns. Inward orientation does not imply closing the economy to foreign trade, but rather a planned expansion of domestic services and production to increase employment and meet social needs. This would also entail establishing controls over capital movements. The institutions governing the international economy need to develop policy capacities to reinforce stable and pluralistic national macroeconomic conditions rather than impose the singularity of the neo-liberal model of development. For example, it is quite possible to imagine international financial institutions working to reinforce nationally based capital controls while also working to enforce the transfer of technological capacities as part of performance requirements imposed on the foreign investments of multinational corporations. The problems of solvency of financial institutions, and the sharp economic contraction that has ensued, suggest that nationalization of the banking system has become imperative, not just to prevent the crisis from getting deeper but to re-think what production and services will most meet social needs.

Finally, neoliberal policies dominate this phase of capitalism and attempt to spread market processes. Any alternative would have to make redistribution the central social and economic policy. It would have to entail a radical redistributional shift in power, resources, and new institutional structures: from the traded goods sector to the local and national economies; from the highest paid to the lowest paid; from those with too many hours of work to those with too few; from management-dominated to worker-controlled labour processes; and from private, consumption-led production to ecologically sustainable economies.

These types of economic strategies pivot around political capacities that might allow workers and their communities to control and disengage from market imperatives and impose democratic and collective priorities. These ideas—or ones similar to them—have been emerging from the political struggles of unions and workers in many parts of the world. But the weakened state of workers and the union movement in the new economy of neoliberalism has made their generalization into new social and workplace practices fraught with difficulty.

The search for alternatives has been further complicated by the political impasse of left-wing political parties (Sassoon 1996; Carroll and Ratner 2005). This has meant that even when social democratic parties have come into power, they have had little success reversing the policies of the neoliberal governments of the political right, or in changing the social outcomes produced by the new economy. Indeed, social democratic parties themselves have moved to the political right and have come to embrace many of the policies of neoliberalism, whether this be the backing of international trade agreements or restraints on the expansion of the public sector. They have abandoned the more radical political alternatives forming in the social and union movements. The failure of the traditional electoral option of voting for a social democratic party in order to produce new policy options has had several consequences for progressive politics. It has led many into isolated single-issue campaigns, sporadic attempts at community-wide organizing, and wider dissent expressed in loose social-justice networks such as the World Social Forum (the annual international social-justice fair for union, ecology, and anti-globalization activists from around the world).

But, after many years of these efforts, it is now quite evident that political and economic alternatives today are going to depend upon breaking out of these constrained political options. The economic recession is allowing more radical political options to be envisioned once again. Union renewal is one critical component; so are campaigns on issues such as Employment Insurance reform that form the deeper connections of anti-neoliberal alliances across unions and civil society movements. These two developments will depend in turn, it now seems clear, upon a new period of democratic organizational experimentation in movements linked to parties of a new kind. Such an alternative project will necessarily address the scale and spaces of economic activity and democracy. In a sense, the task is to invert the dominant logic of the new economy of this phase of capitalism by expanding the scale of democracy while reducing the scale of dependence on market activities. Such an alternative will produce not merely a "new economy," but an entirely new social order.

Discussion Questions

1. Why does capitalism always seem to produce a new economy, and what are some of its features today?

2. Technology and new labour processes are two key features of different phases of capitalism. How should we compare the postwar period and the contemporary period in terms of these features? And how do they influence some of the other features of different phases of capitalism?

3. Technological change under capitalism tends both to increase labour productivity and to be labour-saving, always leaving the possibility of increasing real wages for workers. But why might it also reduce wages and increase working hours, or lead to more precarious forms of work?

4. What are some of the alternatives that might be possible in contemporary capitalism? What different unions or civil society movements might be attracted to pursue some of them?

References

Albo, Gregory. 2008. "Neoliberalism and the Discontented." In Leo Panitch and Colin Leys (eds.), *Socialist Register 2008: Global Flashpoints: Reactions to Imperialism and Neoliberalism*. London: Merlin. 354–62.

——. 1997. "A World Market of Opportunities? Capitalist Obstacles and Left Economic Policy." In L. Panitch (ed.), *Ruthless Criticism of all that Exists: Socialist Register 1997*. London: Merlin. 5–47.

Carroll, William, and R.S. Ratner (eds.). 2005. *Challenges and Perils: Social Democracy in Neoliberal Times*. Halifax: Fernwood.

Dicken, Peter. 1998. *Global Shift*. New York: Guilford.

Glyn, Andrew. 2007. *Capitalism Unleashed: Finance, Globalization and Welfare*. Oxford: Oxford University Press.

Gorz, Andre. 1999. *Reclaiming Work*. Oxford: Polity.

Harvey, David. 1982. *The Limits to Capital*. Chicago: University of Chicago Press.

Henwood, Doug. 2003. *After the New Economy*. New York: New Press.

Hermann, Christoph. 2006. "Labouring in the Network." *Capitalism, Nature, Socialism* 17 (1): 65–76.

Huws, Ursula. 2003. *The Making of a Cybertariat: Virtual Work in a Real World*. New York: Monthly Review Press.

ILO. 2001. *World Employment Report 2001: Life at Work in the Information Economy*. Geneva: International Labour Office.

Lipietz, Alain. 1987. *Mirages and Miracles*. London: Verso.

Marx, Karl. 1867 [1967]. *Capital, Volume One*. New York: International Publishers.

Moody, Kim. 1997. *Workers in a Lean World*. London: Verso.

Saad-Filho, Alfredo (ed.). 2003. *Anti-Capitalism: A Marxist Introduction*. London: Pluto.

Sassoon, Donald. 1996. *One Hundred Years of Socialism*. New York: New Press.

Smith, Adam. 1776 [1976]. *An Inquiry into the Nature and Causes of the Wealth of Nations*. Chicago: University of Chicago Press.

2. Work, Welfare, and the New Economy
The Commodification of Everything[1]

DAVE BROAD AND GARSON HUNTER

A significant component of the new economy is neoliberal state policy. In this essay we will examine the impact of this new economy ideology on social welfare policy. Our focus is on the changes wrought by corporate globalization and the new economy on work and on state policy related to work, specifically the shift from welfare to workfare. We will begin by presenting our conceptualization of the new economy. We will then turn to an examination of neoliberalism and its impact on state policy regarding work and welfare. We will end with some thoughts on prospects for moving beyond neoliberalism and the new economy. Central to our argument is the proposition that an important historical element of the welfare state has been a partial *de*commodification of labour. Consequently neoliberalism, as the policy of the new economy, is essentially about the *re*commodification of labour. We might, in fact, say that neoliberal globalization is the highest stage of the capitalist commodification of everything on the planet.[2]

The New Economy

Since its advent in the 1990s, we continue to hear about this new economy, the alter ego of globalization. Most accounts of the new economy
say it is based on advanced information and communication technologies (ICTs). Drawing on the early work of Daniel Bell (1973), many
authors have argued that we are witnessing an industrial revolution
driven by computerized production of both goods and services. One
of the first people to use the term "new economy" was Canadian management guru Nuala Beck (1992), who actually trademarked the term.
Alan Murray, a leading proponent of the new economy, has described it
in glowing terms:

> The New Economy ... is like the Istanbul bazaar, that five-hun-
> dred-year-old covered maze where thousands of vendors sell
> carpets and curios, icons and samovars. The orderly world of
> a generation ago, with its limited choices and fixed prices and
> clear lines of distribution, is being transformed into a chaotic,
> bustling, teeming global marketplace. Countless sellers court
> countless buyers, with an array of merchandise. Prices aren't
> fixed. Each merchant tries to extract the highest price for his
> wares; but each customer has the power to walk to the next
> booth in search of a better deal. (2000: 7)

Murray goes on to tell us approvingly that "globalization, deregulation,
and digitization are turning the entire world into a modern version of
the Istanbul bazaar."

As Murray's definition indicates, this new economy is, first of all,
global. The ICT revolution has made possible changes in communication,
production, and transportation, so economic structures are no longer
constrained by geography (or political boundaries). Virtually everyone
around the world is tied into one global economy. The impact on work
has been equally as dramatic. ICTs and globalization have transformed
work processes and both created and destroyed jobs. For example, bank
machines have replaced bank tellers, while opportunities have opened up
for computer programmers and operators. Not only have the kinds of
jobs changed in the new economy, but the nature of work has also been
altered. For example, we are often told that the days of having a lifelong career with one employer are long gone. Finally, the nature of government has changed with the emergence of the new economy. Owing to
globalization, the role of government in the new economy is supposedly
much more minimal than in the years up to the 1970s. Government is

supposed to provide the conditions for international economic competitiveness, and reduce barriers to economic globalization and be less concerned about individual citizens' social welfare, which, ostensibly, will be
taken care of by economic growth. In other words, government is supposed to be a midwife to the new economy.

Therefore, the new economy has three key features: a newly globalized economy; restructured—i.e., new forms of—work (both supported and driven by the new electronic technologies); and a new form
of politics. Each of these key features, in turn, consists of several important elements. There is considerable agreement about the features of the
new economy, but there is also considerable debate about its nature and
effects. In very general terms, there are two main schools of thought on
the new economy.

According to one kind of assessment and analysis, the new economy
is a good thing. It will promote economic growth in part by increasing labour productivity. As to the overall economic benefits, promoters
believe that the new economy will reboot the world economy to promote economic growth, just as rebooting our computers will clear out
whatever is impeding the workings of the system. In particular, promoters state that the new economy will provide new and exciting employment opportunities. There will be plenty of work for everyone, work will
be flexible and well paid, and it will consume less and less of our time.
This rebooting of the economy and work is aided by neoliberal public
policy change. According to the proponents of the new economy, and to
use another computer analogy, governments will eradicate system viruses
like environmental, labour, and tax regulations that impede the free flow
of capital. Governments that do not act in this way will be condemning
their populations to the deprivations of global uncompetitiveness and,
ultimately, to the "recycle bin" of history.

Thomson (1999: 400) explains the "conventional economic wisdom"
favouring globalization: "In policy terms, it is widely accepted that if
governments acted to ensure unimpeded free trade in goods, services,
capital and technology, then an integrated capitalist global market would
stimulate competition and spur productivity thus raising living standards, particularly for the aspiring citizens of the developing countries."
Neoliberal economist Richard Easterlin (1998) favourably sees this as
"growth triumphant," with economic cycles resulting from old economic
"laws" of capitalism being superseded. Equally, this growth and expansion is driven by the spread of new technologies (ICTs) throughout the
production processes of the new economy. By adhering to neoliberal values of market freedom, privatization, and deregulation, governments can
support new economy growth.

Others disagree with this scenario. Authors and researchers in a second school of thought argue that while ICTs have indeed had a significant impact, the global economy is deepening, and governments' behaviour is changing, we are not, in fact, witnessing the emergence of a truly new economy. Rather, we are in thrall to an old economy—the same old capitalism based on fundamental social inequalities—redeveloping and attempting to recharge itself. Further, proponents of the second school of thought argue that neoliberal economic restructuring has produced at least as many negative as positive results, with the positive ones most often not being evenly distributed (Broad and Antony 2006).

New economy government is much in evidence. Critics of the new economy point out that governments in almost all industrial countries have cut back on the social safety net—witness the cutbacks to education, social assistance, health care, and environmental protection and the constant drive to cut taxes. But unlike new economy promoters, critics regard these changes as actually making the situation worse for the majority of citizens whose lives have already been made more precarious by the economic and work changes in the new economy. In fact, most critics would argue that, far from minimizing their impact on the lives of citizens and their economies, governments have been willing and necessary partners in the emergence of the new economy.

New technologies, accompanied by economic globalization and the shift from social welfare to neoliberal state policies, have led to increased employer strength and weakening trade unions, to a faster pace of work and unhealthy work environments, and to increasing unemployment and underemployment, while state regulation and the provision of social welfare benefits have been eroded. In short, the capital accumulation process is being rebooted at the expense of workers, their families, and their communities. Critics believe it is unlikely that the global new economy will indeed reboot the capital accumulation process in the long run. In fact, after the "dot-com" crash of 2000–2001, some observers pronounced the new economy dead (Henwood 2003).

To put it most simply, the new economy is not really new. There have been some economic changes in recent years, and some changes that are significant to the lives of many people. But the new economy is really just capitalism with a new face. All the inequalities, exploitation, and conflicts that are part and parcel of capitalism have not been superseded. In fact, what globalization and the new economy are all about is the recommodification of labour and the continuing commodification of everything, as Wallerstein (1983) has put it. These are the particular consequences of neoliberal policy changes undertaken to free up the market and deregulate labour and social policy.

Despite the exaggerated claims about the new economy, we cannot simply write these trends off as pure rhetoric. Globalization and the new economy may not really be new, and new economy industries may not have produced the sort of economic and employment growth that promoters wish us to believe they have; but they have been promoted so strongly by business and government that their impacts on workers, their families, and their communities are significant.[3] Neoliberal policy has been used to shift the role of the state away from promoting social welfare, as under Keynesianism, to promoting privatization and deregulation of the economy. We are constantly being told that we must improve our individual and collective productivity to be more competitive in the global market. In the workplace, this means constantly pushing workers to exceed production targets by "re-engineering" production processes. Meanwhile, neoliberal governments have shifted from a focus on ensuring social rights to promoting individual "responsibilities." Social assistance is being replaced by "workfare" as we are all exhorted to increase our economic productivity. Let us examine this shift in the role of the state.

From Welfare to Workfare: Public Policy for the New Economy

To fully comprehend the effects of the new economy on the modern welfare state requires an understanding of the relationship between governments and business in Western industrialized nations. A clear definition of the welfare state is crucial to understanding the development of social and public policies in capitalist economies. This applies whether the economy is labelled as industrial, post-industrial, or "new." "Social policies" are the activities and principles that guide the ways in which the members of society intervene in and regulate the relationships among individuals, groups, communities, and institutions to generally determine the distribution of social resources and the level of citizens' well-being (Barker 1995: 355). "Public policies" are, more specifically, created by governments and the state, and they most often reflect compromises in the conflicts between different groups in society as represented by political parties and social and political interest groups: "That is, social reforms have been defined and administered as national programs; they have represented the political compromise between a national capitalist class and resistance to its particular forms of exploitation by sections of a national working class or social movements; and they have depended partly on the kind and degree of political alternatives that have evolved in particular nations" (Teeple 2000: 17). These compromises are unstable situations that are always open to change due to the power shifts among (unequal) groups. This essay is concerned mainly with public policy, and more specifically with welfare policy or that set of policies and practices that is often called the welfare state.

What is referred to as a welfare state is defined here as the welfare effort, or legislatively sanctioned and publicly or quasi-publicly administered spending on welfare benefits (health, education, social assistance, unemployment, pensions, etc.) (Hicks 1999: 168–69). The modern welfare state (often referred to as the Keynesian welfare state[4]) refers to a pattern of expansion and development of public policies and services within particular industrialized nations since World War II. The modern welfare state refers to political and policy development in only certain industrialized nations, as not all industrialized nations in fact have a welfare state.[5] Welfare states exist in countries with capitalist economies where "the welfare state can also be seen as a capitalist society in which the state has intervened in the form of social policies, programs, standards, and regulations in order to mitigate class conflict and to provide for, answer, or accommodate certain social needs for which the capitalist mode of production in itself has no solution or makes no provision" (Teeple 2000: 15).

International research has indicated that a key factor in the early development of a welfare state is the degree of working-class mobilization. Hicks (1999: x), for example, concludes that "labor organizations and their politics built the welfare state by exploiting—sometimes quite fortuitously, sometimes most deliberately—the political opportunities offered to them." Therefore, central to the development of a welfare state is an industrialized economy with some history of working-class mobilization. The development of a modern welfare state within a structure of industrialized capitalism and organized labour should therefore more accurately be referred to as "welfare capitalism," and its policies as "capitalist public policy" rather than "public policy."

The Creation of the Modern, Keynesian Welfare State

Following the depression of the 1930s and the rise of labour militancy, governments introduced a number of social programs (for example, the New Deal in the United States) to alleviate the threat of further social disruption. Again, the inability of private charity to deal with poverty and misery was evident. Public works projects appeared again, similar (although much larger in scope) to those of the depression of 1893. The main contribution of the New Deal, however, was "to assert the primacy of government in the field of social welfare" (Katz 2001: 142).

At the end of World War II, the lessons that governments had learned from dealing with worker militancy and social unrest during the 1930s were not lost: "All western countries [introduced] income protection programs, won in response to the political mobilization of poor and working people over the course of the twentieth century" (Piven 2002: 19). These income-protection programs took many forms, including unemployment insurance, medicare and government health insurance, and enhanced forms of social assistance to those unable to work. In general terms, these programs, often referred to as an entitlements-based approach, were based on three principles. First, they were social entitlements—that is, citizens were entitled to these protections simply by virtue of being citizens. Second, they were based on need only—that is, all people, even the able-bodied unemployed, were eligible for funding simply by being unable to provide for themselves. Third, the programs were based on labour-market exclusion—those who did not have jobs were eligible simply because they were unemployed; looking for a job was not the basis for receiving benefits. In some important ways, this kind of welfare policy actually contributed to economic redistribution by transferring income, through taxation and social assistance programs, from those who were comfortable and those who were well off to those who did not have enough to live on. It is also important to point out, as noted above, that the welfare state contributed to a degree of *de*commodification of labour.

Based on a general consensus, during and immediately after World War II, Western governments adopted a more interventionist, or Keynesian, approach to the economy. This is the period during which "economic statism" developed, as governments took a direct role in regulating the economy. They did this by providing various kinds of incentives for business investment, including vast amounts of military spending, especially in the United States. Along with business and economic development subsidies, governments also dramatically increased spending on roads, infrastructure, and the sub-urbanization of metropolitan areas. This pattern continued from the 1940s through the 1970s.

Moscovitch and Drover (1987: 13) suggest that Canada's state expenditures can be explained by two hypotheses: "1) the necessity of state intervention to assure continued private capital accumulation and profitability, and 2) the necessity of state social intervention, including expenditures on social welfare programs, to regulate labour in the workplace and at home by diminishing the cost to capital of a mobile, available, and appropriately educated labour force." Social expenditures therefore reduce the costs of production, which assists private capital accumulation, and the expenditures legitimize the social order. Conversely, the more stable and potentially less volatile the industrialized country is, the less need there is for social programming. It is within the state (legislative, judicial, and executive branches) that the struggles between big and small capital, finance and industry, rulers and the ruled are resolved, "reflecting the interests of the most powerful and dominant factions while at the same time attempting to secure the collective rule of the whole" (Jones and Novak 1999: 114).

During these first decades after World War II, the modern, Keynesian welfare state developed to better complement the employment needs of the capitalist labour market. But the economic expansion due to the government interventionist expenditures of this period began to slow down in the mid-1970s. The next upswing of profits in the business cycle was to result from a dramatic lowering of corporate income taxes, the shedding of labour and the de-unionization of large segments of the labour force, the development of "free trade" agreements that allowed capital access to high-profit sectors in other nations, and the government advancement of the so-called new economy.

As noted above, a contingent, flexible workforce and free trade (the globalized economy) are tools of business in the new economy. The new economy welfare state reflects and supports these economic changes. Public policies of the welfare state are being modified to adapt to the current labour force needs of capital, shifting from a Keynesian welfare approach to a neoliberal, workfare approach that has modified public policy to fit the desire of business for a "flexible workforce" (Broad 2000). Within the period of neoliberal dominance, with unregulated market interests being the major priority of nearly every government, public policy has been redefined.

Third Way Welfare Policy

New economy public policy is changing the face of the welfare state. However, the current restructuring of welfare policy is not, in terms of the fundamental goals and effects, a qualitative break from the "old" or Keynesian welfare state and a shift to something new. Rather, new economy public policy simply continues the pre-welfare state policy: "The workfare offensive against the [Keynesian] welfare state and its rights-based benefits is an effort to construct a new system of labor regulation, to enforce work under the new conditions of casualisation, falling wages and underemployment that characterizes postindustrial labor markets" (Piven and Cloward 2001: x). The modern welfare state is being redesigned to accommodate employers' needs for economic restructuring in the so-called new economy. More specifically, in refashioning welfare funding structures and program delivery, modern welfare states have moved from needs-based eligibility, social entitlement, and labour-market exclusion programs to models that emphasize selective entitlements, active programming, and maximum participation in wage labour (Theodore and Peck 1999: 488). "Active" welfare programming implies that national, standardized programs for welfare have been replaced by local experiments in delivery. This shift, in our view, is not fundamentally new, contrary to the claims made by new economy public policy analysts that theirs is a *new* approach to public, specifically welfare, policy. We propose that this shift in vision and functioning of welfare programming is designed to meet the needs of the economy and employers, thus conforming to a long-standing capitalist political dynamic. Here is how it works.

In the United States, the active welfare programming model is viewed as the "work-first approach" (Peck 2001; Theodore and Peck 1999) or "third way neo-liberalism" (Platt 2003: 21), and in Britain the model is viewed as "Third Way" policy making (Holden 1999; Jordan and Jordan 2000; Callinicos 2001). The term "Third Way" generally refers to the search for a political road somewhere between capitalism and socialism, a long-term quest of social democrats. Welfare change in Canada is a hybrid Third Way policy that combines both the features of US policy and the welfare ideology of Britain (Hunter and Miazdyck 2003). In this essay, we refer to the recent changes to the modern welfare state as Third Way public policy which serves the new economy. In defending changes to public policy, two arguments are used: (1) that government intervention and economic redistribution are wrongheaded; and (2) that globalization forces us to minimize government spending, accept a weaker labour position, and cut back social programs. The message is that there is no alternative; we must adjust and adapt. We will comment below on how the current global economic crisis affects these arguments.

Advocates believe that a Third Way approach is needed because the entitlement-based approach has failed to acknowledge the importance of the market system in the new global economy (Callinicos 2001). With the economic consequences of global integration, the autonomy of nation-states has been greatly reduced. Therefore, the economic statism of a particular form of entitlement-based eligibility welfare system has been rendered obsolete. Economic statism is an approach that points in the wrong direction, for the economic game has changed. Social assistance, a system designed to help the resourceless unemployable, is instead now portrayed as trapping the employable on a "welfare treadmill." As the Canadian federal government states, "... too many recipients spend many years on social assistance even though, with the right sort of employment and training support, they could successfully make the transition from welfare to work, from dependency to self-sufficiency" (Government of

Canada 1994a: 72). Welfare is presented as a system that has inadvertently promoted dependency among people who are actually employable, so a different policy approach is called for.

New economy public policy is viewed as an approach to rectify some of the mistakes of the old welfare state. Public policy during the modern Keynesian welfare state was based primarily on the concept of entitlement, with little to say about responsibility, the assumption being that the state has a duty to offer assistance to citizens with no other resources or options for support. According to its Third Way detractors, the policy of entitlement was a "passive" income support that did little to stimulate employment. Today the Organization for Economic Co-operation and Development (OECD) wishes to see what it terms an "active society," which represents a wide range of reforms that include linking cash benefits (welfare) to work-oriented incentives across a broad range of options (Gilbert 2004).

The OECD's employment agenda is clearly articulated in *The OECD Jobs Study* (OECD 1994), which puts forth ten criteria for its jobs strategy:

1. Set macroeconomic policy such that it will both encourage growth and, in conjunction with good structural policies, make it sustainable, i.e., non-inflationary.
2. Enhance the creation and diffusion of technological know-how by improving frameworks for its development.
3. Increase flexibility of working-time (both short-term and lifetime) voluntarily sought by workers and employers.
4. Nurture an entrepreneurial climate by eliminating impediments to, and restrictions on, the creation and expansion of enterprises.
5. Make wage and labour costs more flexible by removing restrictions that prevent wages from reflecting local conditions and individual skill levels, in particular for younger workers.
6. Reform employment security provisions that inhibit the expansion of employment in the private sector.
7. Strengthen the emphasis on active labour market policies and reinforce their effectiveness.
8. Improve labour force skills and competencies through wide-ranging changes in educational and training systems.
9. Reform unemployment and related benefit systems—and their interactions with the tax system—such that society's fundamental equity goals are achieved in ways that impinge far less on the efficient functioning of the labour markets.

10. Enhance product market competition so as to reduce monopolistic tendencies and weaken insider-outsider mechanisms while also contributing to a more innovative and dynamic economy. (restated in OECD 1997: 4–5)

These proposals all point to the sanctity of the capitalist market economy and emphasize the neoliberal priorities of privatization, deregulation, and downsizing of government.

The first item tells us that economic growth should be the beginning point for public policy, which is one of the fundamental assumptions of post-World War II modernization theory. The second item accords with a core belief of the new economy, namely that technology is the key to economic growth, from which all else flows. Items 3 and 5 reflect the current neoliberal promotion of labour-market flexibility with respect to working hours and wages, which includes the lower minimum wages for youth that we see in some jurisdictions, but Item 5 even challenges notions such as minimum wage. Item 7 supports the shift from welfare to workfare policies that we see in many countries, Item 8 refers to the move away from notions of liberal education toward market-oriented skills training, and Item 9 reflects the assumption that state benefit programs such as unemployment insurance must be "reformed" because they create "dependencies" on social welfare programming.

In its reports on implementing the jobs strategy, the OECD claims that the countries following its prescriptions have been making great headway in creating employment. The United States is often held up as an example because its labour productivity has been higher and official unemployment numbers lower than those in most other Western countries. But labour productivity gains can be a simple outcome of forcing people to work longer and harder, and official unemployment statistics generally mask a lot of unemployment (Yates 1994).

The Canadian government adopted the entire OECD jobs strategy following its social security review and budget program of 1994. Ostensibly, the review was a public consultation into the wishes of Canadians regarding public policy and social programming. But critics have argued that the review was really a front for selling the neoliberal agenda, as reflected in the OECD *Jobs Strategy*, to Canadians (Pulkingham and Ternowetsky 1996). The two main documents outlining the Canadian government's direction sport the banner "Agenda: Jobs and Growth" (Government of Canada 1994a, 1994b). According to *A New Framework for Economic Policy*, the policy-making setting includes economic globalization, competition from developing countries, and the information economy. To address these issues, we are told, "Productivity growth is the foundation of economic progress and must therefore be the primary focus of economic policy" (Government of Canada 1994c: 16). The government's proposed framework for achieving this objective is stated as one that will help Canadians acquire skills, encourage them to adapt to change, get government right, provide leadership in the economy, and create a healthy fiscal and monetary climate. The presumption is that this will lead to innovative combinations of people, capital, and ideas, which will produce stronger economic growth, resulting in more and better jobs (Government of Canada 1994c: 36–37).

The flaw in this argument is that economic growth *per se* does not necessarily lead to the sort of social development that might include more and better jobs. If we want more and better jobs, determinants for the ingredients of a development program that might result in those jobs must be built into policy proposals from the start. Economic growth in a capitalist market economy is not primarily oriented toward creating good jobs and satisfying human needs, but rather toward selling commodities at the highest possible profit to promote the accumulation of capital. One result is the decent work deficit, which, according to the evidence we have presented, is exacerbated by neoliberal policies proposed by the OECD and followed by Western governments. Meanwhile, "getting government right" has included targeting social programs for supposedly allowing workers to become dependent on social welfare, the implication being that they are lazy. So a residual policy of cuts to social programs has accompanied the trend toward fewer and worse jobs, creating yet more hardships for workers and their families, and exacerbated by the shift from welfare to workfare.

Britain, Australia, New Zealand, the United States, Canada, and the Scandinavian countries have all developed work-oriented welfare policies. Along with the transition from passive to active policies, programs have moved from a "needs-based" approach (the financially destitute having a right to social benefits) to one focused on the responsibilities of recipients to find work, to be self-sufficient, and to lead a productive life. Speaking from a Canadian perspective, Chris Axworthy (1999: 279), former federal member of Parliament, former Saskatchewan justice minister, and Third Way advocate, observes: "Not much has flowed from this [passive] approach other than entitlement to receive a cheque—no responsibility to prepare for old age, look for work, seek the skills needed for the workplace, relocate to a job, provide for our children, etc. Worse yet, there has been no empowerment." The assumption is that entitlement-based social programs of the modern welfare state create dependency among the recipients; they are passive programs that do not work.

Axworthy and other Third Way advocates see the continuation of entitlement-based public policy without responsibilities as unworkable. Canada and the rest of the world, we are told, must face and adjust to the new global economy: "Social programs must change to keep up with new realities—realities around a changing economy, around unmanageable public debt and around problems with the programs themselves" (Axworthy 1999: 283). The public policy solution to the challenges presented by the new global economy is to give people receiving government assistance "the chance to acquire the skills inventory they need for the current workplace and the chance to be as independent as possible—a hand up rather than a handout" (283). The commitment from government welfare recipients, then, in their quest for self-sufficiency, is to become employed within the labour market: "For those able to take advantage of expanded, enhanced employment, education and training opportunities, it will be imperative that they do" (283). Accordingly, work in all its forms is good, and the quality of that employment is not an issue for welfare programmers.

The language of social inclusion is being adopted as a justification for workfare (Hunter and Donovan 2007). To be without employment, apparently, unless one is rich or disabled, is to be outside of the community. The corollary that people on welfare are excluded from full citizenship has its genesis in conservative ideology. Jones and Novak (1999: 188) comment:

> The primary aim of social inclusion and cohesion is therefore to bind the excluded back into the labour market as a solution to the problem. That this may result in their continuing poverty is conveniently overlooked, since it is their inclusion (whether self-imposed or structural) that is the problem rather than their poverty.

New economy advocates of rights and responsibilities have not extended their analysis to members of society who benefit immensely from the tax laws and publicly subsidized loans that allow them to accumulate considerable wealth. They do not mention that group's responsibilities to the community for receiving a "hand up." Gilbert (2004: 65) comments:

> ... the discourse on balancing rights and responsibilities has not concentrated on the diverse obligations that might attend the full spectrum of benefits derived from social rights. Rather, the moral calculus of this equation has been applied almost exclu-

sively to the unemployed poor—whose rights to social benefits are being weighted against the recipient's efforts to be financially self-supporting.

Within the logic of new economy public policy, citizenship for individuals and families is defined as having a job, being self-sufficient, contributing to society, and having access to education, health care, and security (Government of Saskatchewan 1999). Typical of neoliberal states, according to the Government of Saskatchewan this is "A New Way of Doing Business." Seemingly at odds, however, with the goal of individual self-sufficiency, if the work is poorly paid, with few or no benefits, the government will offer programs that support that work and, hence, the individual's or family's community integration. But neither the contradictions between self-sufficiency (i.e., the individual pursuit of wealth in a market-based society) and membership in a community, nor the additional responsibility and obligations of welfare recipients to the community are explained. Moreover, the idea that self-sufficiency is contrary to human nature is totally ignored.

We see what in essence is a shift from welfare to workfare priorities because, for new economy public policy advocates, global changes and markets have created a need for the change. The old way of delivering programs is supposedly no longer viable and thus requires change. According to Third Way new economy advocates, if state management of the economy was ever a feasible idea, it is now certainly a discredited one, although this view is being challenged by the current global economic crisis. Anthony Giddens, a prominent British academic and Third Way advocate, observes, "The left has to get comfortable with markets, with the role of business in the creation of wealth, and the fact that private capital is essential for social investment" (cited in Callinicos 2001: 8).

It is more than just interesting to note Giddens's claim. In his argument that the Third Way is new, he is actually saying it is not, for he is insisting that public welfare policy must conform to the dictates of the (new) economy—that the left must get "comfortable with markets." But this is not new—as our historical discussion above shows, public policy in capitalist society has conformed to the needs of the economy (read: capitalists and markets) for centuries. Therefore, Giddens and other Third Way proponents are really only advocating for a new face on a very old policy. As we have argued, the "new" in new economy and new public policy is fundamentally the same old capitalism. Ultimately, what the Left has to offer to the new economy that separates and defines it from the Right are alternative values (Callinicos 2001: 8), through stressing community, opportunity, fairness, and social justice. Phrasing this another way, Piven and Cloward assert that "the key to an understanding of relief-giving is in the functions it serves for the larger economic and political order, for relief is a secondary and supportive institution" (1971: xiii). These authors maintain that welfare policies are expanded during times of unemployment and civil disorder but are restricted at other times to enforce work norms (xiii). Therefore, the main functions of welfare are to maintain civil order and to enforce work discipline, both of which serve capitalism. These priorities have become clear with new economy public policy, in the drive to *re*commodify labour and *re*habituate workers to the labour market.

The Third Way, Globalization, and Free Trade

The second reason that Third Way advocates have offered for moving away from an entitlement-based welfare state is that globalization is inevitable. Opinions on the consequences of globalization are varied, but the common thread in Third Way literature is that the welfare state must accommodate this new "reality." However, the ability of national governments to enact policies is curtailed by globalization. Commenting on public policy changes in Canada, Graham and Al-Krenawi (2001: 417) write, "As companies compete in an increasingly international marketplace, the demands upon national governments to restrict welfare may grow." For an export-driven economy such as Canada's, trade is crucial, and in the 1980s the focus of business was to maximize Canada's potential as a trading partner. McQuaig (2001: 55) argues that the impetus for a free trade agreement came from corporate leaders in the United States who were set on ending government protectionism of the service industry and reducing corporate responsibility to meet "performance requirements." With very few protectionist measures in place in Canada in the first place, it was obvious that there was more at stake for business to push the 1988 Free Trade Agreement (FTA) between Canada and the United States than simply reducing tariffs. Merrett (1996: 15) argues that the desire "to restructure the Canadian economy along neoconservative lines," that is to enshrine corporate rights, limit the power of labour, and reduce the welfare state, was the real reason for originally pushing for free trade with the United States.

The 1994 North American Free Trade Agreement (NAFTA), signed by the participating governments of Canada, Mexico, and the United States, allows businesses to ask their respective government to seek formal resolutions against other governments if local policies or trade decisions are undesirable to those businesses: "The treaties contain clauses used as levers to extend the agenda of [corporate] capital against state intervention, including measures to decrease or erase welfare statism" (Collier 1997: 89). Altering domestic economic and public policies and programs to suit business interests creates a harmonization of policy within the partners' trade agreement (Swenarchuk 2001).

The pressure to adopt this new economy public policy in Canada is largely a direct consequence of the business lobby that led to the creation of NAFTA. Peck (2001: 215) comments:

> For all the talk of globalization in Canada, much of the competition the country faces is originating from just south of the border. And just as the *North American Free Trade Agreement* (NAFTA) has accelerated and deepened the process of economic continentalization, so also it seems that pressures are mounting for a "downward convergence" in public policy.

However, by strategically citing the ethereal concept of "globalization," rather than trade agreements, as the reason for policy change, leaders have brought Third Way public policy to Canada and other countries. The effect of this new, Third Way economy has not been benign, but has involved an imposition of neoliberal policies such as deregulation, trade liberalization, and privatization by those with economic power. It remains to be seen whether this trend continues after the current debate over free trade globalization versus protectionism, and government interventions to bail out failing banks and industries.

The Future of Social Welfare

With the economic restructuring that has been occurring since the early 1970s and a business community that increasingly seeks to impose "flexible employment," with low wages, no job security, and little in the way of benefits, we see the income-support programs of the welfare state being adjusted accordingly. It has become increasingly difficult for those in welfare programs to eke out a decent living, with grossly inadequate benefits, time limits, and workfare or constant work-search requirements. Essentially, they are designed to keep people off social assistance by forcing them into low-income, insecure employment that provides enough of an income supplement to disqualify families from welfare. This thereby assures business the "flexible" labour force it desires for profit, especially in service-sector and temporary employment. In effect, current welfare programming is subsidizing the wages for the low-income labour force: "Under conditions of falling wages, chronic underemployment, and job casualisation, workfarism maximizes (and effectively mandates) participation in contingent, low-paid work by churning workers back into the bottom of the labour market, or by holding them deliberately 'close' to the labour market in a persistently 'job-ready' state" (Peck 2001: 13–14).

Even the International Monetary Fund (IMF), one of the foremost promoters of globalization, admits that globalization may indeed hurt the poor (Prasad et al. 2003; 50 Years Is Enough 2004). Juan Samavia, Director-General of the International Labour Organization (ILO), has referred to a global "decent work deficit." "A survey of the world we work in today points to an inescapable conclusion.... There is a profound concern about a global decent work deficit of immense proportions, reflecting the diverse inequalities of our societies. Unless we tackle this deficit, the goal of social justice will remain beyond our grasp" (ILO 2001: 5).

For all its faults, modern Keynesian welfare policy was a step in the right direction. Even though the fundamental goal of Keynesianism was to preserve capitalism, the labour and social-movement unrest of the post-World War II era did provide, at least, a human face for capitalism through some degree of *de*commodification of labour (Esping-Anderson 1990; Teeple 2000). The actual policies and programs resulting from the belief that social welfare benefits are rights, not privileges to be earned, not only provided the poorest of the poor with some modicum of dignity and less-than-abject poverty, but the so-called social safety net that developed in that era also benefited working people in their struggles with employers because they had less to fear from the age-old threat of unemployment. These ideas came under attack in theory and practice by new economy welfare policies.

Canada has not gone far down the road to its own new economy welfare state, so it is difficult to predict the outcome. It is not our intent to suggest that the modern welfare state represents the "good old days" to which we could return to solve current problems. However, the movement toward new economy public policy certainly represents a significant regression in social welfare policy and programming. The Third Way or new economy welfare policy changes have become a *Poor Law* for the twenty-first century (Jones 2001). There is no easy solution to the growing disparity between the haves and the have-nots in the new economy welfare state: social welfare programs should, of course, be defended and improved, but a larger set of struggles is required to move beyond the current state of social welfare.

Generally, we can conclude that, while producing significant effects like the recent wave of globalization and the spread of ICTs, the new economy is not a step beyond capitalism. We must keep in mind that the world system is still a capitalist socio-economic system, not a post-industrial or post-modern utopia. It is not human need but the incessant drive to accumulate capital that says we must continue to produce more, faster, at lower costs of labour and resources, with no apparent end in sight (Altvater 2001). Karl Marx (1867: 742), the foremost student of capitalism, characterizes the imperative of the system thus: "Accumulate, accumulate! That is Moses and the prophets!" Yet in the last few years we have increasingly seen signs that neoliberalism and the new economy have already begun to run their course and will not reboot the capital accumulation process (see Amin 2004; Henwood 2003; and Wallerstein 2008a). And in the longer run, some economists have identified a systemic trend toward economic stagnation that will continue to plague the capital accumulation process (see Steindl 1952; Baran and Sweezy 1966; Foster and Szlajfer 1984; Foster and Magdoff 2009).

The full onset of a global economic crisis in late 2008 has shown both the fallibility of the capitalist market economy and the hollowness of neoliberal promises about globalization and the new economy. While mainstream economists and politicians are avoiding the term, some critics argue that we are moving into a full-fledged economic depression, not just a recession (Wallerstein 2008b). The situation has become severe enough to cause conservative French President Nicolas Sarkozy to call for "a new capitalism" (CBC 2008). Even in the extreme free-market United States we see increasing state intervention in the economy, promotion of protectionist trade policies, and even near-heretical suggestions of nationalizing banks. Still, labour is being assaulted and pushed to make further concessions to secure state bailouts of businesses like the "Big Three" automotive manufacturers (Chrysler, Ford, and General Motors). Now the need for an alternative to "business as usual" is even more pressing.[6] Fortunately, we are seeing people's hopes for humanity expressed in social justice struggles taking place every day, in all parts of the world. The World Social Forum, for example, with its clarion call "Another World Is Possible" and its self-declared struggle against neoliberal globalization, is a positive development (Fisher and Ponniah 2003; Santos 2006). As policies of neoliberal globalization and the new economy continue to unravel, more space will open up for the progressive "*alter*globalization movement" (Wallerstein 2008a) to push toward a non-commodity-based society.

Discussion Questions

1. What role has the Canadian state played in the development of the new economy?

2. How is neoliberal ideology reflected in current welfare-state policy?

3. Is a return to Keynesian-style welfare policies a wise or necessary step toward the "non-commodity society" alternatives that are advocated by the authors?

4. Can the movement against neoliberalism and "the commodification of everything" serve to link the environmental movement, the labour movement, and the struggle to preserve and improve the welfare state? Could this link foster the kind of alterglobalization movement that is being advocated in this chapter?

Notes

1 The authors wish to thank Wayne Antony and Dionne Miazdyck-Shield for their assistance with the material presented in this essay.

2 Capitalism's tendency to commodify everything is a trend that has been noted throughout history (Marx 1867; Polanyi 1957; Braverman 1974; Wallerstein 1983). Examples of the current rush to commodify everything on the planet are easy to find. A look through one issue of *The Globe and Mail*, 31 May 2008, reveals three glaring cases. A news story in the business pages discusses the global food crisis, partly the result of land formerly used for food production being turned over to growing corn to produce ethanol to feed automobiles. But the article points out the often overlooked problem of deregulation of grain markets, and the move from forward marketing to futures marketing and speculation (Stewart and Waldie 2008). Agriculture in this neoliberal world is obviously not about producing food, but rather about producing profits. Another story deals with the supposed "discovery" of an uncontacted tribe of indigenous people in the Amazon jungle. Apparently anthropologists have known of this group and others for some time, but the Brazilian government is now releasing photos of these people because of concern for their welfare as loggers and oil exploration companies encroach on their territory (Astor 2008). A third story in this same issue of *The Globe* reports on a recent meeting of western Canadian premiers in Prince Albert, Saskatchewan. The story, titled "Premiers Vow to Help Bring Boom to the Arctic," reports on the premiers' plan to "share" the western Canadian economic boom with the northern territories now that global warming will allow the building of more roads and ports to exploit northern oil and other resources (Walton 2008). So, rather than showing any concern about exacerbating the negative effects of climate change in the Arctic, it's "full speed ahead and damn the torpedoes" in the pursuit of economic growth and profits.

3 A search of the University of Regina library holdings, for example, shows recent publications with titles such as *New Economy and Macroeconomic Stability* (Togati 2006), *Academic Capitalism and the New Economy* (Slaughter and Rhoades 2004), *Environmental Regulation in the New Global Economy* (Jenkins et al. 2002), *Female Enterprise in the New Economy* (Hughes 2005), and *Aboriginal Economic Development in the New Economy* (Anderson 2005).

4 Many attribute the main features of the modern welfare state to the theorizing and policy development of the British economist John Maynard Keynes.

5 The industrialized nations of Japan, South Korea, and Indonesia have not developed welfare states similar to those in Scandinavia, Britain, Australia, New Zealand, Canada, and, to a lesser extent, the United States. Additionally, no developing country has produced a welfare state based upon the above definition. Therefore, being an industrialized nation appears to be a necessary condition for the development of a welfare state, but is not a sufficient condition for that development.

6 For a fuller discussion of alternatives see Broad and Antony (2006).

References

Altvater, E. 2001. "The Growth Obsession." In L. Panitch and C. Leys (eds.), *The Socialist Register 2002*. London: Merlin Press.

Amin, S. 2004. *The Liberal Virus: Permanent War and the Americanization of the World*. New York: Monthly Review Press.

Anderson, R.B. 2005. *Aboriginal Economic Development in the New Economy*. Regina: Saskatchewan Institute of Public Policy.

Astor, M. 2008. "Brazil Sheds Light on the People that Time forgot." *The Globe and Mail* 31 May: A3.

Axworthy, C. 1999. "A Modern Socialist Approach: R and R for Social Policy." In D. Broad and W. Antony (eds.), *Citizens or Consumers? Social Policy in a Market Society*. Halifax: Fernwood.

Baran, P.A., and P.M. Sweezy. 1966. *Monopoly Capital: An Essay on the American Economic and Social Order*. New York: Monthly Review Press.

Barker, R. 1995. *The Social Work Dictionary*. Washington, DC: NASW Press.

Beck, N. 1992. *Shifting Gears: Thriving in the New Economy*. Toronto: HarperCollins.

Bell, D. 1973. *The Coming of Post-Industrial Society*. New York: Basic Books.

Braverman, H. 1974. *Labor and Monopoly Capital: The Degradation of Work in the Twentieth Century*. New York: Monthly Review Press.

Broad, D. 2000. *Hollow Work, Hollow Society? Globalization and the Casual Labour Problem*. Halifax: Fernwood.

Broad, D., and W. Antony (eds.). 2006. *Capitalism Rebooted? Work, Welfare and the New Economy*. Halifax: Fernwood.

Callinicos, A. 2001. *Against the Third Way*. Cambridge: Polity Press.

CBC (Canadian Broadcasting Corporation). 2008. "'A new capitalism' on the agenda." <www.cbc.ca/world/story/2008/10/15/eu-summit.html>.

Collier, K. 1997. *After the Welfare State*. Vancouver: New Star Books.

Easterlin, R.A. 1998. *Growth Triumphant: The Twenty-first Century in Historical Perspective*. Ann Arbor: University of Michigan Press.

Esping-Anderson, G. 1990. *The Three Worlds of Welfare Capitalism*. Princeton: Princeton University Press.

50 Years Is Enough. 2004. "IMF Report: Globalization May Hurt Poor." <www.50years.org/cms/updates/story/21>.

Fisher, W.F., and T. Ponniah (eds.). 2003. *Another World Is Possible: Popular Alternatives to Globalization at the World Social Forum*. Halifax: Fernwood.

Foster, J.B., and F. Magdoff. 2009. *The Great Financial Crisis: Causes and Consequences*. New York: Monthly Review Press.

Foster, J.B., and H. Szlajfer. 1984. *The Faltering Economy: The Problem of Accumulation Under Monopoly Capitalism*. New York: Monthly Review Press.

Gilbert, N. 2004. *Transformation of the Welfare State: The Silent Surrender of Public Responsibility*. New York: Oxford University Press.

Government of Canada. 1994a. *Agenda Jobs and Growth: Improving Social Security in Canada, A Discussion Paper*. Ottawa: Human Resources Development Canada.

——. 1994b. *Agenda Jobs and Growth: Improving Social Security in Canada, Discussion Paper Summary*. Ottawa: Human Resources Development Canada.

——. 1994c. *Agenda Jobs and Growth: A New Framework for Economic Policy*. Ottawa: Finance Canada.

Government of Saskatchewan. 1999. "Building Independence—Investing in Families." Saskatchewan Employment Supplement; Saskatchewan Child Benefit; Family Health Benefits; Provincial Training Allowance; Youth Futures [Brochures].

Graham, J., and A. Al-Krenawi. 2001. "Canadian Approaches to Income Security." In J. Turner and F. Turner (eds.), *Canadian Social Welfare*. Toronto: Pearson Education Canada.

Henwood, D. 2003. *After the New Economy*. New York: The New Press.

Hicks, A. 1999. *Social Democracy and Welfare Capitalism*. Ithaca, NY: Cornell University Press.

Holden, C. 1999. "Globalization, Social Exclusion and Labour's New Work Ethic." *Critical Social Policy* 19 (4): 529–38.

Hughes, K.D. 2005. *Female Enterprise in the New Economy*. Toronto: University of Toronto Press.

Hunter, G., and K. Donovan. 2007. *Social Exclusion and the Justification of Welfare-To-Work Programs in Saskatchewan*. Ottawa: Canadian Centre for Policy Alternatives.

Hunter, G., and D. Miazdyck. 2003. *Current Issues Surrounding Poverty and Welfare Programming in Canada: Working Paper No. 20*. Regina: University of Regina, Social Policy Research Unit.

ILO (International Labour Organization). 2001. *Report of the Director-General: Reducing the Decent Work Deficit—A Global Challenge*. Geneva: International Labour Organization.

Jones, C. 2001. "Voices from the Front Line: State Social Workers and New Labour." *British Journal of Social Work* 31 (4): 547–62.

Jones, C., and T. Novak. 1999. *Poverty, Welfare and the Disciplinary State*. London: Routledge.

Jordan, B., and C. Jordan. 2000. *Social Work and the Third Way: Tough Love as Social Policy*. London: Sage.

Jenkins, R.O., J. Barton, A. Bartzokas, J. Hesselberg, and M. Knutsen. 2002. *Environmental Regulation in the New Global Economy: The Impact on Industry and Competitiveness*. Cheltenham: Edward Elgar.

Katz, M. 2001. *The Price of Citizenship: Redefining the American Welfare State*. New York: Henry Holt and Company.

Marx, K. 1867. *Capital: A Critique of Political Economy*. Vol. I. Harmondsworth: Penguin Books/New Left Review.

McQuaig, L. 2001. *All You Can Eat: Greed, Lust and the New Capitalism*. Toronto: Penguin.

Merrett, C.D. 1996. *Free Trade: Neither Free nor About Trade*. Montreal: Black Rose Books.

Moscovitch, A., and G. Drover. 1987. "Social Expenditures and the Welfare State: The Canadian Experience in Historical Perspective." In A. Moscovitch and J. Albert (eds.), *The Benevolent State: The Growth of Welfare in Canada*. Toronto: Garamond Press.

Murray, A. 2000. *The Wealth of Choices: How the New Economy Puts Power in Your Hands and Money in Your Pocket*. New York: Crown Publishers.

OECD(Organisation for Economic Co-operation and Development). 1997. *Implementing the OECD Jobs Strategy: Lessons from Member Countries' Experience*. Paris: Organization for Economic Co-operation and Development. <www.oecd.org/dataoecd/42/52/1941687.pdf>.

——. 1994. *The OECD Jobs Study: Facts, Analysis, Strategies*. Paris: OECD Publications. <www.oecd.org>.

Peck, J. 2001. *Workfare States*. London: Guilford Press.

Piven, F. 2002. "Welfare Policy and American Politics." In F. Piven, J. Acker, M. Hallock, and S. Morgan (eds.), *Work, Welfare and Politics: Confronting Poverty in the Wake of Welfare Reform*. Eugene: University of Oregon Press.

Piven, F., and R. Cloward. 2001. "Foreword." In J. Peck, *Workfare States*. London: Guilford Press.

Platt, T. 2003. "The State of Welfare: United States 2003." *Monthly Review* 55, 5 (October): 13–27.

Polanyi, K. 1957. *The Great Transformation*. Boston: Beacon Press.

Prasad, E., K. Rogoff, S.J. Wei, and M.A. Kose. 2003. *Effects of Financial Globalization on Developing Countries: Some Empirical Evidence*. Washington, DC: International Monetary Fund.

Pulkingham, J., and G. Ternowetsky. 1996. *Remaking Canadian Social Policy: Social Security in the Late 1990s*. Halifax: Fernwood.

Santos, B. de S. 2006. *The Rise of the Global Left: The World Social Forum and Beyond*. London: Zed Books.

Slaughter, S., and G. Rhoades. 2004. *Academic Capitalism and the New Economy: Markets, State, and Higher Education*. Baltimore: Johns Hopkins University Press.

Steindl, J. 1952. *Maturity and Stagnation in American Capitalism*. New York: Monthly Review Press.

Stewart, S., and P. Waldie. 2008. "The Byzantine World of Food Pricing: How Big Money is Wreaking Havoc." *The Globe and Mail* 31 May: B1, B6–7.

Swenarchuk, M. 2001. "Civilizing Globalization: Trade and Environment Thirteen Years On." Canadian Centre for Policy Alternatives, Briefing Paper Series: Trade and Investment, 2, 6.

Teeple, G. 2000. *Globalization and the Decline of Social Reform: Into the Twenty-First Century*. Toronto: Garamond Press.

Theodore, N., and J. Peck. 1999. "Welfare to Work: National Problems, Local Solutions?" *Critical Social Policy* 19 (4): 485–510.

Thomson, J.W. 1999. "Globalization: Obsession or Necessity?" *Business and Society Review* 104, 1 (Winter): 397–405.

Togati, T.D. 2006. *The New Economy and Macroeconomic Stability: A Neo-modern Perspective Drawing on the Complexity Approach and Keynesian Economics*. London: Routledge.

Wallerstein, I. 2008a. "2008: The Demise of Neoliberal Globalization." *MRZINE*, 1 February. <www.monthlyreview.org/mrzine/wallerstein010208.html>.

———. 2008b. "The Depression: A Long-Term View." *MRZINE*, 16 October. <www.monthlyreview.org/mrzine/wallerstein161008.html>.

———. 1983. *Historical Capitalism*. London: Verso Books.

Walton, D. 2008. "Premiers Vow to Help Bring Boom to the Arctic." *The Globe and Mail* 31 May: A12.

Yates, M.D, 1994. *Longer Hours, Fewer Jobs: Employment and Unemployment in the United States*. New York: Monthly Review Press.

3. Restructuring Work and Labour Markets in the New Economy
Four Processes

WALLACE CLEMENT, SOPHIE MATHIEU, STEVEN PRUS, AND EMRE UCKARDESLER[1]

Introduction

The idea of the new economy has been central to many arguments: technologically-driven high productivity and economic growth, global economic integration, the "dot-com" boom, creative and flexible jobs, the same old capitalism, and new forms of exploitation. Despite the popularity of the term "new economy," only a few thorough definitions are available. "New" does not accurately identify the characteristics of what is emerging.

In this paper we suggest a framework for identifying the content of the new economy. We argue that four processes are primarily restructuring work and labour markets today: (1) the unfolding of *post-industrialism*, marked by a sectoral analysis of the rise of the service economy and a massive entry of women into the paid labour force; (2) the large-scale utilization of *new technologies*, i.e., the computerization and digitization of work; (3) the emergence of a *knowledge economy or society*, meaning a focus on education and vocational training; and (4) the rise of *precarious employment*, characterized by the deteriorating quality of jobs, working conditions, pay, and benefits under neoliberal pressures. The new economy represents a combination of these processes, especially as they have occurred since the 1980s. The role of each process varies across different sectors and countries, but they are observable almost everywhere.

We are aware that some of these four processes, especially post-industrialism and the knowledge economy/society, have been associated with problematic claims such as the end of capitalism, the end of class, and the end of arduous work. Rather than taking these processes as self-evident realities, we take them as elements of a conceptual toolkit to understand changing labour markets. This paper has two purposes: first, to identify the substance of the new economy through four processes; second, to reflect on both the nature of these processes, and how best to approach them, from a critical social-science perspective.

Concepts of Critical Social Science and Processes of the New Economy

The four processes take place in contexts of welfare-state regimes, industrial relations, and macro-economic policies. The challenge is to see how these processes can be approached in ways that are conceptually informed, so that the social structures of the new economy, especially inequalities, can be demonstrated and comparatively informed, revealing cross-national and cross-sectoral similarities and differences in the way the new economy is experienced. A conceptual framework provides a holistic perspective to the analyst by prioritizing particular aspects of social phenomena under investigation. Using comparative cases enables a wider perspective on the phenomenon and its variations.

We believe that central concepts of critical social science, i.e., class, gender, and heritage,[2] are relevant for a conceptual and comparative analysis of the new economy. As Carroll (2004) aptly says, critical research allows the researcher to connect several sides of the social world and reveals the relations that generate injustices. In this regard our analysis of the four processes of the new economy is geared toward emphasizing what Acker (2006: 441) calls *inequality regimes*, i.e., "the interlocked practices and processes that result in continuing inequalities in all work organizations." Class practices include the wage-setting mechanism, low-pay and low-status jobs, as well as "class controls, directed at maintaining the power of managers, ensuring that employees act to further the organization's goals, and getting workers to accept the system of inequality" (454). Class practices at the workplace are embedded with patriarchal and ethnic-discriminatory assumptions, wage-setting systems, and divisions of labour. Patriarchy in the household is also not separate from the patriarchy in the labour market. For example, in an analysis of European labour markets, O'Dorchani (2008) finds that it is not motherhood *per se* but the patriarchal mechanisms of labour markets (treating all women as potential mothers) that is used to justify paying women low wages. Furthermore, "motherhood status generally worsens women's wages whereas being a father tends to have a positive impact on men's wages" (1).

The substances of critical social-science concepts are dynamic, not frozen across time and space. Consider the following example: Although increasingly a large part of contemporary work is characterized correctly as precarious, we must remember that contingencies have long characterized women's working lives. A Canadian study reports that almost two-thirds of women with paid employment have had their work interrupted for six or more months. This is in contrast to just over a quarter of the men. What is crucial is that whereas family (gender: women doing unpaid domestic or childcare work) was the main reason for such interruptions in the 1950s (88 per cent), by the 1990s this fell to almost half (47 per cent); economic reasons such as layoffs (class: the declining power of employees, and gender: women being laid off first) accounted for nearly a quarter (22 per cent) (Fast and Da Pont 1997).

What attracts our attention in the new economy is the increasing complexity of class relations as well as the nexus of class, gender, and heritage. An outstanding attempt to map the social structures of the new economy is offered by Leslie McCall's analysis of the United States. In *Complex Inequality: Gender, Class and Race in the New Economy* (2001), McCall takes on a complex sociological issue, intersectionality, alongside the topic that motivates her project: the new economy. As the economy is restructuring—i.e., becoming more high-tech, international, flexible, and service-oriented—the wages and social security of most workers are declining. McCall's central claim is that "race, class, and gender are interrelated and constituted in historically and contextually specific ways" (12). She develops a diligent gender and race analysis; her notions of class inequalities, however, are inadequate since they are limited to income and educational attainment. Larger explanatory richness in class analysis is sacrificed to the available aggregated data. Despite these limitations, McCall shows that patterns of racial, gender, and class inequalities are significantly different across the United States. Unionized blue-colour cities with a recent history of deindustrialization, such as Detroit, exhibit modest class and racial wage inequality among employed men yet are marked by significant gender and class inequality among employed women. In contrast, a post-industrial city such as

Dallas is marked more by class and racial inequality than by gender inequality.

To give a Canadian example of the unfolding of the new economy, one strong pattern of change in Canada's labour force during the free trade era was the rise of self-employment, accounting for three-quarters of all new jobs created between 1989 and 1997. This brought the number of self-employed to 18 per cent of Canada's labour force. Nine out of ten of these new jobs were located in the service sector (especially in business, health, and social services). Earnings by self-employed workers are more polarized than for paid work: according to 1998 figures, 45 per cent of self-employed workers earned less than $20,000, compared to 26 per cent of the paid workers; while only 1 per cent of the employed earned over $100,000 annually, 4 per cent of self-employed earned this much (Statistics Canada 1998: 28). A hybrid of the "old" and "new" middle classes is emerging in the form of some contract workers who are formally "self-employed" but who in practice are dedicated to single employers through contingent arrangements and poor benefits. Some of these contract workers are also working-class. Although nominally self-employed, they are directed in their employment by the companies hiring them and have no significant supervisory or administrative responsibilities, representing a form of "disguised wage labour." As more workers become self-employed, fewer can rely on employment-based benefits. And as the state sheds universal forms of coverage, there is more pressure on individuals to cover their own social-welfare costs. Indeed, self-employment constitutes an important part of the present precarious employment landscape. (Other forms of precarious employment are analyzed in the fourth section of our paper.)

It is important to note that the "new" middle class stands as a significant actor in modern society by virtue of its size, character, and strength. By "new" middle class we mean those standing "between employers and workers" in the organizations of advanced industrial society. They are the employees who both exercise the rights of employers to supervise and organize the work of others but who do not themselves set policy or determine the direction of the organizations (which are the responsibilities of executives). They are distinct from the "old" middle class, whose members are independent (self-employed), often owning the means of realizing their labour power—such as farmers, shopkeepers, and traditional professionals (doctors, dentists, accountants, etc.) who work for themselves. Ideologically, the new middle class is located between capital and labour and has the potential to form an alliance with either side on several issues. Keeping these aspects of this class in mind provides additional insight into the four processes analysed in this paper.

1. *Post-industrialism Enriched*

The term "post-industrialism" became popular with Bell's *The Coming of Post-Industrial Society* (1973). There is some difference, however, between contemporary usages of the term and Bell's definition. For Bell, post-industrialism meant the replacement of mechanical labour with intellectual labour and an increased role played by theoretical knowledge, as opposed to socio-economic class, as the basis of social stratification. Optimistic about the virtues of higher education, Bell argued that human capital constitutes the foundation for privilege in post-industrial societies. Today most people refer to post-industrialism as labour markets characterized by service-sector jobs combined with the massive entry of women into labour markets. Bell thought post-industrialism would modify the central feature of capitalism, i.e., economic class relations, and this has proven to be incorrect. However, he did foresee a number of issues, such as the intersection of technological developments with social stratification, human capital, and skills formation, many of which are central to new economy debates. In this section our use of post-industrialism is limited to its contemporary usage. Our overall perspective on the new economy, as a combination of processes, nonetheless acknowledges the original contribution of Bell.

There are many important observations to be made about the extent and nature of the service sector. OECD (2000) data show that the service economy, once a residual category, has grown to include almost three-quarters of all employment in most capitalist countries. The increase in the service sector's share of total employment represents a reduction in the number of jobs involving the direct production of goods. Although this share has become more similar across countries, national differences in the *composition* of service jobs persist. In other words, the unfolding of the service industry, as one important component of post-industrial society, is experienced differently across developed countries.

Service jobs can be classified into different categories (see Table 3.1). "Personal" services are usually regarded as providing the "bad jobs" found in the hospitality services of hotels, bars, and restaurants. In the mid-1980s, Australia, Canada, and the United States had a larger share of these jobs than other developed countries; however, these differences have diminished over time. Conversely, many "good jobs," which provide high income and job security, are found in the "social" service category (such as in health and education). In the late 1990s, the Scandinavian countries, Belgium, France, and Luxembourg had the highest share of social-services jobs in developed countries. Producer services have generally provided the high-skill jobs, mostly occupied by men, whereas distributional services, dominated by retail trades, have been low-skill and low-paid, and mainly occupied by women.

Table 3.1   Characteristics of Services

PRODUCER SERVICES	DISTRIBUTION SERVICES	PERSONAL SERVICES	SOCIAL SERVICES
· Business and professional · Financial · Insurance · Real estate	· Retail trade · Wholesale trade · Transport services · Communications	· Hotels, bars, and restaurants · Recreation, amusements, and cultural · Other personal	· Government proper (civil or military) · Health · Education · Miscellaneous
Knowledge economy	Communication and transportation; capital-intensive	Generator of "bad jobs." Demand for these jobs is very sensitive to labour costs.	"Good" jobs; welfare-state jobs
High skill, men, women	Retail low-skill, women	Low-skill, women	High-skill, women

Source: Based on OECD (2000), Table 3.1, p. 83.

Post-industrialism has brought changes not only in the nature of work, but also in the social composition of workers. Education levels are considerably higher in the service sector than in the goods sector, even though there are variations in different categories of service (personal-service jobs tend to be filled by less educated workers, while many social-service jobs require university degrees). The expansion of the service sector has been accompanied by a gender shift from a predominantly male workforce to a more gender-mixed labour force.

The rise of female employment, as well as declining fertility and the increase of marital disruptions, has forced welfare states to redefine their role. In industrial societies, "old social risk" (OSR) policies were designed to support a traditional family at times of income interruption due to unemployment, sickness, or retirement (Taylor-Gooby 2004). The combination of post-industrial labour markets and contemporary family structures, however, has created a new risk configuration. Full time and permanent "standard" employment is no longer available on a mass scale, and women's advancement in education and employment has created strains on caring responsibilities. "New social risks" (NSR), on the other hand, are situations in which individuals experience a welfare loss. This occurs in families (and even more so in single-parent households), which are challenged to reconcile earning and caring responsibilities (for children, the disabled, and the elderly); in labour markets, for people lacking the skills or experience necessary to gain access to an adequately paid and secure job; and with regard to social security for individuals following "atypical" career patterns (as pension coverage is often optimal for continuous full-time workers) (Bonoli 2006; Taylor-Gooby 2004; Esping-Andersen 1999). Younger people, women, and low-skill workers are particularly at risk, as NSR are particularly high upon entering and maintaining a place in the labour market, and in meeting care responsibilities at the stage of family building. The timing of new risks is therefore entirely different from that of old risks, such as health-care needs and retirement, which are experienced at an older age (Bonoli 2006; Taylor-Gooby 2004).

The capacities of states to adapt to post-industrial changes, and the extent to which governments are able to reduce the risks of citizens, differ across welfare regimes. In the Nordic countries, for example, the risk of being unable to reconcile work and family life is cushioned by an existing state commitment to high levels of wide-ranging social supports, thus making these risks more potential than actual (Taylor-Gooby 2004). Generous family services and benefits in these countries allow women to be active in the labour market while maintaining relatively high levels of fertility. Conversely, the liberal model that is found in the United States tends to offer solutions that can be purchased from private caregivers so that access to care is unequal, further excluding and marginalizing vulnerable groups.

2. New Technologies

New technologies emphasize the diffusion of hardware and software into work processes. This has implications for the execution, autonomy, and supervision of work. Information and Communications Technologies (ICTs) have a prominent place in popular debate, but the topic of new technologies is not limited to them. Similarly, reducing the ICT-driven work debate to call centres, for instance, would be misleading as it conceals changes in other areas.

New technologies are altering the structure of work not only within but also between firms. Outsourcing, sub-contracting, partnerships, and on-call work, among other practices, are embedded in the capitalistic reorganization of work and its cost-cutting and competitive enterprises. Yet it is new technologies, such as just-in-time inventory, computer-aided product design and customization, broadband communication, online ordering, and online product delivery, that make many new inter-firm relations possible. These work processes require new tasks and skills from employees and place new burdens on them.

We can discern four principal opinions regarding new technologies. First, *economistic optimists* see new technologies as a way to achieve higher growth and productivity, at both the firm and national levels (Jorgenson, Ho and Stiroh 2004). Second, *economistic skeptics* believe that the influence of technological changes on growth and productivity are exaggerated (Farrell 2003). Third, *sociological optimists* claim that new technologies pave the way for creative jobs, higher skills, and possibly more equality in at least some—if not all—areas of class, gender, and heritage (Florida 2002; ILO 2001). Finally, *sociological pessimists* argue that new technology in capitalist labour markets leads to a deskilling of workforces, worse jobs, intensified supervision, and deeper class and gender inequalities (Benner 2002; Head 2003).

How valid are such generalizations when cross-sectoral and cross-national variations are considered? Why are there so many different points of view? An explanation can be found in the way analysts frame their research. Researchers investigating if technological change increases productivity find contradictory answers depending on whether the "firm" or the "economy" is their unit of analysis. Because of this, the term *productivity paradox* was coined: the productivity impact of new technologies is larger at the firm level than at the national level. It is also wrong to simply associate unemployment with technological developments (Carnoy 2000). The fact that our times witness both rising unemployment and technological advances does not suggest that the two are straightforwardly connected. Most decisions leading to changes in employment rates and work quality are driven by market-competitive, managerial motives rather than being results of technology. Powell and Snelmann (2004) provide a fundamental but often-neglected insight: significant productivity gains are achieved only when new technologies are combined with organizational changes, such as employee participation in decision making, greater autonomy, and profit-sharing plans.

Productivity is not a sufficient framework for a sociological account; hence we see sociologists analysing job quality, workplace autonomy and supervision, the work–life balance, and pay gaps. High-quality ethnographic research exists on how high-tech, self-employed, contract, call-centre, and on-call employees work and how they strive to reconcile work, home, and caring for others (Rogers 2000; Greenbaum 2004). The main problem with various studies of new technologies is that they are not commensurable. For, as Brown and Campbell (2002: 26) explain, "National-level studies do not incorporate the impact of human resource practices as an intervening variable, which has been found to be important in case studies." Similarly, we observe that there exist "international" studies on the impacts of new technologies, but they are not "cross-national" since they aggregate data rather than differentiate. Therefore, ethnographic, international, and national levels of analysis have not yet led to a comprehensive understanding of the impacts of new technologies.

In studying technology and its influence on work it is important to start with the awareness that technological developments are not forces on their own but are mediated through existing social institutions. A technological change can have egalitarian or inegalitarian, autonomy-increasing or autonomy-decreasing effects depending on what kind of legal environment, extent of union protection, or managerial culture it takes place within.

Tremblay (2003) suggests that there are three spheres to analyse when considering the role of technological developments: business strategy, the human resources strategy of firms, and national labour-market policies. She shows that changing forms of the gender division of labour in Canada are outcomes of both computerization and organizational restructuring. For example, the introduction of multi-skilling by means of computerization has given women an opportunity to move into nontraditional jobs in some Quebec firms, whereas in others, despite their successes in multi-skilling, women have remained in traditional jobs.

Frenkel et al. (1999) compare the organization of front-line work in Japan, the United States, and Australia. They argue that in the information economy, "work is becoming more *complex*, rather than more *routinized* in a single direction" (266; emphasis in original). Contemporary forms of technology-driven work, they suggest, should be analysed in five spheres: work relations, employment relations, control relations, co-worker relations, and customer relations. They rank contemporary work practices in terms of income, job autonomy, skill levels, and the degree of computerization. As a result, they suggest, there are three types of contemporary front-line work: mass-customized service work, sales-work, and knowledge-work. Whereas mass-customized service workers have the lowest income, least autonomy, and least computerization, knowledge-workers enjoy the highest levels in all categories. Nevertheless, as Frenkel et al. (1999) observe, national contexts of class and gender relations and valuations of work produce complex outcomes. For example, Japanese mass-customized service workers have the least job satisfaction and commitment compared to their counterparts in the United States and Australia. This is caused by higher gender discrimination in the Japanese mass-customized service work-place as well as the inferiority of mass-customized service work to sales-work and knowledge-work. Thus, we see the interplay of a relatively national-context-free valuation of different front-line jobs in capitalist labour markets (knowledge work being the most valued and rewarded) and a national-context-dependent (i.e., gender in Japan) valuation of women's work. Frenkel et al. (1999) note that the diffusion of computers was least in Japanese mass-customized service work, since this type of work has low market-value and priority for managers. This situation also intensifies the gender-based exercise of power and supervision in the workplace. Frenkel et al.'s (1999) finding parallels England's (1979) and Clement and Myles's (1994) observations that resistance to gender equality is greatest in situations of face-to-face contact in the workplace.

Despite limitations for cross-national comparisons, statistical analyses of new technologies demonstrate a fundamental aspect of the new economy: increasing wage inequality on the basis of skill levels. Although this is not equal to a class analysis, it is a significant insight. There is one more layer of the puzzle: the ideological construction of the notion of *skill* conceals the deeper complexities of labour markets. For instance, in their study of low-skill (low-paid) jobs, Borghans and ter Weel (2005) find that at the bottom of the labour market wage differentials are not determined simply by skill differentials. The cost of computerization relative to wages is the main determinant of computerization in low-paid sectors. Therefore, not merely technology or individual skills, but also managerial decisions shape the way in which technology is utilized and employees are rewarded.

Autor, Levy and Murnane's (2002) analysis of computerization is noteworthy in demonstrating the socially determined interplay of technology and work organization. The introduction of digital cheque imaging in two departments of the bank they examined led to the emergence of two different forms of non-computerized work. Although the computerized task is pursued similarly in both departments, each department had different managerial choices on the execution of the non-computerized task. One was Taylorist, divided into narrower steps with less skill content; the other was less divided, demanding that each employee use broader knowledge and exercise greater control. Unsurprisingly, the latter produced more job satisfaction and higher productivity.

The interaction of technology with gender presents another challenge. Feminist scholarship shows how technology is gendered: patriarchy is embedded in the design, usage, and cultural associations of technological artefacts at work and home (Faulkner 2001). However, women are not passive subjects of technology; the gender-technology interaction is complex. Eriksson-Zetterquist (2007) suggests that an alternative way of understanding this interaction is to approach technology as composed of different nodes in a network. Each node, such as technological education and research, inventions, manufacturing, implementation, and interpretations, is gendered but also creates openings for alternative gender constructions, i.e., it has potentialities to challenge patriarchy and use technology to increase women's power, autonomy, and discretion at work. Changes in one node can possibly affect not only other nodes but also the social relations of technology. An early work, Pat Armstrong's *Labour Pains* (1984), showed that technology in the workplace brings about increased managerial supervision but also offers new opportunities for female workers. Then, during the 1990s, post-industrialism in general and ICT developments in particular first generated optimistic accounts of technology for gender equality (Eriksson-Zetterquist 2007).

However, recent research also demonstrates that gender equality is still far from realized, even in ICT jobs. Ben (2007) finds that 60 per cent of the group in data-processing training in Germany are female, but only 15 per cent of software developers are women. Furthermore, although in 1982 20 per cent of students in computer-science departments in Germany were women, in 2002 this proportion dropped to 16 per cent. In Canada about 25 per cent of ICT workers are female, and the proportion of women in computer-science programs at Canadian universities is declining too (Cukier 2007). The difference between German and Canadian figures could possibly be explained by the fact that the German labour market is more segregated than the Canadian one. However, the lower representation of women in ICT jobs in both countries could be explained by the gendered structure of ICT jobs regardless of national context. The distribution of jobs, wages, and careers across jobs made possible by new technologies is still disappointingly gendered, just like the labour markets of industrial capitalism.

3. The Knowledge Economy/Society, Skills, and Training

Today everyone talks about knowledge *something*. These knowledge discussions are about the restructuring of labour markets, vocational training programs, new priorities in public education, job-creation subsidies, and, not surprisingly, university research grants. Information and Communications Technologies (ICTs) again have a prominent place in this preoccupation with "knowledge," since some ICT jobs are viewed as knowledge-intensive. Knowledge-based skills are deemed crucial for successful careers, but these skills and careers are not limited to ICTs as there is a broader role for knowledge in the contemporary world of work. Not only does the knowledge (and hence the skills) of hardware and software matter, but so does the knowledge of customer service, goods and services sales, retail, the modern assembly line, and child care, among others. The changing valuation of work and skills via an emphasis on knowledge blurs the demarcation between so-called hard (job-specific) and soft (teamwork, initiative, and networking) skills. Employees are now under pressure to be successful in both.

Webster (2004: 160) states that a knowledge society is one in which human capital, knowledge, and expertise are central to the conduct of business and to the performance of work. Brint (2001) observes that three conceptions of knowledge are in use: first, knowledge is conceived of as any impression-making information; second, it is seen as the organization of understandings and processes intended to yield constant product innovation; third, it means economically relevant systems of thought generated and transmitted in higher education. In all three accounts, education, learning, and training dominate the agenda.

Esping-Andersen (1993) writes that the entry to employment and subsequent job mobility are dictated by education and training programs. Such a meritocratic assignment introduces a new class filter: those with few or outdated qualifications are blocked from upward mobility. Thus, Esping-Andersen notes, education may even promote a class divide, but the severity of this filter depends on the nature of the educational system. If access to credentials is broad and if a public system of continued training exists, the polarizing effect of meritocracy may be lessened. On the other hand, a rigid education system is likely to result in class closure. The important point Esping-Andersen makes concerns the socially constructed nature of labour markets and training regimes. National training regimes differ in their abilities to equalize.

In their impressive comparative study of vocational training in several countries, Crouch, Finegold and Sako (1999) make four observations. First, improvements in skill levels have a limited capacity to generate employment, so employment policy cannot depend entirely on education policy. Second, although the acquisition of skills is a major issue for policy makers, vocational training chances are increasingly contingent upon the private sphere of firms that are not always willing to meet public needs. Firms provide training, but only for selected employees. Third, this selectivity limits government action to residual care for the unemployed, which further decreases the capacity of public institutions to contribute to skill policy. Fourth, government action without cooperation from firms could be misleading, while extensive reliance on firms' training agendas curbs the capacity of public policy in the area of employment and training. Despite the cross-national differences in the role of public education, the state, local agencies, unions, and firms, Crouch, Finegold and Sako (1999) observe a general pattern in vocational training: the excessive focus on education and training for knowledge is fed by an emphasis on global competitiveness and knowledge production. However, they remind us, sectors that provide high-skill and knowledge-based employment and those that provide competitive advantages in the global economy are not one and the same.

In a recent report, the International Labour Organisation (ILO) (2002) observes that the process of learning is increasingly individualized, and it is now individuals who are the architects of their own skills. The report maintains that the emphasis on human capital, the shift from teacher-centred learning to student-centred learning, and ICTs are the major factors affecting the acquisition of skills in the present era. At the same time, the ILO observes that there is a widening gap between social groups in terms of decent work and income and participation in social and economic life. Although total employment has increased, the patterns of employment have shifted. Employers are reorganizing their workforce by dividing them into primary (fixed) and secondary (contingent, peripheral, part-time) segments. In a single firm one sees both segments of the workforce, with each group having a different status and variable access to training. The main losers in such a system are those who are less educated and more low-skilled. This observation is not wrong, but it is incomplete. It assumes that higher skills are the key to decent jobs, yet it understates the fact that managerial-capitalistic decisions interact with workers' skill levels in determining who gets what.

Furthermore, institutional means and forms of training vary across countries. They include student loans, special training funds, trade union and employer partnerships, community-based training, and training vouchers. Collective bargaining, for example, usually enables employees to receive high-quality, long-lasting training and helps allocate training resources across vulnerable groups. The establishment of lifelong learning through tripartite agreements at the national level in Spain in the early 1990s is one of the most apposite examples (ILO 2002). In Japan, the employment insurance scheme has a special account for the vocational development of workers. The scheme finances special training institutions and assistance to authorized private-sector training programs (ILO 2002).

ICTs are not only transforming jobs, but they are also bringing new methods of training. Using broadband Internet techniques, companies create virtual classrooms for their employees across the world. Initially the target groups were well-paid engineers and managers, but currently larger groups of employees receive online training (ILO 2002). Cost-cutting is a significant motive; setting up an online system is less expensive than conventional training methods. Whether it is more effective is yet to be determined. Nevertheless, online training could be helpful in training the self-employed, home-employed, or disabled workers, and it is yet to be fully utilized by public institutions. As they are not covered by collective agreements or company training schemes, self-employed workers are dependent on (expensive) free-market and public programs.

Investigating women's work in the knowledge economy, Webster asks whether women with non-managerial jobs in finance and retail are "really engaged in something that can be called knowledge work" (2004: 161), i.e., work that involves elaborate knowledge of the product and the process. Her findings are significant. Branch-based clerical and customer-service jobs, for example, require more knowledge, especially in Nordic and German finance companies where employees have access to better training. In Italy, Spain, Ireland, and England, however, even in the finance sector, knowledge of administrative tasks overshadows product knowledge. Call centres in the finance sector, she finds, are the most disadvantaged in regard to product knowledge, training, and job upgrading. In retail services, the overall emphasis on product knowledge and training is less than the finance sector everywhere. Nevertheless, cross-national variations do exist, with the best training provisions in Germany and Denmark. Webster notes, however, that the quality and quantity of training are declining everywhere, and especially that interpersonal and persuasive skills are being prioritized over product knowledge. Training and learning opportunities in many non-managerial positions are in decline and are being replaced by women's individual efforts at informal, on-the-job learning, or shadowing their colleagues. The problem with informal training is that qualifications acquired through such methods cannot be recognized in the same way as qualifications gained through formal training. Webster notes that when companies link career progression to formal in-house training, women have better chances of acquiring managerial positions. Yet, Webster adds, "it is not uncommon for women to reject progression because they cannot accommodate the time demands of the [managerial] job with the rest of their lives" (168). Webster finds that women do acquire managerial positions, but this usually happens following an organization's decentralization or the downgrading of some existing managerial positions.

We draw three main conclusions regarding the valuation of knowledge and the emphasis on learning and training in the new economy: first, learning is increasingly deemed to be an individual issue; second, the discursive overvaluation of knowledge and skills may not always be realized in job markets, especially when job creation is at the discretion of private firms. Third, not all social groups have equal access to training, and work is becoming more segmented within and across sectors.

4. Precarious Employment

Since the 1980s, scholars have questioned whether there has been a shift from standard employment, where the worker maintains a stable, full-time, 9-to-5 job with statutory benefits. Non-standard jobs, defined by the absence of these features, are likely to be held by women, youth, immigrants, and poorly educated individuals. It is unclear, however, whether it is the jobs, work arrangements, labour markets, sectors, or particular people (with regard to their class, gender, or heritage) that are non-standard. Furthermore, comparatively measuring non-standard work practices is difficult, given the varieties of non-standard employment and the diversity of definitions used by different countries. These forms of employment are sometimes characterized as "part-time," "casual," "contingent," "temporary," or the concept we choose to use, "precarious." The novel contribution of the concept of precarious employment has been to capture the diversity within non-standard employment and the deteriorating quality of standard jobs, along with the classed, gendered, and racialized nature of these processes (Cranford, Vosko and Zukewich 2003).

An important issue is to locate part-time work within non-standard work. Part-time work, albeit non-standard by definition, is not always precarious. Part-time work is ambiguous: sometimes it is progressive, sometimes regressive, and it can be both precarious and permanent (Clement and Prus 2004). In some cases, even when the hours worked do not constitute a full-time schedule, the working arrangement may not be precarious. In some countries part-timers are even entitled to the similar rates of pay, protection, and benefits as full-timers. This is the case in Sweden, where part-time is in some cases an earned status based upon entitlements that may be achieved through full-time employment.

Some prefer to use the duration of work, rather than the occurrence of part-time work, as an indicator of instability. For the ILO (1993), casual workers or seasonal workers are considered non-standard employees. Similarly, the OECD refers to "temporary" employment as an umbrella term for "jobs that provide little or no prospect of a long-lasting employment relationship" (2002: 132), which includes fixed-term contracts, temporary agency work, seasonal work, on-call work, and trainee positions. Others use the degree of uncertainty of job tenure as the central characteristic of work that falls outside the realm of standard work. Polivka and Nardone (1989), for example, argue that the most salient characteristic of "contingent work" is the low degree of job security. Any work arrangement that does not contain a commitment between the employee and the employer for long-term employment has to be considered contingent. Polivka and Nardone (1989) explain that the variability and unpredictability of working hours can make the work contingent (since unpredictable working hours can be more disruptive than the number of hours) and that workers' access to benefits—especially health benefits—affects the contingency and quality of work.

Another definition is provided by Rodgers and Rodgers (1989), who use the concept of "precarious job." Precariousness depends on four factors: the degree of certainty of continuing employment; the control over the labour process, i.e., the presence or absence of a trade union, and control over working conditions, wages, and pace of work; the degree of regulatory protection, i.e., the extent to which workers are protected against discrimination, unfair dismissal or unacceptable working practices; and the element of income, as even a secure long-term job may be labelled "precarious" if it keeps one poor.

As these definitions demonstrate, there is no consistency between scholars on how to define work that is not standard. We choose to use the concept of precarious employment precisely because it embeds other concepts such as "casual," "contingent," or "temporary." We suggest that precarious work should be defined as a form of employment involving one or a combination of the following: atypical employment, in the form of temporary, casual, seasonal, short-term or low-security work; persistently low earnings that are insufficient to independently support oneself; a limited number of key fringe benefits, such as paid vacation leave, paid sick leave, unemployment insurance, and a pension plan; and a working environment where employees are not in a position to defend their interests in terms of working conditions and practices, wages, and discrimination. The novel contribution of the concept of precarious employment is to capture the diversity within non-standard employment and, as we will see below, the deteriorating quality of standard jobs along with the classed, gendered, and racialized nature of this process (Cranford, Vosko and Zukewich 2003).

We believe that precarious employment is related to the new social risks (NSR) of post-industrialism. The shortcomings of welfare states in protecting citizens against NSR force people to develop individual strategies to cope with precariousness. This might be asking grandparents to care for children, buying private pensions, or returning to school. Post-industrialism also involves the massive entry of women into labour markets. As a consequence, women are overrepresented in all forms of precarious employment. For example, Cranford, Vosko and Zukewich (2003) demonstrate the overall growth of precarious employment in Canada. Precarious employment, they write, increases along the continuum in the following order: full-time permanent, full-time temporary, part-time permanent, and part-time temporary employees. Women are disproportionately represented in the last three categories. Even when women are in the least precarious forms of employment, they are more precarious than men: they have less regulatory protection and fewer means to support themselves and their dependents. The work of Leschke (2008) has shown that women who are already overrepresented in precarious jobs also suffer from a social-protection deficit. As Leschke (2008) explains, part-timers increasingly suffer from unemployment insurance deficit, and the proportion of the unemployed population who are entitled to insurance benefits is declining in several countries.

The perspective of precariousness also reveals a dramatic aspect of the post-industrial era. Fudge and Owens (2006: 12) aptly note, "'Feminisation' has a double meaning and refers both to the increased labour market participation of women and the proliferation of forms of employment historically associated with women, that is, jobs that are part time, temporary, poorly paid, and lacking benefits and collective forms of representation." The concept of gender wage gap, a structural indicator of female precariousness, verifies this clearly. In Canada over the past 25 years, the ratio of young women's to young men's earnings (25–29-year-olds with full-time jobs) increased from .75 to .85. This is an apparently progressive shift, but when one compares the changes in actual earnings, we see that the decline in the gap is due to a drastic decline in men's earnings while women's have also declined (Clement et al. 2009).

Precarious jobs are a significant feature of the employment landscape, but differences across countries are persistent with regard to the incidence, configuration, and consequences of such jobs (Rodgers and Rodgers 1989). OECD (2002) data show that while there is a strong increase in precarious work in France, Italy, the Netherlands, Portugal, and Spain, many countries show mixed trends. A few cases, such as Greece and Luxembourg, have even experienced a decrease in what the OECD refers to as temporary employment. States, markets, and families can be sources of, as well as buffers against, precariousness. For example, in 2000, the gap in poverty rates between children living in two-parent families and those living in single-mother households was 10.6 per cent in Sweden, but 26.7 per cent in Germany and an astonishing 34.7 per cent in the United States. In Sweden, the relatively low poverty rate for unemployed single parents demonstrates the ability of the welfare state to protect against precariousness in labour markets and family life. Indeed, high divorce rates in Sweden are related to the lesser financial penalty that women face for marital disruption, rather than a sign of precariousness (Clement et al. 2009). One strong international demographic pattern is the overrepresentation of younger and less educated workers. Workers aged 15–24 years are three times as likely as older workers to hold a temporary job, suggesting that many students hold these jobs. Workers who have not completed upper secondary schooling have a 60-per-cent higher rate of temporary employment than more educated workers, which indicates long-term traps in precarious work (OECD 2002).

Ethnic background disrupts the association between education level and precariousness, but not in a progressive way. Rather, immigrants are confined to precarious jobs despite their education level. Badets and Howatson-Leo (1999) find that recent immigrants in Canada are over-represented in precarious work. Although recent immigrants speak one of the two official languages and are highly educated, they are more likely to be employed in precarious work and are stuck in these jobs for longer periods of time compared to non-immigrants. Zeytinoglu and Muteshi (2000) note that visible-minority women are disproportionately represented in precarious jobs. Hence the interaction of race, gender, and class accentuates the segregation of certain groups of people—women of colour, for instance—into unstable and less well-paid employment.

Conclusion

We have argued in this paper that the new economy can best be understood through processes of post-industrialism, new technologies, the knowledge economy/society, and precarious employment. We have approached these processes as parts of a conceptual vocabulary to understand the new economy, rather than self-explanatory facts. We have also drawn on critical social-science concepts such as class, gender, and heritage, and used cases from different sectors and countries to inform and widen our perspective. As such, the puzzle of the new economy is the puzzle of a co-articulation of regimes of social inequalities with technological changes, population dynamics, and macroeconomic policies. Post-industrial changes have challenged the "old" division of labour between capitalists, managers, and workers, as well as the gendered composition/organization of the workforce and households. At the same time, technological developments, neoliberal policies, welfare-state cutbacks and insufficiencies, and the decline of stable full-time jobs affect labour markets, the sectors people work in, the way people work, conditions of work, and the quality of lives. These developments involve power relations between employers and employees, men and women, native-born and immigrants, governments and citizens.

Moreover, we have demonstrated that the processes of the new economy are related to each other contingently, rather than deterministically. For example, post-industrial jobs do not have to be precarious, but presently, where a neoliberal ideology of competitiveness is dominant and where the power of organized labour (unions) is comparatively weak in general and service-sector unions are the weakest in particular, many post-industrial jobs become precarious. Similarly, precarious employment is a gendered phenomenon because patriarchal households and labour-market relations distribute these jobs unevenly to members of social groups who either desperately need jobs or have to reconcile their work with their family obligations, especially child and elder care.

Finally, it is clear that there is no linear path for the new economy or its processes. Not dissimilar to the "old economy," there are varieties of work and labour markets in the new economy. At stake is whether these varieties are friendly to the needs and rights of workers over the course of their lives. The new economy is not something uniformly invented and executed by the capitalist class. The new economy, especially the ICT-led growth under neoliberalism, could well be understood as part of a new capital-accumulation strategy. However, the forms that this accumulation takes are contingent upon the relative power and organizing capacity of people and the political representation of socio-economic interests in the state.

Discussion Questions

1. What changes initiated the shift from the "old" to the "new" economy? What processes are involved in characterizing the "new" economy?

2. Why is it useful to distinguish between "precarious" and "non-standard" employment in studying work in the new economy?

3. How has work in the new economy transformed gender roles?

4. Post-industrialism should be defined as the transition to a service economy. True or false? Explain.

5. What are the changes that post-industrialism has imposed on the social composition of workers?

6. What are the old and the new social risks? How are the new social risks related to post-industrialism?

7. Is self-employment precarious?

Notes

1 Authors are listed alphabetically to reflect equal contribution.
2 We prefer the notion of heritage to that of race/ethnicity, in the sense that it is broader and encompasses a variety of issues including language, cultural traditions, and citizenship status not necessarily captured by the notion of race/ethnicity.

References

Acker, J. 2006. "Inequality Regimes: Gender, Class and Race in Organizations." *Gender and Society* 20 (4): 441–64.

Armstrong, P. 1984. *Labour Pains: Women's Work in Crisis*. Toronto: Women's Educational Press.

Autor, D., F. Levy, and R. Murnane. 2002. "Upstairs, Downstairs: Computers and Skills on Two Floors of a Large Bank." *Industrial and Labor Relations Review* 55 (3): 432–47.

Badets, J., and L. Howatson-Leo. 1999. "Recent Immigrants in the Workforce." *Canadian Social Trends*. Catalogue No. 11-008. Statistics Canada.

Bell, D. 1973. *The Coming of Post-Industrial Society: A Venture in Social Forecasting*. New York: Basic Books.

Ben, E.R. 2007. "Defining Expertise in Software Development While Doing Gender." *Gender, Work and Organization* 14 (4): 312–32.

Benner, C. 2002. *Work in the New Economy*. Oxford: Blackwell.

Bonoli, G. 2006. "New Social Risks and the Politics of Post-industrial Social Policies." In K. Armingeon and G. Bonoli (eds.), *The Politics of Post-Industrial Welfare States: Adapting Post-War Social Policies to New Social Risks*. New York: Routledge. 3–26.

Borghans L., and B. ter Weel. 2005. "Computer Adoption and Diffusion at the Bottom of the U.S. Labor Market: Disentangling the Effects of Skills and Wages on Computer Use." <http://www.roa.unimaas.nl/cv/borghans/pdfp/bottom.pdf>

Brint, S. 2001. "Professionals and the Knowledge Economy: Rethinking the Theory of Postindustrial Society." *Current Sociology* 49 (4): 101–32.

Brown, C., and B.A. Campbell. 2002. "The Impact of Technological Change on Work and Wages." *Industrial Relations* 41 (1): 1–26.

Carnoy, M. 2000. *Sustaining the New Economy*. Cambridge, MA: Harvard University Press.

Carroll, W.K. 2004. *Critical Strategies for Social Research*. Toronto: Canadian Scholars' Press.

Clement, W., and J. Myles. 1994. *Relations of Ruling: Class and Gender in Postindustrial Societies*. Montreal and Kingston: McGill-Queen's University Press.

Clement, W., and S. Prus. 2004. The Vocabulary of Gender and Work: Some Challenges and Insight from Comparative Research. Paper presented at the "Gender & Work: Knowledge Production in Practice" conference. York University: 1–2 October.

Clement, W., S. Mathieu, S. Prus., and E. Uckardesler. 2009. "Precarious Lives in the New Economy: Comparative Intersectional Analysis." In L. Vosko, M. MacDonald, and I. Campbell (eds.), *Gender and the Contours of Precarious Employment*. New York: Routledge.

Cranford, C.J., L. Vosko, and N. Zukewich. 2003. "The Gender of Precarious Employment in Canada." *Relations Industrielles / Industrial Relations* 58 (3): 454–82.

Crouch, C., D. Finegold, and M. Sako. 1999. *Are Skills the Answer?: The Political Economy of Skill Creation in Advanced Industrial Countries*. Oxford: Oxford University Press.

Cukier, W. 2007. *Diversity—The Competitive Edge: Implications for the ICT Labour Market*. Ottawa: Information and Communications Technology Council.

England, P. 1979. "Women and Occupational Prestige: A Case of Vacuous Sex Equality." *Signs: Journal of Women in Culture and Society* 5 (2): 252–65.

Eriksson-Zetterquist, U. 2007. "Gender and New Technologies." *Gender, Work and Organization* 14 (4): 305–11.

Esping-Andersen, G. 1993. "Post-industrial Class Structures: An Analytical Framework." In G. Esping-Andersen (ed.), *Changing Classes: Stratification and Mobility in Post-industrial Societies*. London: Sage. 7–31.

———. 1999. *Social Foundations of Post-industrial Economies*. Oxford: Oxford University Press.

Farrell, D. 2003. "The Real New Economy." *Harvard Business Review* 81 (10):104–12.

Fast, J., and M. Da Pont. 1997. "Changes in Women's Work Continuity." *Canadian Social Trends* 46 (Fall): 2–7.

Faulkner, W. 2001. "The Technology Question in Feminism: A View from Feminist Technology Studies." *Women's Studies International Forum* 24 (1): 79–95.

Florida, R. 2002. *The Rise of the Creative Class: And How It's Transforming Work, Leisure, Community and Everyday Life*. New York: Basic Books.

Frenkel, S., M. Korczynski, K.A. Shire, and M. Tam. 1999. *On the Front Line: Organization of Work in the Information Economy*. Ithaca, NY: Cornell University Press.

Fudge, J., and R. Owens. 2006. "Precarious Work, Women, and the New Economy: The Challenge To Legal Norms." In J. Fudge and R. Owens (eds.), *Precarious Work, Women, and the New Economy: The Challenge to Legal Norms*. Oxford: Hart Publishing. 3–27.

Greenbaum, J. 2004. *Windows on the Workplace: Technology, Jobs, and the Organization of Office Work*. New York: Monthly Review Press.

Head, S. 2003. *The New Ruthless Economy: Work and Power in the Digital Age*. Oxford: Oxford University Press.

Leschke, J. 2008. *Unemployment Insurance and Non-Standard Employment*. Wiesbaden: Verlag für Sozialwissenschaften.

ILO. 1993. "Resolution Concerning the International Classification of Status in Employment Adopted by the Fifteenth International Conference of Labour Statisticians." Geneva: International Labour Office.

———. 2001. *World Employment Report*. Geneva: International Labour Office.

———. 2002. *Learning and Training for Work in the Knowledge Society*, Report IV(1). Geneva: International Labour Office.

Jorgenson, D.W., M.S. Ho, and K.J. Stiroh. 2004. "Will the US Productivity Resurgence Continue?" *Current Issues in Economics and Finance* 10 (13): 1–7.

McCall, L. 2001. *Complex Inequality: Gender, Class and Race in the New Economy*. London: Routledge.

O'Dorchani, S. 2008. "Pay Inequality in 25 European Countries." Working Paper No: 08-06.RS. Département d'Economie appliquée (DULBEA), Université Libre de Bruxelles.

OECD. 2000. *Employment Outlook*. Paris: Organisation for Economic Co-operation and Development.

———. 2002. *Employment Outlook*. Paris: Organisation for Economic Co-operation and Development.

Polivka, A., and T. Nardone. 1989. "On the Definition of 'Contingent Work.'" *Monthly Labor Review* (December): 9–14.

Powell, W., and K. Snelmann. 2004. "The Knowledge Economy." *Annual Review of Sociology* 30: 199–220.

Rodgers, G., and J. Rodgers. 1989. *Precarious Jobs in Labour Market Regulation: The Growth of Atypical Employment in Western Europe*. Brussels: Free University of Brussels.

Rogers, J.K. 2000. *Temps: The Many Faces of the Changing Workplace*. Ithaca, NY: Cornell University Press.

Statistics Canada. 1998. *Canadian Social Trends* 48 (Spring).

Taylor-Gooby, P. 2004. *New Risks, New Welfare: The Transformation of the European Welfare State*. New York: Oxford University Press.

Tremblay, D.-G. 2003. "New Ways of Working and New Types of Work: What Developments Lie Ahead?" Research Note no 2003–3A. <http://www.teluq.uquebec.ca/chaireecosavoir/pdf/NRC03-03A.pdf>.

Webster, J. 2004. "Digitizing Inequality: The Cul-de-sac of Women's Work in European Services." *New Technology, Work and Employment* 19 (3): 160–76.

Zeytinoglu, I.U., and J.K. Muteshi. 1999. "Gender, Race and Class Dimensions of Nonstandard Work." *Relations Industrielles / Industrial Relations* 55 (1): 133–67.

4. Global Restructuring of Value Chains and Class Issues[1]

URSULA HUWS AND SIMONE DAHLMANN

We are currently witnessing a global restructuring of work on a historically unprecedented scale, affecting especially, but not exclusively, those jobs that involve the processing of information that can be digitized and transmitted over telecommunications links. The combination of digitization (information technology) and telecommunications (communications technology), often referred to as Information and Communications Technologies (ICTs), brings about changes in the skill requirements of jobs and makes it possible for work to be relocated to any point where there is a ready supply of workers with the appropriate skills and suitable infrastructure, thus opening up vast new potential for restructuring work processes and shifting jobs around the globe. This brings about changes in *who* does *what* work, *when*, *where*, and *how*. In doing so, it challenges some of the most fundamental features of workers' occupational identities, which have in the past been strongly shaped by such factors as what skills are required to do the job, where the job is located, who the employer is, and what relationships these jobs have to those of co-workers or customers. In this chapter we examine how global restructuring is affecting work and what these changes mean for workers' occupational identities, class positions, and class consciousness.

The Importance of Occupational Identities

Whether they derive from a Marxist or a Weberian perspective, or from the more pragmatic approach adopted by national statistical offices, all systems of class categorization use the occupational identity of the worker as the basic marker of class position. This approach raises several problems. One of the most serious of these is that statistics related to employment use the individual worker as the basic unit of analysis, because people enter the labour market as individuals and are recorded as such. However in many other statistics, such as those relating to consumption or social need, the unit at which data are collected is the household. This creates difficulties in assigning a class position to individuals who live in households in which cohabiting adults have occupations that place them in different class positions. The tradition of assigning women to the class positions of their husbands or fathers has, as a result, often had the effect of rendering women's class identities as workers invisible (Huws 2003: 157ff). Although the market-research industry continues to develop new methods for classifying the population according to a range of different variables, including their consumption patterns, place of residence, education, etc., sociology has so far failed to come up with an alternative basis for classification to that of the occupation (the name normally given in any given society to the job that a person does). Even Pierre Bourdieu, who has probably gone further than anyone else toward the development of a complex and nuanced theory of class that takes into account both structure and agency and both "objective" and "subjective" dimensions, insists ultimately on the importance of a classification that is fundamentally rooted in occupational identity:

> A group's presence or absence in the official classification depends on its capacity to get itself recognized, to get itself noticed and admitted, and so to win a place in the social order. It thus escapes from the shadowy existence of the nameless crafts of which Emile Benveniste speaks: business in antiquity and the Middle Ages, or illegitimate activities, such as those of the modern healer (formerly called an "empiric"), bone-setter or prostitute. The fate of groups is bound up with the words that designate them: the power to impose recognition depends on the capacity to mobilize around a name, "proletariat," "work-

ing class," "cadres," etc., to appropriate a common name and
to commune in a proper name, and so to mobilize the union
that makes them strong, around the unifying power of a word.
(Bourdieu 1984: 482)

An occupational identity—and how it is classified—is therefore of
much more than academic or bureaucratic importance. It has the double power both of assigning an individual to his or her "place" in society
("objective class position") and of enabling that individual to develop
a sense of fellow-feeling and identification with others who share some
of the same features ("class consciousness"), which can in turn form
the basis for developing forms of organization through which the common interests of the group can be represented. Occupational identities have historically constituted the building blocks from which class
identities have been built. However, they have also and often simultaneously created divisions within broader classes. Efforts by specific occupational groups to protect the interests of their members, for instance in
order to restrict access to "craft secrets" or qualifications, have not only
often led to the pursuit of narrow sectional interests to the detriment of
broader class interests, but have also been associated with the exclusion
of women or people of particular racial origins from privileged positions
in the workforce.

This contradiction draws attention to the ways in which occupational
identities must be seen as both socially constructed and socially contested. The development of a coherent occupational identity is not a one-
off process but part of a continuing struggle by a group (which is itself
being constantly renewed over time with a new and possibly demographically changing membership) to maintain its position in relation to its
employers on the one hand, and other groups of workers on the other.
(The group may also be involved in other negotiations, e.g., with state or
training authorities over control of qualification systems by which entry
to the group is regulated.) In these processes, the group's formal and
informal rules, its status, and its bargaining power are in a continuous
process of being challenged, adapted, and reproduced. Challenges to the
group's status quo do not arise merely as a result of shifts in the overall
power relationships between it and other social groups, but also because
of technological changes that enable changes in labour processes, thus
calling into question the very nature of the skills and qualifications on
which the occupational identity is based.

Impact of the Introduction of ICTs on Skills and Occupational Identities

The last quarter-century has seen a historically unprecedented transformation of traditional occupational identities in the wake of the introduction of information and communications technologies (ICTs). Several key stages can be identified in this restructuring. The first of these was computerization, which started after World War II with the extension of mainframe computers into banks, universities, process-controlled manufacturing industries, and government bodies and gave birth to some entirely new occupations that were difficult to fit into existing occupational categories. As Ensmenger (2003) puts it:

> Despite their obvious importance to the history of information technology, computer programmers represent a perplexing problem for the historian. Neither labourers nor professionals, they defy traditional occupational categorizations. The ranks of the elite programmers included both high-school dropouts and ex-PhD. physicists. Originally envisioned as little more than glorified clerical workers, they quickly assumed a position of power within the organization vastly disproportionate to their official organizational role. Defined by their mastery of the highest of high technology, they were often derided for their adherence to artisanal practices. (154)

Ensmenger goes on to describe the development of splits between clerical and craft aspects of computer-programming work during the 1950s and further shifts in occupational identities during the 1960s, in particular the development of a perception of programmers as "technicians" who had to be "managed." By the 1970s when one of the present authors (Ursula Huws) began researching this topic in the UK, although there were considerable variations by sector, several distinct groups had emerged. At the bottom of the hierarchy were "key punch operators," considered to be a lowly group of clerical workers and entirely female. Many of them subsequently lost their jobs when the inputting of data to computers by punching holes in cards was replaced by data entry using alphanumeric keyboards. Above them in the hierarchy were "computer operators," who carried out maintenance on the computers. They generally worked round-the-clock shifts, wore overalls, joined the same trade unions as skilled craft workers, and were overwhelmingly male. Also in an intermediate position in the hierarchy, and with a higher social status (because they were "white collar"), but often with lower earnings than the computer operators, were ordinary "computer programmers" whose work ranged from the very routine—carrying out simple coding, troubleshooting existing programs or adapting them to new purposes—to more "creative" systems analysis and contributing to the development of new programs. This group included both men and women and was recruited by a variety of means, including, in the UK, advertisements on the London Underground with IQ test questions designed to convince even arts graduates that they might have an aptitude for the "technical" requirements of a computing occupation. Finally, at the top of the hierarchy were two quite distinct groups, each overwhelmingly male: high-flying computer scientists who were breaking new ground in the development of new computer processes and applications; and senior IT managers. Of these, the former would have been defined as "professional" and the latter as "managerial" according to the official occupational classification system. The relatively small workforce directly concerned with the development and operation of mainframe computers, therefore, already encompassed workers falling into five of the main occupational categories: clerical, craft, technical, professional, and managerial.

With hindsight, this mainframe-related period of development can be seen as very transient, though it has undoubtedly left a long-lasting legacy in structuring broader divisions of labour and the qualification systems associated with them. Further developments in the history of the introduction of ICTs were to bring much more far-reaching changes. The next phase can be traced back to the mid- to late 1970s, when the cost of computing was drastically reduced through the introduction of the silicon chip, and computers became smaller and more ubiquitous. No longer just impacting a small group of specialist workers, computerization spread to a range of functions that had previously been carried out by workers in quite different occupational groups. Prime examples of this included the substitution of word processing for typing on a traditional manual or electric typewriter, and the introduction of computerized typesetting into the printing industry. The former affected a female workforce defined as "clerical," the latter a male workforce defined as "craft" (or, in some designations, "skilled manual") workers. The subjective shock of what was perceived by this latter group not only as deskilling but as threatening to their traditional gender identities was described by Cockburn (1983). In the early 1980s, the introduction of the IBM Personal Computer and the adoption of increasingly standardized Microsoft software helped to accelerate a process by which a high proportion of all workers found their traditional tools replaced by a screen and keyboard linked to a processing unit. Studies carried out at the time (summarized in Huws 1982) found that the main productivity advantages achieved when computers were first introduced stemmed not from the computerization *per se* but from the rationalization and standardization that preceded it. Computerization depended crucially on a prior detailed analysis of labour processes, the codification of the workers' tacit knowledge, and the development of standardized, replicable processes to replace those that had previously relied on individual "craft" or "judgement" (Braverman 1974: 307ff).

The effects of computerization (IT) were dramatically multiplied when added to the potentialities of communications technologies (ICTs). Telecommunications networks that over time became not only cheaper but also capable of carrying larger volumes of digitized data or voice traffic made it possible to link individual computers interactively into broader networks. During the course of the 1980s, as protocols were standardized and software became increasingly generic, these networks became more interoperable. During the 1990s, the introduction of the Internet brought about a new degree of seamlessness, creating an enabling infrastructure for another new phase in the distribution of work involving the processing of digitized information. The use of computers and the Internet spread so inexorably across occupational structures that by 2003, 55.5 per cent of all those employed in the United States used a computer at work and 41.7 per cent used the Internet at work (Bureau of Labor Statistics 2005). Women were more likely both to be using computers at work (at 61.8 per cent, compared with 49.9 per cent of men) and to be using the Internet at work (at 45.1 per cent, compared with 38.7 per cent of men). As in other developed countries, although it was most concentrated among managers, professionals, and other office-based occupations, this usage of ICTs overflowed traditional occupational boundaries, with significant numbers of blue-collar workers also using them.

> Managers and professionals were most likely to use a computer and the Internet; 79.6 percent reported that they used a computer at work and 67.1 percent used the Internet. Sales and office occupations also had high rates of computer and Internet use—over two-thirds reported using a computer at work and nearly half said they used the Internet. In contrast, computer- and Internet-use rates were lower for service workers (27.5 and 15.9 percent, respectively), for natural resources, construction, and maintenance workers (26.4 and 16.6 percent, respectively), and for production, transportation, and material moving workers (26.0 and 13.9 percent, respectively). (Bureau of Labor Statistics 2005)

Cumulatively, this represents an enormous redrawing of job descriptions for the majority of the workforce over the last quarter of a century.

The Introduction of ICTs, the Modularization of Work, and the Restructuring of Global Value Chains

As already noted, the codification of tacit knowledge and the standardization of work processes is an important precondition for computerization. The more standardized each unit of work is, the more easily it can be monitored by results and managed remotely, and the easier it is to fragment what used to form part of a single unified work process into separate modules that can be reconfigured in a variety of different ways. Such reconfiguration may take many different forms, ranging from the reskilling of an existing workforce remaining on the same site and working for the same employer, to offshore outsourcing to another continent (Huws 2006). Table 4.1 summarizes some of these restructuring options, organized in relation to two dimensions: whether or not a *legal* (or contractual) separation is introduced (whether the work is outsourced by the original employer) and whether or not a *spatial* separation is introduced (whether the work is relocated to another site).

As work processes are broken up into separate components and these components are outsourced and relocated, we can say that the organization's value chain becomes more elaborate. A value chain can be defined as the sum total of the processes that go into producing a final product or service. Each link in the chain receives inputs in the form of raw materials, data or components from lower down the chain, adds value to them by processing them in some way, and then passes them up as outputs to another unit with a higher position in the chain (Huws 2007). An alternative way to look at the increasingly complex interrelationships between units is to visualize them as networks (Castells 1996).

Typically this restructuring is experienced by workers as a series of incremental steps. Standardization of processes may be followed by market testing or benchmarking against the service offered by external suppliers, which may in turn lead to a partial outsourcing to a local supplier, which may then lead to larger-scale outsourcing to a supplier in another part of the world. However, there is nothing inevitable about such a sequence. It might also be the case, for instance, that a small-scale experimental outsourcing arrangement with a foreign supplier, if it is viewed as successful, might lead to that foreign company being bought up and becoming integrated into a restructured parent organization. This parent organisation might also have a highly developed international division of labour of its own, with employees in several different countries linked together in complex configurations.

Table 4.1   Different Forms of Work Restructuring

| | | LEGAL DIMENSION | |
		In-house	Outsourced
SPATIAL DIMENSION	On the original premises	Reskilling New working practices Separate cost centre Market-testing Benchmarking	Use of temporary agency staff 'Body shopping' Spin-off company External supplier working on premises Transfer of personnel to outsourcer
	On a remote site	Remote back office Nomadic workers Homeworkers Workers in another branch of same company Own workers working on customer's premises	Individual freelancers / consultants Outsourced: · to dependent company · to SME · to global supplier · to strategic partner · via intermediary

Once processes have been successfully modularized, they can be reconfigured rapidly in different ways, for instance either by centralizing a range of different functions on a single site or decentralizing them to many different sites around the globe (Flecker and Kirschenhofer 2002). Modularization can thus provide the basis either for aggregation or disaggregation. Whatever form it takes, however, because it involves a further fragmentation of labour processes, it can be regarded as contributing to an elaboration of the division of labour and hence a lengthening of value chains. A multiplication of options for employers is paralleled by the increasing replaceability of workers.

Generally speaking, the greater the degree of spatial and/or legal separation from the original site, the longer the value chain can be said to be. Value chains take a number of different forms, many of which are typical of particular industrial sectors (Gereffi, Humphrey and Sturgeon 2005). However, there currently appear to be some general trends that characterize value chains in information services—those business functions that are being most dramatically transformed through the introduction of ICTs. On the one hand, these value chains appear to be becoming longer and more elaborated, with a growing number of steps and an increasing role for intermediaries in smoothing over these steps (Huws and Flecker 2004). However, this is also linked to an increasing centralization of control and to requirements for "seamlessness" in the management of these chains (Gurstein 2007). Greater spatial dispersion of work may co-exist with greater geographical centralization of control. By a similar paradox, even when contractual dispersion is increased, and several different levels of subcontracting lie between the workers at the bottom of the chain and the managers at the top, it might still be the case that the wording of these contracts spells out what they have to do so exactly that the room for autonomy is less than in situations where the work is carried out in-house. Modularization must, however, be viewed as more than just a precondition for the restructuring of value chains. It is also an active driver of further restructuring. Large-scale outsourcing of increasingly standardized functions has enabled the emergence of new and exponentially growing, global outsourcing companies that can achieve considerable economies of scale by carrying out these functions *en masse* (Flecker 2007). These companies have evolved sophisticated internal divisions of labour, commonly known as "global sourcing," taking advantage of a worldwide workforce to put together virtual teams for specific contracts that mix and match particular skills to achieve extremely competitive prices for their customers (Ramioul, Huws and Kirschenhofer 2005). They also need to respond to very large fluctuations in the demand for work. Bombarded by aggressive advertising from these companies, their customers find it increasingly difficult to justify the retention of in-house departments providing bespoke services at a cost that is inevitably higher than those on offer from these global suppliers. The customers are then faced with the alternative of outsourcing to these suppliers or finding ways to cut the costs of their internal services, for instance by relocating to a cheaper site, by using migrant workers or by introducing new working practices to ratchet up the productivity of their existing workforce. Standardization and modularization can thus be seen as driving a "snowball effect" whereby global sourcing acts as an accelerator of further global sourcing (Ramioul and Huws [forthcoming]).

What is clear is that in this enormous global reshuffling of work, upheavals do not take place only at the level of companies or regions. They also take place in the labour processes of the individual workers whose outputs form the building blocks of these value chains. As this occurs, occupational identities, which have been shaped over many years—in some cases centuries—by regional cultures, national institutions, the results of past tussles between workers and management, and the specific nature of the ethnic and gender division of labour in the locality, have been transformed almost beyond recognition. Whether this transformation represents a move upwards or downwards in the local occupational hierarchy will vary depending on these different variables. Likewise, its implications for workers' abilities to "place" themselves in relation to each other and maintain or develop forms of collective identification and allegiance will also vary.

In the rest of this paper, we draw on recent empirical work to try to identify, first, what overall occupational changes have taken place in developed economies and what this might mean in terms of the "objective class position" of the information-processing workers whose labour lies at the heart of the current restructuring maelstrom, and second, what this means for their subjective perceptions of the change that has taken place in their occupational identities.

Changes in "Objective Class Position"? The Increasing Unclassifiability of Classifying Occupations

This section of the paper draws on a research exercise that was carried out as part of the STILE project. The starting point for the research was a frustrated realization, arrived at in previous research projects, that the existing labour-market statistics were inadequate for measuring occupational changes in the development of what might be called the "e-economy"—the jobs most affected by the introduction of ICTs. Attempts to plot the growth in, for instance, call-centre work or work involving website design were impossible because specific occupational categories did not seem to exist for them (or, when they did exist, did not appear to be used[2]). Under which categories were they concealed? The only way to find out seemed to be to reconstruct the process by which the statistics were created. We found some typical job descriptions of such workers and then, having anonymized them, gave them to experienced coders in national statistical offices in four EU member states (Hungary, Ireland, the Netherlands, and the UK) in order to see how they would be coded using the International Standard Classification of Occupations (ISCO)[3] developed by the International Labour Organisation (ILO).

This exercise was based in a recognition that several trends have converged to render obsolescent many of the stable occupational identities which, in the past, young people entered when they left school or college and then maintained for a whole working lifetime. In some cases, the death of the old occupational identity was brought about directly by the obsolescence of old technologies. In other cases, boundaries between older occupational identities became blurred in reaction to increasing demands from employers for multiskilling, and to the rapid speed of technological change that created continuous demands for new skills while simultaneously bringing about convergence between old ones. The use of a computer, generally using standard software, has become so generic a feature of so many professional, managerial, technical, and clerical jobs that it has now become increasingly difficult to draw a clear boundary between those features of the job that are content- or employer-specific and those that require a general ability to use ICTs effectively. It might be argued that generic ICT skills are now as essential as basic literacy and numeracy and should therefore be discounted. In practice, however, it is clear that there are some jobs in which ICTs actually form the content itself, or for which knowledge of a particular technology (e.g., a specialist software package) is the essential requirement. There will, therefore, probably remain an uneasy overlap between jobs that are defined by their use of ICTs and those that, although involving extensive use of it, continue to be defined in relation to some other function. This raises fundamental questions in the classification of occupations: should an occupation be defined in relation to the qualifications required to do it? (e.g., a doctor or an accountant); to the tools used to carry it out? (e.g., a lathe operator or a forklift-truck driver); to the level of seniority of the incumbent? (e.g., a supervisor or a managing director); to the sector in which the work is carried out? (e.g., an insurance salesperson or a civil servant); or to some combination of these? (as frequently happens in practice).

The exercise was intended to address some specific problems: a very rapid obsolescence of a range of traditional occupational groups defined in relation to tools and technologies that have now been replaced by ICTs; the increasing need for multilingual skills and communications skills in occupations involving cross-border communication in a global economy, skills that rarely figure in traditional occupational descriptions; the increasing requirement for generic skills related to the use of ICTs, which themselves become obsolete very quickly; the blurring of boundaries between occupations because of increasing requirements for multi-tasking; the effects of "de-layering," i.e., blurring the distinctions between different levels of seniority (e.g., between "managers," "supervisors," and "team leaders"); and the effects of outsourcing from one sector to another, which means, for instance, that workers formerly defined as "civil servants" may have become transformed into specialists within a business outsourcing company.

In order to carry out this exercise, real-life examples were sought of occupations that illustrated some of these problems. These came from a number of sources, including business directories, job advertisements, and cases from past surveys carried out by the research team (including cases known to have been involved in offshore outsourcing). Many of the job descriptions were drawn from databases held by the Irish national government's training body, FÁS, (Foras Áiseanna Soathair) and its planning body, Forfás.[4] These were all carefully anonymized before being circulated and used. The National Statistical Offices in Ireland, Hungary, the Netherlands, and the UK agreed not only to participate in the coding experiment but also to discuss with the team the normal coding practices in each institution so that the material could be provided in the form that most closely mirrored the information they typically handled. These practices turned out to be extremely diverse, however, so it was not possible to find a single form that matched all their normal criteria.

These variations, and the fact that in many cases in the real world, coders would have been able to question respondents more deeply as an aid to coding, meant that the exercise cannot be regarded as strictly representative of the everyday reality of the construction of national statistics. As far as we are aware, this is the first exercise of its kind, so it should be regarded more as a pilot experiment than as a definitive study. It represents something of a step into the dark, and we must begin by acknowledging the limitations of the methodology. Some of these, perhaps, can offer lessons for the design of further studies in this area, using larger samples and controlling for some of the unexpected problems that we encountered.

First, the descriptions used as the raw material for this exercise were not as complete as those normally found at a national level in most countries and reflected the Irish provenance of many, but not all, of the cases. It was sometimes difficult to translate the terminology used to describe enterprises and occupations from one language to another. Each local economy and labour market also had unique features that could make it difficult to transpose definitions that were developed elsewhere. Despite some convergence, much of it due to the development of a global information economy, it is clear that there remain strong differences across countries in the ways in which the economy is organized and occupational identities constructed. It is inevitable that coders' experience and expectations will reflect this diversity, and it is in some ways unfair to expect them to code material that is so different from what they encounter in their everyday work. Nevertheless, with the spread of globalization, it is to be expected that multinational companies will be increasingly likely to spread their normal practices (and terminology) across national borders and that, especially in jobs involving intensive use of ICTs, job descriptions will have more in common in the future.

Second, it was recognized that variations in the results of the coding exercise would not necessarily shed light on particular classification problems. A number of possible causes for coding variations could exist, including the following: variations in practice by an individual coder; variations between different coders within a team, perhaps reflecting differences in training, background, experience, seniority, or just individual preference; variations between different coding teams, perhaps reflecting explicit or tacit institutional rules, perhaps simply the preferences or experience of the manager or trainer, or the priorities of different government departments; variations between countries resulting from different national traditions, qualification systems, and coding schemes; variations between countries resulting from the effect of translation of international terminology into the national language(s); variations between countries resulting from the ways in which national codes are converted into international ones; and variations resulting from inherent ambiguities in the international classification system itself.

Despite these reservations, the results do seem to tell us something quite dramatic about a major mismatch between the contingent realities of job requirements in the global "new economy" and the stable universe imagined by those who design the classification scheme, rooted, as still seems to be the case, in a view of the world in which continuity is the norm and change the exception.

The results were astonishing in their diversity. The ISCO classification scheme is a hierarchical one, in which the first digit (numbers 1–9) represents one of the major occupational categories (managerial, professional, clerical, etc.) into which the workforce is divided, and each subsequent digit adds an extra level of detail. Of the 157 job descriptions the coders were presented with, only forty (25.5%) were even given the same single (first) digit by coders in each of the four participating countries. At a two-digit level, this number fell to 23 (representing only 14% of cases) with a further fall to 18 cases (11.6%) at three digits. In some cases, each of the four national teams assigned a different code, and there were many cases where there was agreement between only two out of four. Table 4.2 illustrates some of these cases; a key to the ISCO codes assigned in this table is given in Table 4.3. A detailed analysis of these divergences (Huws and Van der Hallen 2004) failed to find any consistent patterns in these codings other than the fact that coders showed a strong tendency when confronted with a "new" occupation to avoid using newer coding categories in favour of the nearest match they could find to a traditional occupational category. For instance, a telesales agent in a call centre was likely to be viewed, first and foremost, as a salesperson rather than a call-centre worker, although this was not applied consistently, as the examples of the "call centre agent–travel sales" and "online marketing account manager" in Table 4.2 demonstrate. These divergences in coding (which we do not discuss further here for reasons of space) make it very difficult to assess whether class shifts have been taking place in the developed economies of the world as a result of the general decline in blue-collar occupations and the rise in white-collar ones. There is, in general, little agreement about the class position of office workers. Do they form a "white-collar proletariat"? Are they part of what Marxists term the "petit bourgeoisie"? Do they form part of a new technical-professional middle class with ambiguous allegiances? Or is the category so large that it needs to be subdivided to encompass several different identities (Huws 2003)?

Table 4.2   Coding of Selected Job Descriptions in Four European Countries

JOB TITLE	JOB DESCRIPTION	UK	ISCO CODE IE	HUN	NED
International product manager	I work for an international software company. My job is to develop, define and localize the products, liaising with developers and carrying out market research on competitors. I also have to support the sales cycle with literature, support material and training. I travel regularly to company HQ in the US.	123	123	341	241
Call centre agent–travel sales	I work in a call centre handling calls from US members regarding timeshare properties. I provide information on travel requirements and sell them travel and insurance products, working to meet sales targets.	911	911	341	422
Team leader in order management department	I'm team leader in a shared services centre for a pharmaceutical company. I check on ordering problems, identifying possible risks and bottlenecks and initiating corrective action, communicating with other teams and management. I support the sales and sales support agents on operational issues and advice on process improvement initiatives. The order management agents report to me. I use SAP, QMS VAntive and Excel in my work.	413	419	341	122
Customer relations team leader	I head up the "win back" team for the call centre of a financial services company. I coach and motivate a team of agents trying to persuade customers to return to our service.	422	419	123	122
Team leader in sales call centre	As a team leader I supervise the shift arrangements for the team, and monitor attendance, holidays etc. We work in a sales call centre. I have to ensure my team meets targets and goals. I handle time-consuming customer contacts, and coach and develop team members as well as arranging necessary training with the training manager.	911	419	343	122
Contact centre team leader	As a team leader in a contact centre I carry out monitoring of calls to assess quality levels and use software to predict call loads and arrange staffing levels. I train new recruits and existing staff. I work to maintain motivation of the agents and to improve customer satisfaction. The centre handles holiday reservations.	422	419	343	122
Online marketing account manager	I am responsible for selling online marketing services to business customers in Ireland, the UK and the US. The services include search engine optimization, banner advertising, email marketing and consultancy services on design and revenue generation options.	123	123	241	522
Template designer	I design templates for online training courses that can include text, pictures, audio and video. The templates are used by programmers and content editors to prepare the completed courses.	213	347	312	235
Documentation scanning administrator	I scan documents received by post onto a computer system. I quality check the documents to ensure accuracy and legibility. I also retrieve documents from the system and print them out to order. I keep records of tasks completed each day.	915	414	411	419
Mac operator	I'm a Mac operator and I use Illustrator, Artpro and Photoshop to prepare artwork for reproduction via litho, gravure and flex services. The work involves making editorial revisions and keeping records of client contacts and order changes.	347	734	245	734
Supply chain analyst	As a supply chain analyst I maintain and control the master production schedule according to the business plan using a computerized system. I track actual build against planned build and highlight the supply and demand issues which result. I work to overcome any problems with marketing, purchasing and operations. I analyse inventory to make projections on obsolescence and future supply plans.	341	122	341	311
Database manager	I manage a computer database to record customer details and purchases. The database produces monthly sales reports and stock analysis.	312	123	312	419
Spam manager	I work for an ISP tracking down and removing subscribers who are spamming. This involves tracing senders, checking whether their return address has been used illegally, blocking email addresses and advising end-users on how to avoid spam.	123	213	343	312

Source: Huws and Van der Hallen 2004: 175–95.

Table 4.3 Key to ISCO Codes

LEGISLATORS, SENIOR OFFICIALS AND MANAGERS

122 = 'production and operations department managers'

123 = 'other departmental managers'

PROFESSIONALS

213 = 'computing professionals'

235 = 'other teaching professionals'

241 = 'finance and sales associate professionals'

245 = 'writers and creative or performing artists'

TECHNICIANS AND ASSOCIATE PROFESSIONALS

311 = 'physical and engineering science technicians'

312 = 'computer associate professionals'

341 = 'finance and sales associate professionals'

347 = 'artistic, entertainment and sports associate professionals'

343 = 'administrative associate professionals'

CLERKS

411 = 'secretaries and keyboard-operating clerks'

413 = 'material recording and transport clerks'

414 = 'library, mail and related clerks'

419 = 'other office clerks'

422 = 'client information clerks'

SERVICE WORKERS

522 = 'shop salespersons and demonstrators'

CRAFT AND RELATED TRADES WORKERS

734 = 'printing and related trade workers'

ELEMENTARY OCCUPATIONS

911 = 'street vendors and related workers'

915 = 'messengers, porters, doorkeepers and related workers'

Source: International Standard Classification of Occupations (ISCO), International Labour Organisation, 2004.

Most systems of classification (be they Marxist, Weberian, or bureaucratic) would agree at the minimum that managers and professionals (denoted in ISCO at a single-digit level by the numbers 1 and 2) belong to the upper and middle classes; and that agricultural workers, craft workers, assemblers, and "elementary occupations," (numbers 6–9) belong to the working class, with the main areas of ambiguity falling in the intervening numbers, 3–5 (technicians and associated professionals, clerical workers, and service and sales workers). The results of our research, unfortunately, shed little light on these questions, showing that some workers may be assigned occupational identities that cross even the basic demarcation lines of this tripartite division (for instance, the "team leader in sales call centre"—coded as 9, 4, 3, and 1—and the "Mac operator"—coded to 7, 3, and 2—in Table 4.2). However, our results do illustrate very graphically what a high proportion of the workforce now occupies the ambiguous intermediate terrain.

Figure 4.1 shows the breakdown of the UK workforce in 2006 according to these single-digit ISCO categories. Even if we accept that categories 1–2 and 6–9 have clear class allegiances (which our results suggest is by no means warranted), no less than 38 per cent of women and 37 per cent of men fall into the contested intermediate category, a result that is not untypical of developed Western economies. How do these workers themselves view their occupational identities? That is the question we focus on in the final section of this paper.

Figure 4.1   Breakdown of UK Workforce* by Occupation, 2006

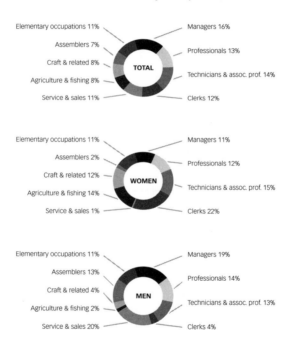

* "Workforce" is defined as all in employment.
Source: UK Labour Force data, January–March, 2006, analysis by Ursula Huws.

Changes in Class Consciousness? The Subjective Experience of Changing Occupational Identity

We now turn to how workers subjectively experience these changes, using three contrasting case studies as illustrations. The first of these, carried out within the scope of the Asian EMERGENCE[5] project, concerns skilled editorial workers in the UK whose jobs were transferred to India and who were faced with the choice of retraining or going freelance. The second, carried out within the scope of the WORKS[6] project, concerns IT workers in the public sector who were transferred, with their jobs, to private-sector companies as part of an outsourcing deal. The third, also carried out within the scope of the WORKS project, also involved public-sector workers, but this time they were clerical workers whose jobs involved dealing with the public. Under an e-government initiative, their tasks were transformed into call-centre jobs, managed under a public–private partnership. These cases demonstrate very clearly not only the changes in occupational identity experienced by workers when restructuring takes place but also the ways in which these are shaped by gender, by the traditional "place" of their work in the division of labour, and by the specific conditions pertaining in the local labour market. The quotations that follow are taken from transcripts of interviews carried out by one of the authors (Simone Dahlmann) in the scope of these projects.

The fieldwork for the first case[7] was carried out in 2003 in a British university town, at the headquarters of a well-established and prestigious publisher of academic books and journals. The editorial staff were mostly older women, with long experience in their jobs (the average job tenure was 20 years), who belonged to a generation that entered the publishing industry as graduates between the 1960s and 1980s. At that time, publishing was a well-respected field of work that was hard to enter, one of the few to offer intellectually satisfying work to highly qualified women. In addition to formal academic qualifications, these copy-editors and readers had undergone a three-year apprenticeship. According to ISCO, they should have been classified as "associate professionals." In the public perception (and their own) they would have been regarded as firmly ensconced in the professional middle class.

When it was announced that their work was going to be relocated to India, their first reaction was one of disbelief. As one employee commented, "It seemed so impossible, reading being done in India, I guess we always thought we were doing a privileged job that could not be done anywhere else, especially not by non-native speakers." While a few staff were kept on in quality-control roles, to check on the work being done in India, the majority were offered the choice of taking redundancy or retraining to do typesetting. Although greatly transformed by the introduction of computerization during the 1970s (Cockburn 1983), typesetting had a very different occupational identity, having evolved as a "craft" carried out by skilled male workers regarded as manual workers and generally considered to be part of the working class, albeit forming part of a "labour aristocracy" within it. In fact, the relationship between the stereotypes of the predominantly female copy editors (genteel, but relatively low paid) and those of the male typesetters (well-paid rough-and-ready tradespeople) in the 1970s could be regarded as a paradigmatic example of the contradictions between class and gender in the formation of occupational hierarchies. Not surprisingly, the majority of the copy-editors in our case study rejected the option of becoming typesetters: "In this area people are in their 40s and 50s, they have no IT skills and are used to reading. There was no appeal in retraining to work with computers." Instead, they chose to accept voluntary redundancy and enter the precarious field of freelance editing.

The change left them feeling shocked and betrayed, both by their management and by their trade union. However, they still felt a strong pride in their work and were concerned that the quality would drop when the work was offshored; and, interestingly, they still identified strongly with their employer's "brand": "I am worried about the future, quality, the company's reputation and what our customers think about us." It was clearly difficult to separate their sense of their own expertise and pride in their skills from a nationalistic identification with the English language and tradition. One respondent said of the Indian workers, "Being a graduate does not necessarily mean they're good at proof-reading. I know there still will be mistakes. I am English, that's why I don't get it wrong; my superiors don't want to see that." Interviews carried out in the Indian locations to which the work was transferred indicated that even though in principle the wage gap between the two countries should have eased the pressures on workers at the new sites, in fact the opposite had happened. The Indian workers were under considerable stress to meet tight deadlines and work to rigid standards. As a result, typical job tenure was only three years, compared with the more or less lifetime employment pattern back in the UK. The new sense of precariousness and replaceability experienced by the British workers had, it seemed, been exported along with the jobs (and even intensified). There was no evidence that the Indian workers had developed any identification with or loyalty to the "brand."

Our second case study, carried out in 2007 in the UK,[8] concerned IT professionals employed in local government whose jobs had been outsourced to large global IT service providers. Interviews were carried out in two cities, one in Wales and one in the Midlands. In the first case, the trade union had originally opposed the outsourcing, and there had been a strike that had favourably affected the terms under which the workers were transferred to their new employer (Company A). In the second case, the work had been outsourced three years earlier to another global IT company (Company B), which had subsequently lost the contract when it came up for renewal, the contract going instead to a British company that had offered a lower price (Company C). Of the workers who had been transferred in the original outsourcing deal, some were absorbed into Company B, some were recruited by Company C, and some took redundancy. Subsequently, Company C was bought up by a US-owned global company (Company D). Some of the workers interviewed in the second city had therefore had the experience, over a period of three years, of being employed by four different employers (the City Council, Company B, Company C, and Company D) while still doing essentially the same work.

These workers were predominantly male but included several women. Although from diverse backgrounds, most of them had made a conscious decision to work in the public sector, valuing its lack of commercialism, the feeling that they were doing some good in the world, and the knowledge that the public sector offered a less cut-throat pace of work, with more security and a better work–life balance than the private sector, even if this meant lower earnings. In the words of two employees of Company A,

> I had the choice to be working for a private service provider in a bigger town, for example London. If this is what I wanted I'd have made that choice ... I thought it was a job for life. I liked IT and that is why I got a job as an IT support technician with [name of city council]. I progressed and now everything has changed and IT is not a job for life anymore. (software developer, Company A)

> We made a choice for working in the public sector and if we wanted to work elsewhere we could have made that choice but we didn't want to; we preferred to work for the council because it was a job for life. (IT technical manager, Company A)

Some of the women, in particular, valued the fact that the public sector had a tradition of offering family-friendly policies (including flexitime, the opportunity to work part-time, and childcare facilities) that made it easier for them to combine parenthood with a career. It was seen as acceptable to be relatively unambitious.

Transferring from this kind of working environment to the private sector has meant a complete change of culture:

> I'm not ambitious, I never wanted to go into management which is not an attitude that is liked in [Company D]. They

want young, hungry [people] trying to get up the ladder. (female programmer, Company D)

Workers in Company D told us that their new employer (like Company C for whom they previously worked) is vehemently opposed to the idea of part-time working or flexibility. When one worker asked to be allowed to work from home (in line with UK government policy, which stipulates a right for parents of young children to request flexible working arrangements),

> My line manager passed on the request but it was rejected by [his more senior manager]. He said that: "If your whole team can work from home then their jobs can be outsourced to India." (project manager, Company D)

Such statements exacerbate the general anxiety around further restructuring and increase the feeling that workers should "keep your head down, get on with the job, but ask for nothing," "keep your head down and hope you will keep your job for another year," and "get the job done, no matter what" (IT workers in Company D). Employment in these global IT companies is not just perceived as being more precarious and less sympathetic to work–life balance issues; it is also seen as having different values, which has made employees reconsider their commitment to the work:

> I do my work, I don't slack but you have to look for meaning outside. I walk out and switch off. It is hard to get recognition here. You don't get credit for your work so that is why I can't be bothered. If I lose this job I'll go find another one somewhere else. I am not bothered. I have other things going on. (project manager, Company D)

> I am less tempted to stay in IT because it got too cut-throat and has become a risky industry. (account maintenance manager, Company A)

> The way they do things just makes you want to come into work, do your job and go home. (project manager, Company D)

Some of the workers interviewed told us of colleagues who had already left the industry, in some cases to do skilled manual work in the construction industry. Others were planning to do so. One woman was hoping to find another job in the public sector, not caring whether it involved IT or not. A man who had reached a stage in his life with more financial options (his children had left home and his mortgage was paid off) was planning to make his living by buying up run-down properties to renovate and sell on.

Even if these workers have not formally changed their class position, it is clear that they have undergone a profound change in their commitment to their work, their motivation, and their sense of a secure and permanent occupational identity. Some of their attitudes reflect those found in a study of new media workers in New York by Andrew Ross (2003), who speaks of the way in which many of these workers are not so much interested in financial rewards but "have a nostalgia for an irresistible work environment" and a resistance to being "branded" by large corporations (15). Here, the scale of their disillusionment seems to go beyond mere nostalgia and some give the sense of participating in the death of the occupation they joined, typically one or two decades earlier.

Our third case also involves local government workers involved in what might be regarded as a commercialization, if not an outright outsourcing, of public services. This case, however, did not involve transferring personnel to a private-sector employer, but rather entailed a form of "secondment," whereby employees retained their formal contractual employment with the local government body but were moved under the managerial control of a newly formed "public–private partnership" with the strong involvement of a large private telecommunications company.[9] This company had reached similar arrangements with several different local councils in the UK. Our interviews were carried out in 2007[10] in two different locations, one in a relatively prosperous rural county in the east of England, and one in a relatively depressed "rustbelt" town in the north of England with high unemployment levels due to the decline of its traditional manufacturing and resource-based industries.

In contrast with the workers in the previous two cases, who could be classified as associate professional or technical workers, most of the workers involved here had previously held clerical jobs in local government. As part of an e-government initiative, call centres were opened to provide a "one-stop shop" whereby local citizens could access any of the approximately 400 services provided by local councils by calling a single phone number or attending a drop-in centre. In effect, the workers were transformed from department-based specialists into generalists working out of communal offices where call-centre work was combined with providing face-to-face services. The vast majority of these workers were women, most of whom had chosen public-sector work because it offered good working conditions and flexible working time arrangements, making it easy to combine their work with parenting. Few were ambitious; most saw their primary role as that of housewife and mother and the job as a way of providing extra income to supplement their partners' earnings.

In the rural county in the east of England, most workers were fairly satisfied with the change. Many felt they had been able to acquire new skills, and they enjoyed working in teams. Some considered that the work had been enhanced.

> I don't think, well from my point of view, serving the customer is any different. We can give them more information now which is something we couldn't do before. It was always "oh I'm sorry, you've got to go here, or you've got to go there." Whereas now you can actually answer 99.9% of the questions that they have, because you've got the tools to do it.

Although they now had to work to more rigid "service-level agreements" than before, as a result of working under the terms of a contract between the council and the public–private partnership, this had not yet put them under the kinds of pressure experienced in comparable studies of public-information call-centre workers in other countries (Pupo 2007). For instance, when a customer was distressed,

> You can say "right, come back in the back office," you can take them in there, get them a drink, you can sit there for an hour and a half with a box of tissues, nobody's on your back saying "get rid of that customer." There's no pressure like that at all.

Their main complaints related to the increased rigidity in working hours. Previously, most employees had been able to work flexitime, but there were now requirements for the phones to be covered at set times, including Saturday mornings, which meant they had to work shifts that sometimes interfered with domestic plans. Restrictions had also been placed on their ability to take vacations with their families during the school summer holidays.

Viewed objectively, the workers interviewed in the north of England had had a more negative work experience: there had been a difficult transition period when the scheme was first introduced because there was a severe shortage of staff and the workers were put under considerable stress. However they were, if anything, even more positive in their responses than the workers in the east of the country. This is, perhaps, in part a reflection of the lack of alternative choices on the local labour market and a sense that it is necessary to be realistic about what is possible. Here, where unemployment was higher, there were more men in the call-centre workforce, perhaps reflecting a lack of attractive alternative options. One of these (a stepfather of two) told us that he was happy with the work–life balance the job gave him and that, although it was not the "dream" career he had once envisaged, he felt satisfied with his work. Unlike the women interviewed, he had expectations that he would be able to work his way up to a management job within five years. In strong contrast with the IT workers in our second case, he saw the job as much more secure than previous employment. He had previously worked at a large bank call centre and wanted to move into the public sector because he felt that there was "greater stability" there since it was working, as he saw it, for the government. He thought of it "as a job for life" and thought that the public-service aspect of the job was worthwhile. His career trajectory was interesting and fairly wide-ranging: he had done a stint at college studying graphic design but had left before completing the course. He expressed some regret at this; it would have been his ideal job. There followed a range of stop-gap jobs: he had worked in a sewing factory as general labourer, in warehouse work, and on construction sites.

A female interviewee said that she "loves the job" and "goes home happy." Her career trajectory also exhibited the ups and downs of life in a precarious labour market. After leaving school she had worked for two different electricity boards as a clerical worker. Then came marriage and two children, which meant no paid employment for the next 14 years. To get back into the labour market, she went on a community-care-practice course and decided that something in the public sector would suit her. When she secured her job, she found it "ideal." She felt she was doing something "worthwhile." For her, there is a type of personality that best suits the work: being "interested in people" and being willing to take time and "connect" were important qualities. "Taking the trouble and not being judgmental" were important attributes. She felt that this job enabled her to exercise all of these attributes. Again, this is in strong contrast with our second case, where the "caring" aspects of the job were perceived as having been squeezed out by the commercial pressures of the private sector.

These cases make it clear that occupational identities cannot be viewed outside the context of the alternatives available to the worker, alternatives that are shaped both by the nature of the local labour market and by personal attributes, including gender, qualifications, and experience. The first case represented a drop in status and job satisfaction for a group of middle-class female professionals; the second also represented a drop, in terms of both job security and job satisfaction, for a group of male professional/technical workers; in the third case, entry to the world of ICT-related work represented a step up the occupational ladder for a group of relatively low-qualified workers whose career prospects had in the past been severely limited, either because they were women workers in dead-end clerical jobs stereotyped as being for "secondary earners" or because they had previously only been able to obtain contingent work in an area of high unemployment and few opportunities.

Conclusion

These snapshots provide no easy general conclusions. It is clear that major upheavals are taking place in occupational identities across a broad swathe of employment as a result of the restructuring of global value chains. It also seems to be the case that this represents a deterioration in job security and job satisfaction for more highly skilled professional workers, as well as a routinization of many aspects of their work.[11] However, these changes must be viewed relative to their previous conditions and to the alternatives available, factors that are affected by gender and other variables. For groups that have been disadvantaged in the past, the impacts may be more contradictory. Still, a great deal of further research will be required to establish how permanent these impacts are and what this means for workers' perceptions of their class positions and interests. Meanwhile, the speed of change of global restructuring, combined with a lack of clarity in the definition of the new occupations, leaves both workers and those who analyse them at a loss. As Bourdieu would perhaps say, there is an urgent need, both objectively and subjectively, for a nomenclature for this new breed of workers, to give them a place in the social order.

Discussion Questions

1. What is the significance of "occupational identity" to one's "class" and "class consciousness"?

2. What are the limitations in using "occupational identity" to define class and class consciousness?

3. How has the restructuring of work through ICTs had an impact upon workers' occupational identities, class positions, and class consciousness?

4. How are conceptualizations of class complicated by occupational classifications in the new economy?

Notes

1 This paper was originally presented at the International Sociological Association Conference, *Work and Employment: New Challenges*, at the University of Quebec at Montreal, 28–30 August 2007. We would like to thank Peter van der Hallen, Imogen Bertin, Tomas Koltai, Nicola Tickner, and Roel Verlinden for their help with the analysis of occupational coding by national statistical offices from the STILE project, and Alison Gosper and John Kirk for their assistance with the qualitative interviews with call-centre workers carried out as part of the WORKS project.

2 In the UK, the category "call centre worker" was introduced for the first time in the 2000 revision of the occupational classification, SOC2000. However there is some evidence that workers do not identify with such new job titles (or their interviewers fail to acknowledge them), which leads to considerable underestimation of their numbers. In spring 2003, the UK Labour Force Survey recorded numbers in this category that grossed up to only 81,000 nationally, although it is known from other sources (such as industry estimates derived from shipments of workstations) that there were more call-centre workers than this in a single British city such as Leeds or Liverpool, with the total number of such workers in the UK estimated conservatively at well over 1 million in that year (Paul and Huws 2003:11).

3 See <http://www.ilo.org/public/english/bureau/stat/isco/index.htm>.

4 See <http://www.forfas.ie>.

5 See the EMERGENCE website at <http://www.emergence.nu>.

6 See the WORKS website at <http://www.worksproject.be>.

7 This case is discussed more fully in Huws and Dahlmann (2007).

8 This case is discussed more fully in Dahlmann (2008).

9 By ensuring that the workers remained technically the employees of the local authority, this arrangement avoided the application of the TUPE (Transfer of Undertakings [Protection of Employment] Regulations, 1981) regulations, which offer some specific forms of protection of employment rights to workers who are transferred from one employer to another.

10 This case study was also carried out as part of the WORKS project. See n.6, above.

11 For reasons of space we have not elaborated on this aspect of our case studies here. For further information, see forthcoming publications from the WORKS project at <http://www.worksproject.be>.

References

Bourdieu, P. 1984. *Distinctions: A Social Critique of the Judgment of Taste*. Cambridge, MA: Harvard University Press.

Braverman, H. 1974. *Labor and Monopoly Capital: The Degradation of Work in the Twentieth Century*. New York: Monthly Review Press.

Bureau of Labor Statistics. 2005. *Computer and Internet Use at Work Summary*. Washington, DC: Bureau of Labor Statistics. <http://www.bls.gov/news.release/ciuaw.nr0.htm>.

Castells, M. 1996. *The Rise of the Network Society: Economy, Society and Culture*. Oxford: Blackwell.

Cockburn, C. 1983. *Brothers*. London: Pluto Press.

Dahlmann, S. 2008. "The End of the Road: No More Walking in Dead Men's Shoes: IT Professionals' Experiences of Being Outsourced to the Private Sector." *Work Organisation, Labour and Globalisation* 2 (2): 148–61.

Ensmenger, N. 2003. "Letting the 'Computer Boys' Take Over: Technology and the Politics of Organizational Transformations." In A. Blok and G. Downey (eds.), *Uncovering Labour in Information Revolutions*. International Review of Social History Supplements 11. Cambridge and New York: Cambridge University Press. 153–80.

Flecker, J. 2007. "Network Economy or Just a New Breed of Multinationals? Relocation of eWork as a Window to the Restructuring of Value Chains." *Work Organisation, Labour and Globalisation* 1 (2): 36–51.

Flecker, J., and S. Kirschenhofer. 2002. *Jobs on the Move: European Case Studies in Relocating eWork*. IES Report 386. Brighton: Institute for Employment Studies.

Gereffi, G., J. Humphrey, and T. Sturgeon. 2005. "The Governance of Global Value Chains." *Review of International Political Economy* 12 (1): 78–104.

Gurstein, P. 2007. "Navigating the Seamless Environment in the Global Supply Chain: Implications for Canadian Regions and Workers." *Work Organisation, Labour and Globalisation* 1 (2): 36–51.

Huws, U. 1982. *New Technology and Women's Employment: Case Studies from West Yorkshire*. Manchester: Equal Opportunities Commission.

——. 2003. *The Making of a Cybertariat*. New York: Monthly Review Press.

—— (ed.). 2006. *The Transformation of Work in a Global Knowledge Economy: Towards a Conceptual Framework*. Leuven: Hooger Institute Voor der Arbeid.

——. 2007. "Defragmenting: Towards a Critical Understanding of the New Global Division of Labour." *Work Organisation, Labour and Globalisation* 1 (2): 1–4.

Huws, U., and S. Dahlmann. 2007. "Sunset in the West: Outsourcing Editorial Work from the UK to India—a Case Study of the Impact on Workers." *Work Organisation, Labour and Globalisation* 1 (1): 59–75.

Huws, U., and J. Flecker (eds.). 2004. *Asian EMERGENCE: The World's Back Office?* IES Report 409. Brighton: Institute for Employment Studies.

Huws, U., and P. Van der Hallen. 2004. *Opening the Black Box: Classification and Coding of Sectors and Occupations in the eEconomy*. Leuven: Hooger Institute Voor der Arbeid.

International Labour Organisation. 2004. International Standard Classification of Occupations (ISCO). <http://www.ilo.org/public/english/bureau/stat/isco/index.htm>.

Paul, J., and U. Huws. 2003. *How Can We Help? Good Practice in Call Centre Employment*. Brussels: European Trade Union Confederation.

Pupo, N. 2007. "Behind the Screens: Telemediated Work in the Canadian Public Sector." *Work Organisation, Labour and Globalisation* 1 (2): 36–51.

Ramioul, M., U. Huws, and S. Kirschenhofer. 2005. *Offshore Outsourcing of Business Services*. Dublin: European Foundation for the Improvement of Living and Working Conditions.

Ramioul, M., and U. Huws. (Forthcoming). "The Snowball Effect: Global Sourcing as an Accelerator of Economic Globalisation." Submitted to *Journal of Architectural and Planning Research* (under review).

Ross, A. 2003. *No-collar: the Humane Workplace and its Hidden Costs*. New York: Basic Books.

Part II. Transformations in Work and Labour Processes

5. Labour Casualization in the Public Sector

JANE STINSON[1]

One of the most significant changes in employment over the past decade, and a prominent aspect of the so-called "new" economy, has been in the casualization of labour. Casualization here refers to the erosion of a standard employment relationship where full-time, full-year, long-term, or permanent jobs are eliminated and replaced by work that is part-time, temporary, and/or self-employed. These jobs provide precarious, uncertain employment rather than stable, ongoing, full-time, waged work.

The implications of the shift away from standard employment have been the subject of a fair amount of research and debate over the past decade (e.g., Cranford, Vosko and Zukewich 2003; Cranford, Fudge, Tucker and Vosko 2005; Lowe and Schellenberg 2005; Vosko 2007). Many analysts have looked at this trend in the Canadian labour market overall or, in some cases, in the private sector specifically. The rapid growth of self-employment, in place of a standard employment relationship, has been noted extensively. Casualization within the public sector has not received as much specific attention in the literature. Yet, as my analysis reveals, the extent and nature of casualization in the public sector in Canada are significantly different from those in the private sector.[2]

The key difference is that casualization in the public sector has taken place primarily through the growth of temporary full-time employment between 1997 and 2007, whereas in the private sector the growth in casualization has been mainly in temporary part-time work.[3] Over the decade from 1997 to 2007, temporary full-time work has squeezed out permanent part-time employment as the main form of casualized labour in the public sector.[4] The number and proportion of temporary full-time workers increased significantly more than the number of permanent part-time workers in the public sector in the decade between 1997 and 2007. This caused the number of permanent part-time workers to decline as a proportion of the total, from 11.3 to 10 per cent. During the same time, temporary part-time employment increased in the public sector both in numbers and as a proportion of the workforce (Statistics Canada 2007/2004). Together these trends indicate greater precariousness in public-sector employment overall, as temporary work (both full- and part-time) with little or no job security replaced secure, permanent positions (both full- and part-time).

Analysis of the labour-force data shows that the rise in temporary work was due largely to the growth of full-time term or contract employment and secondly to the growth of casual (and other) employment. In the public sector, these new casual jobs were mainly full-time, while in the private sector they tended to be part-time. What is behind these different trends in employment in the public and private sectors? While a number of factors are at play, in this paper I argue that the main reason for the difference is the higher union density in the public sector, which creates conditions for public-sector union strategies to counter employers' efforts to use casual employment as a cheap source of labour.

Why Does Public-Sector Casualization Matter?

A narrow definition of the public sector encompasses governments at all levels: federal, provincial, territorial, and local. Together, governments are among the largest employers in the country, employing 1.3 million workers directly in 2008 (Statistics Canada 2009a). However, the scope of the public sector is even broader than direct government employees alone. Statistics Canada's definition of the public sector includes educational institutions such as school boards, universities, and colleges, as well as health and social-service institutions and government business enterprises. This brings the total number of Canadian workers employed in the broader public sector to 3.5 million in 2008 (Statistics Canada 2009a).

Knowing more about public-sector casualization is important for many reasons. The public sector represents almost one-quarter of the workforce in the Canadian labour market: 23.5 per cent of 14.5 million jobs in May 2008, according to Statistics Canada (2009b). Public-sector jobs are predominantly held by women (61 per cent in 2004). The erosion of full-time, full-year jobs in the public sector is therefore important for women since this sector is such a crucial source of employment for them. Understanding why casualization is less pronounced in the public sector can also provide insights to limit the growth of casual labour in the private sector. Moreover, shifts in the standards of government employment arrangements affect not only over 3 million workers employed in Canada's broader public sector, but additionally can have direct and indirect implications for private-sector labour. Alongside its responsibility for regulating the conditions of work and protecting the rights of all workers, government also sets national and provincial standards through its own employment practices.

Furthermore, all Canadians rely upon public-sector services, most visibly health care, social services, education, and municipal services. Employment conditions profoundly affect the quality and accessibility of these services, for which the government is accountable. Therefore all citizens can be affected by casualization, since changes to public-sector employment relations may affect the quality of public services. For example, employment conditions that contribute to high staff turnover can profoundly affect the quality of public service. This has been extensively documented for child-care services (Doherty and Forer 2003; Hale-Jinks, Knopf and Kemple 2006), and the same argument applies to other jobs that require training and provide direct services to the public, such as social services, health care, and education. Thus, the casualization of public-sector employment has negative consequences for citizens who rely on these services, as well as for workers who rely on wages from these jobs. In both cases these are most often women, who, as mentioned above, form the majority of workers in public services, but who also tend to be more responsible than men for the domestic labour (e.g., housework) and social labour (e.g., caring for the sick and elderly) that is provided or assisted through public services.

For all of these reasons, then, an understanding of the extent and nature of labour casualization in the public sector is critical to developing an appropriate response.

Data Insights and Limitations

This analysis relies on data from Statistics Canada's Labour Force Survey (LFS) to explore changes to the standard employment relationship in the public sector. The LFS is a long-running survey that provides, on a monthly and annual basis, the most comprehensive information available on employment trends in Canada. However, certain questions related to casualization, such as information on job permanency, were not included until 1997, as public concern rose about the growth of non-standard employment. As a result, in this paper 1997 is the base year for analyzing changes in casualization for public-sector employees.

Statistics Canada's Labour Force Survey tracks two dimensions that are central to an analysis of casualized labour and that form the basis of this inquiry into trends in the public-sector labour market. The first dimension is *weekly hours worked*, divided into full-time and part-time employment status. This measure helps in the analysis of one form of casualization, where full-time jobs are replaced with jobs with fewer paid hours of work. For the LFS, those who regularly work 30 hours per week or more are considered full-time; those who work less are classified as part-time. The second dimension of casualization tracked by Statistics Canada is the *expected duration of employment*, which distinguishes between permanent and temporary work. The LFS defines temporary employment as work for which there is a predetermined end date or which is expected to end when a specified project is completed. By contrast, permanent work is defined as employment that is anticipated to last as long as the employee wants, if business conditions permit.

These two dimensions of casualization are not mutually exclusive. For example, in 2007, 10 per cent of public-sector workers were permanent and part-time. We can get a clearer idea of how the two dimensions interact by combining them to form four distinct types of work: permanent full-time, permanent part-time, temporary full-time, and temporary part-time. While these categories are helpful in the analysis of these dimensions of casualization, they do not tell the whole story. Certain groups of workers are left out of the analysis entirely. For example, the LFS data refer only to workers classified as employees, which is the case for all workers in the public sector, but which excludes self-employed individuals in the private sector, a growing segment of the labour market. Further, in cases where labour-force participants hold multiple jobs, the LFS collects detailed information only on the main job held by each participant. The following analysis is therefore based on the main or only job indicated by respondents. It is hard to know how certain forms of casualized work are captured and categorized. For example, when public-sector work is contracted out to a private firm, the duration is subject to periodic renewal agreements. But since this work does not always have a predetermined end date and is ongoing as long as business conditions permit, does it get classified as temporary or permanent? As public-sector or private-sector? The blurring of these distinctions makes it hard to analyze casualized work and its links to privatization and outsourcing.

Despite these grey areas, Statistics Canada's Labour Force Survey does distinguish between public- and private-sector employment. Demographic information such as gender and age is also available. Unfortunately, the LFS does not gather information on race, making a much-needed racial analysis of this important labour-force trend impossible using this otherwise extensive data source.

Data on Types of Work

The original hypothesis of this research project was that we would find a public-sector pattern of casualized employment similar to the private-sector norm, where temporary part-time jobs were replacing permanent full-time ones. Instead, the data analysis revealed a very different pattern in the public sector: one where temporary full-time jobs are growing, replacing permanent part-time jobs as the main type of casualized labour. What do the data say about what was going on with casualized employment in the public sector between 1997 and 2007? And what explains the divergent trends? In what follows, I explore different patterns of casualization between the public and private sectors, noting gender and age differences. I then discuss possible causes for the different trends, noting the role of unions and high union density in the public sector. I begin by examining more closely what has been happening to the standard employment relationship (full-time, permanent) and changes to the main categories of casualized employment in the public sector.

STANDARD EMPLOYMENT

Permanent full-time work, considered the standard employment relationship, still accounted for almost three-quarters of all jobs in both the public and private sectors in 2007. But between 1997 and 2007, non-standard jobs grew at a faster rate than standard ones. Most of the 3.28 million public-sector jobs in Canada were full-time (83.5%) or permanent (83.1%) in 2007. Almost three-quarters (73.1%) were both permanent and full-time, which represents the traditional standard employment relationship. Substantially fewer jobs were non-standard, i.e., not full-time or permanent. This included permanent part-time jobs (10% of all public-sector jobs in 2007), temporary full-time (10.4%), and temporary part-time (6.5%). Among temporary positions, most were categorized as contract or term, followed by casual or other temporary work, with seasonal jobs constituting the smallest category of temporary employment.

Both standard and non-standard employment in the public sector is gendered: for instance, while both the majority of men and women work full-time in the public sector, in 2004 fully 92 per cent of men's jobs were full-time, compared to only 78 per cent of women's jobs. In addition, women account for the majority of employees in all the non-standard categories.

As indicated, however, non-standard work grew at a faster rate than standard employment, accounting for almost half (43%) of all new public-sector positions between 1997 and 2007. The number of public-sector jobs rose by 33 per cent, or over three-quarters of a million positions (808,800). This growth was fuelled primarily by a much higher rate of growth in certain forms of temporary work. Specifically, the number of contract/term jobs increased by 70 per cent from 1997 to 2007 (approximately 150,000 jobs), followed closely by a 57-per-cent increase in jobs classified as casual/other (approximately 50,000 jobs). In relation to total public-sector growth, contract/term positions accounted for 18 per cent of all new public-sector jobs, while casual/other comprised 6 per cent of new positions. The growth of temporary employment overall far outstripped the growth of traditional permanent, full-time jobs in the public sector from 1997 to 2007. A 64-per-cent rise in temporary employment compared to a 28-per-cent increase in permanent employment caused a disturbing erosion in the share of permanent employment in the public sector as it fell 3 percentage points as a share of total employment between 1997 and 2007. Public-sector employment grew over the decade, in both categories, but temporary employment grew faster than permanent employment.

TYPES OF NON-STANDARD EMPLOYMENT

Part-time work is the most prevalent form of casualized work and, as mentioned earlier, is somewhat less common in the public sector than in the private sector (16.5% vs. 18.2% in 2007). There has been a slight decline in the proportion of part-time employees between 1997 and 2007 in the public and private sectors. Considering the size of the workforces, however, even a 1-per-cent change in proportion represents over 30,000 public employees and over 100,000 private employees. Between 1997 and 2007 there was a decrease of 0.2 per cent in the public sector and 0.8 per cent in the private sector in the proportion of workers in part-time positions. This was not due to the number of part-time workers decreasing, but rather because their rate of increase was not as high as that of full-time workers. Women hold most (about 80%) of the part-time jobs in the public sector. But over recent years, the rate of growth for men being employed in part-time public sector jobs is higher than for women. Between 2000 and 2004, part-time jobs held by men grew at almost twice the rate (15.9%) than for women (8.9%). And the increase in the number of men with permanent jobs was much lower (3.6%) than the overall growth rate in public-sector employment (10%) from 2000 to 2004. This indicates that men are also being affected by an erosion of the standard employment relationship in the public sector.

Temporary work, is more common in the public than the private sector, accounting for 17 per cent of public-sector employment and 12 per cent of private-sector employment in 2007. Temporary work has grown faster than permanent work in both sectors. For example, the number of workers in temporary positions in the public sector grew by 63.5 per cent between 1997 and 2007, whereas the number of employees in permanent positions increased by only 27.8 per cent in that decade. The increase in temporary employment is more pronounced in the public sector, where temporary work accounted for over one quarter (26.6%) of the growth between 1997 and 2007 (195,350 jobs). Just under half of all non-standard jobs in the public sector were temporary full-time positions in 2007 (160,118 jobs). Again these temporary jobs are gendered, with almost twice as many women in them than men (311,400 women compared to 172,800 men in 2004) (Harrison 2007).

Temporary full-time work is more common in the public sector than in the private sector, accounting for 10 per cent of all public-sector work but only 7 per cent of all private-sector work in 2007. The number and proportion of temporary full-time employment have increased in both sectors. The increase is more notable in the public sector, where the main growth in non-standard work between 1997 and 2007 was due to temporary full-time work, which grew by 79 per cent over that decade, taking over as the most prevalent form of casualized work in the public sector. In the private sector, temporary full-time work grew by only 33 per cent during that period; in contrast, temporary part-time work grew by 45 per cent over that same period.

Another indication of the large and growing proportion of part-time jobs in the private sector, is that permanent part-time jobs are twice as common as temporary full-time jobs. Permanent part-time jobs represented 13.4 per cent of the private-sector workforce and temporary full-time jobs accounted for only 7 per cent in 2007. In contrast, in the public sector, temporary full-time jobs have become more common than permanent part-time jobs over the decade from 1997–2007. There were 362,374 temporary full-time positions compared to 329,579 permanent part-time jobs in the public sector in 2007. Ten years earlier, there were fewer temporary full-time jobs (202,255) than permanent part-time jobs (279,192). Temporary part-time employment is the least common form of casualized work, in both the public and private sectors. It represents less than 5 per cent of work in both sectors (4 per cent in the public sector and 3.3 per cent in the private sector in 2007). Gender differences are emerging as temporary work increases in the public sector. Temporary work for men grew more as a proportion of public-sector employment (2.7%) than it did for women (1.6%) between 1997 and 2004 (Harrison 2007, Table 4.1.B).

To sum up, proportions of temporary forms of casualized work are increasing in both sectors. Part-time work has grown most when it is also temporary. In the public sector, full-time temporary work has grown most, while in the private sector, part-time temporary work has grown most from 1997 to 2007. And in the public sector, more men have been employed in non-standard temporary and part-time positions over that decade. Proportions of part-time work are higher than proportions of temporary work for both sectors, the difference being more notable in the private sector. Therefore, part-time employment is a much more common form of casualized work than temporary employment in the private sector, while this is only marginally apparent in the public sector.

TYPES OF TEMPORARY EMPLOYMENT

There are several kinds of temporary employment arrangements. The Labour Force Survey uses the following three categories of temporary work: seasonal, term or contract, and casual or other temporary work.

Seasonal employment is the smallest category of temporary work in the public sector, representing 1.8 per cent of employment in 2007. It is more common in the private sector, where it accounted for 3.3 per cent of positions in 2007. There has been little change in the share of seasonal work as part of total work in both sectors. Seasonal part-time employment in the public sector from 1997 to 2007 grew significantly— it almost doubled with 81-per-cent growth—but it still accounted for only 0.6 per cent of the total public-sector workforce.

Term or *contract work* is the largest category of temporary employment. It was about twice the proportion of public-sector jobs, accounting for 11 per cent of employees, than in the private sector, where it accounted for 5.2 per cent of employees in 2007. Proportions of term/ contract work have increased in both sectors from 1997 to 2007, but more so in the public sector, where contract jobs grew by 70 per cent compared to a 43-per-cent rise in private-sector contract jobs. In the public sector, full-time contract jobs grew the most (by 79 %). In the private sector, part-time contract jobs grew the most (by 50%) from 1997 to 2007.

Casual or *other temporary employment* is the only category of temporary labour where there were more part-time than full-time jobs. In the other forms of temporary work—contract and seasonal—there were more full-time than part-time jobs in 2007. (There were 74,661 part-time casual jobs in the public sector compared to 57,458 full-time casual jobs in 2007. In the private sector there were 255,727 part-time casual jobs compared to less than half that number—103,183—of full-time casual jobs in the private sector. In other words, 71.3 per cent of casual/other positions in the private sector were part-time, compared to 56.5 per cent in the public sector in 2007. Overall, casual jobs accounted for a slightly higher proportion of work in the public sector than in the private sector, accounting for 4.2 and 3.3 per cent of the respective workforces in 2007. However, from 1997 to 2007 casual work grew at a faster rate in the public sector (57%) than in the private sector (39%). But in breaking down the data, we can see that in the public sector full-time casual jobs grew at three times the rate (66%) than they did in the private sector, where full-time casual jobs grew by only 29 per cent from 1997 to 2007. Part-time casual jobs grew at a slightly higher rate in the public sector (51%) than in the private sector (44%) from 1997 to 2007.

In summary, in the public sector the growth of temporary employment has mainly been in terms of full-time term or contract work. In the private sector, in contrast, the growth of temporary employment has mainly been in part-time term or contract work. In the public sector, there has been more growth in full-time casual temporary employment than in part-time casual employment. In the private sector, in contrast, part-time casual employment grew faster than full-time casual employment from 1997 to 2007.

QUALITY OF TEMPORARY WORK IN THE PUBLIC SECTOR

In theory, casualized work can be beneficial by providing flexibility that facilitates employment for those who are unable to participate in a traditional schedule of work. The reality of casualized labour, however, is often reduced quality of work. In this section I focus on indicators of work quality associated with temporary or casualized work in the public sector, including union coverage, wages, hours of work, and job tenure.

Union coverage is associated with increased job security and regulatory protection, control over terms and conditions of work, and advantage in wages and benefits. Temporary workers in the public sector have lower proportions of union coverage than permanent workers (57.9% vs. 77.9% in 2007). Of the different types of temporary employment, the highest proportion of union coverage is observed in work classified as casual/other and the lowest proportion of union coverage is evident in seasonal work. Even at the lowest level, more public-sector temporary workers are unionized than are permanent, private-sector workers, since only around 19 per cent of private-sector jobs have union coverage (Bickerton and Stinson 2007).

As one component of income, wages are related to a worker's ability to maintain an adequate standard of living for themselves and their dependents. Average hourly wages in the public sector were lower for temporary employees than permanent employees ($20.39 vs. $26.69 in 2007). Temporary workers earned 76 cents for every dollar earned by permanent workers. Among temporary workers, seasonal work is associated with the lowest average hourly wage and term/contract work with the highest. Specifically, seasonal workers earned 55 cents, casual/other workers 72 cents, and term/contract workers 81 cents for every dollar earned by permanent workers in 2007.

Low Paid Employees (LPEs) are those earning less than two-thirds of the national median hourly wage. LPEs are more likely to be found in temporary public-sector employment than in permanent public-sector jobs. The 2007 median hourly wage was $18, so two-thirds of that median is $12. Just under one-quarter of permanent employees (22.9%) and almost half of all temporary employees (45%) made under $12.

Hours of work are an important component of income, as employees working fewer hours per week have a lower income capacity than employees working more hours per week. Part-time work is by nature more vulnerable to low working hours than full-time work, but within part-time work there is also a range in the number of hours usually worked per week. Within part-time work, temporary employees worked only 81.6% as many hours per week, on average, as permanent employees in 2007. Of the different types of temporary work, part-time seasonal employment is associated with the fewest weekly hours (13.7 hours in 2004) and part-time term/contract is associated with the most weekly hours (15.6 hours in 2004) (Harrison 2008). Temporary part-time workers are more likely than permanent part-time workers to work fewer than 15 hours per week. Specifically, 53.7 per cent of temporary part-time workers usually worked under 15 hours each week in 2007, compared to 34.1 per cent of permanent part-time workers.

Tenure refers to the length of consecutive time employed by a current employer. It is associated with job stability and security through seniority. In 2007 most temporary workers were employed for fewer than three years with the same employer. But a surprising percentage of temporary workers (7.3%) had been with the same employer for ten or more consecutive years. They are considered Long Term Employees (LTE) by Statistics Canada definitions. This is temporary employment only in that there is no guaranteed job security. Among temporary employees, casual employees (with no fixed hours of work or duration of employment) are the most likely to work for ten years or more with the same employer. Contract employees (who have a fixed term) are the least likely to have Long Term Employment of ten consecutive years or more.

Traditionally, in a standard employment relationship, longer job tenure has meant less precariousness and more job security. This does not apply, however, to long-term temporary employees whose continued employment is not guaranteed but must be continually renegotiated. The job insecurity of temporary work is being extended for long periods of time for some workers now.

Summary of the Data

The pattern of precarious employment in the public sector is strikingly different than in the private sector. Temporary full-time or contract work predominates in the public sector, but in the private sector, temporary part-time work is the largest and fastest growing form of precarious work.

Higher union density in the public sector may partly account for the higher growth of temporary work that is full-time, rather than part-time, as it is in the private sector. First, public-sector unions often try to limit the growth of part-time employment in favour of creating more full-time jobs. As well, public-sector unions have negotiated the right for permanent employees to take various forms of long-term leave and return to their job. For example, many public-sector employees have the right to a lengthy period of time for maternity and parental leaves of absence, up to three years in some cases. Those who have a serious illness or are disabled by their job often have the right to be away from work for a long time and return to their former job or equivalent. These various scenarios give rise to the need for workers to replace them on a temporary basis, since they have the right to return to their job or an equivalent position, and these types of absences may also partly explain the higher rate of full-time term and contract employment in the public sector.

Regardless of whether it is full-time or part-time, temporary employment is more precarious than permanent employment in terms of wages, hours, job security, and control over working conditions. Compared to permanent employees, temporary workers in the public sector have lower hourly wages and fewer weekly work hours. Therefore, the earning capacity of temporary employees is dramatically limited compared to permanent employees. Furthermore, temporary workers are less likely to have the protection and control over work conditions afforded by union coverage. Finally, lengths of tenure indicate that temporary positions are not as short-term as might be expected, so the precariousness of these positions is a long-term reality for many of these workers.

Why the increase in casualization? Casualization provides an opportunity for employers to lower labour costs in many different ways, for example, by cutting weekly hours, or hiring workers for a specific project rather than on a permanent basis. Temporary, casual, contract, and term employees may not be paid the same wage rate as permanent employees. They are also are far less likely to have extended health benefits or a pension plan. These benefits can easily add 20 to 30 per cent to the wage bill. Inferior employment conditions for casualized jobs provide employers with cheaper labour than the standard employment norm of full-time, full-year jobs. Therefore there is an economic incentive for employers to replace full-time jobs with casualized ones.

Union Resistance to Casualization in the Public Sector

The primary reason for the different patterns of casualization between the public and private sectors lies in a key factor: that the public sector is much more highly unionized than the private sector (74.5% for the public sector and 18.7% for the private sector in 2007). Public-sector unions have used collective bargaining, legislation, and their power to organize collective protest actions to establish a stronger set of rights and higher wages for workers (full- and part-time, permanent and casualized) than is the norm in the non-unionized private sector. Canadian unions have worked toward establishing greater equality between workers, for example by raising the wages of low-paid workers (Jackson 2003: 11) such as part-time and casual workers.

Canadian public-sector unions have been concerned about the growth of a cheaper, precarious labour force replacing long-term, full-time "good jobs" with short-term, cheaper casual employment. One way they have sought to restrict employers' use of this cheaper labour is by raising wages for temporary and part-time workers, ideally to the same level as that of permanent part-time workers. Another way has been to negotiate benefit coverage for part-time and temporary workers in order to ensure that such casual labour will not be as cheap an alternative to permanent full-time work (and because these workers need benefits too).[5] Some unions have also tried to negotiate specific employer restrictions on the use of part-time, temporary, or casual work. For example, the Canadian Union of Postal Workers negotiated full-time to part-time staff ratios requiring Canada Post to convert part-time jobs to full-time ones once the number of part-time hours is at a certain level (CUPW 2007). Other public-sector union strategies include challenging the definition of who is considered an employee in order to include under collective agreements and conditions of employment those who work for a temporary agency, a contract employer or are considered self-employed.

In New Brunswick, the Canadian Union of Public Employees (CUPE) has been challenging the provincial labour legislation that excludes casual employees from belonging to a trade union, thus preventing the union from bargaining on their behalf to improve their conditions of employment and compensation. These workers had no rights, lower wages, and no benefits (CUPE 2009). CUPE was successful with a complaint it took to the International Labor Organization (ILO) in 1999 based on the fact that these casual workers were denied the fundamental right of freedom of association as members of a trade union (ILO 2001). Since this international success, CUPE has launched domestic legal action against the government, arguing that these workers should have the rights of freedom of association to be members of a union (CUPE 2007). In June 2009, CUPE finally won its case. Justice Paulette Garnett of the New Brunswick Court of Queen's Bench ruled that the *New Brunswick Public Service Labour Relations Act* is contrary to section 2(d) of the Charter of Rights, which protects the right to freedom of association. The judge found that the province, as an employer, had subjected casual workers to unfair practices and gave the province one year to remedy the situation (CUPE-NB 2009).

The Canadian Union of Postal Workers (CUPW) was recently successful with a campaign for rural-route mail carriers, who were seen as independent contractors and therefore not considered employees who could be represented by a union. After a long-term union campaign to have the legislation changed and during which the union started to represent these workers in various ways, CUPW was finally successful in having rural-route mail carriers recognized as employees and negotiated a collective agreement in 2003 that guaranteed future employment, hours of work, paid holidays and vacations, benefits, and more (Bourque and Bickerton 2004).

Contracting out is another way in which public-sector employment is being casualized. Contracting out occurs when a public-sector employer contracts with a private company to provide services. Often this means that a private contractor hires its own workers to provide the service. Their future employment is subject to that contractor's ability to renew its contract, so there is no long-term job security. And often contractors will lower labour costs by cutting hours for employees so they work less than full-time, another dimension of casualization. These and other consequences have been documented in the largest wave of public-sector contracting out in Canada, which occurred in the British Columbia health services field in 2003–04 (Stinson, Pollak and Cohen 2005; see below).

Negotiating prohibitions to stop employers from contracting out or hiring contract employees is very hard to achieve. According to some public-sector legislation, it may even be beyond the scope of bargaining. But many public-service unions have negotiated some language in their collective agreement that restricts their employers' unilateral right to replace employees with contract workers. These collective-agreement provisions include, at minimum, advance notice that the employer is considering contracting out, and may also establish wage and other employment conditions for contract employees. For example, the Ontario Council of Hospital Unions of CUPE established in the collective agreement with its employer that while services may be contracted out, the employees providing those services must be guaranteed the same employment conditions and rights as regular employees (OCHU 2008). By undercutting contract workers as a cheap source of labour, the union has reduced the incentive for the hospitals to replace regular full-time employees with contract employees.

The recent Supreme Court of Canada decision concerning the largest wave of contracting out in Canada—of primarily cleaning, food, and security services in British Columbia health services—clearly established that a government's decision to contract out cannot be taken so quickly and without proper notice to the unions representing the affected workers. The BC government was censured by the Supreme Court for its actions and forced to negotiate after the fact with the unions affected (Norman 2008). These negotiations resulted in a $75-million compensation package for the employees who lost their jobs, and training opportunities for them to find alternative employment (HEU 2008).

Conclusion

High union density in the public sector, collective-bargaining, and legislative strategies that public-sector unions have used are key factors explaining the different pattern of casualization in the public sector compared to the private sector. While I have listed some of the measures taken by public-sector unions to deal with casualization, there are many more examples. As attempts to casualize the workforce intensify, public-sector unions will have to find innovative ways to defend their members from casualization and continue to draw upon a range of already proven strategies to protect jobs and services. Examples of such strategies include the following:

- Collective bargaining to influence the extent and forms of casualized labour.
- Organizing workers into unions when union jobs have been contracted out (and are no longer covered by a collective agreement), as well as expanding unionizing efforts into unorganized workplaces where public-sector work is being performed.
- Launching legislative campaigns and/or challenges to pressure governments to extend employee status to all workers so that they are covered by labour legislation.
- Actively advocating for legislative improvements to labour laws to afford greater protection and rights to all workers.
- Campaigning to resist employer attempts at casualization, such as through privatization and contracting out of public-sector work. Particularly effective have been campaigns that have produced research showing the link between casualization and the erosion of services, adverse effects on women (the group of workers most likely to be in casual public-sector jobs and to use public services), and the lack of public accountability when work is contracted out or privatized.

It is clear that where there is significant union density, as in the public sector, unions can make a difference by protecting workers against the erosion of rights, working conditions, and income that are common effects of the casualization that is a prominent feature of the transformation of work in the new economy.

Discussion Questions

1. Do you think the growth of less than full-time, full-year employment in the public sector is a concern? Why or why not? What are the implications?

2. Who is most disadvantaged and advantaged by the growth of casual employment in the public sector?

3. How are the needs of casual workers best met?

4. What is union density, and why and how has it affected the development of casualization in the public sector?

Notes

1 I would like to thank Joy Harrison for the tremendous data analysis and thorough reports that informed this article, Rosemary Warskett for her assistance in overseeing the initial research, Sylvain Schetagne for help updating the data, and Bozica Costigliola for her assistance with the final revisions. I would also like to acknowledge financial support from the Social Sciences and Humanities Research Council for the Centre for Research on Work and Society's Restructuring Work and Labour in the New Economy (RWL-INE) project of which this research was a part.

2 The Statistics Canada definitions of sectors are used here. The public sector includes employees in public administration at the federal, provincial, and municipal levels as well as in Crown corporations, liquor control boards, and other government institutions such as schools and universities, hospitals, and public libraries. The private sector includes all other employees and self-employed owners of businesses (including unpaid family workers in those businesses), and self-employed persons without businesses (Statistics Canada 2009a).

3 Temporary full-time employment includes employees working for a specified period of time, for example, term and contract workers.

4 This is what can be stated based on the data captured by the Labour Force Survey (Statistics Canada 2007/2004, 2009b). There may be more forms of casualized labour that are not captured there.

5 Benefits include a broad range of items that represent a significant cost to the employer, such as a pension plan; extended health-care benefits such as drug plans, vision care, dental care, physiotherapy, and other specialized forms of health care; paid holidays and vacations; overtime pay; and shift premiums. However, despite many unions' efforts, most part-time and temporary workers still have inferior benefits compared to permanent full-time workers.

References

Bickerton, G., and J. Stinson. 2007. "Challenges Facing the Canadian Labour Movement in the Context of Globalisation, Unemployment and the Casualisation of Labour." In A. Bieler, I. Lindberg, and D. Pillay (eds.), *Labour and the Challenges of Globalization*. London and Ann Arbor, MI: Pluto Press. 161–77.

Bourque, D., and G. Bickerton. 2004. *Stepping Out of the Legal Framework: Organizing Rural Route Couriers*. Montreal: Centre de Recherche Interuniversitaire sur la Mondialisation et le Travail / Interuniversity Research Centre on Globalization and Work, 2004. Also available at <http://www.crimt. org/2eSite_renouveau/Samedi_PDF/Bourque_Bickerton.pdf>.

Cranford, C.J., J. Fudge, E. Tucker, and L.F. Vosko. 2005. *Self-Employed Workers Organize: Law, Policy, and Unions*. Montreal and Kingston: McGill-Queen's University Press.

Cranford, C.J., L.F. Vosko, and N. Zukewich. 2003. "Precarious Employment in the Canadian Labour Market." *Just Labour* 3 (Fall): 6–22.

CUPE (Canadian Union of Public Employees). 2007. "CUPE in Court for Casual Workers' Rights." 11 September. <http://www.cupe.ca/bargaining/ CUPE_back_in_Court_f>.

CUPE-NB (Canadian Union of Public Employees—New Brunswick Division). 2009. "CUPE Wins Major Victory for Casual Workers' Rights." 17 June. <http://nb.cupe. ca/casuals/cupe-wins-major-victory-for-casual-workers-rights/>.

CUPW (Canadian Union of Postal Workers). 2007. "Agreement between Canada Post Corporation and the Canadian Union of Postal Workers. Expires: January 31, 2007." Appendix P. <http://www.cupw.ca/multimedia/website/publication/English/ PDF/2004/urban_ca_eng_2003_2007.pdf>.

Doherty, G., and B. Forer. 2003. *Unionization and Quality in Early Childhood Programs*. Ottawa: Canadian Union of Public Employees.

Hale-Jinks, C., H. Knopf, and K. Kemple. 2006. "Tackling Teacher Turnover in Child Care: Understanding Causes and Consequences, Identifying Solutions." *Childhood Education* 82 (4): 219–26.

Harrison, J. 2006. "Casualization in the Public Sector: A Problem of Temporary Proportions." Unpublished paper. Presentation to the CRWS conference on Restructuring Work and Labour—Initiatives in the New Economy. York University, Toronto.

———. 2007. "Trends in the Casualisation of Public Sector Labour." Unpublished research paper for the Restructuring Work and Labour in the New Economy initiative organized through the Centre for Research on Work and Society at York University and funded by the Social Sciences and Humanities Research Council of Canada.

HEU (Hospital Employees' Union). 2008. "Bill 29 Settlement Includes New Rights, $75 Million for Compensation and Training." Bill 29 Update. 28 January. <http://www.heu.org/%7EDOCUMENTS/2008_Newsletters/bill29updatejan28.pdf>.

ILO (International Labor Organization). 2001. 324th Report of the Committee on Freedom of Association. GB280-9-2001-03-0213-1-EN.Doc. CASE NO. 2083. Para 235–56. <http://www.ilo.org/public/english/standards/relm/gb/docs/gb280/pdf/gb-9.pdf>.

Jackson, A. 2003. '*In Solidarity': The Union Advantage*. Ottawa: Canadian Labour Congress. <http://www.canadianlabour.ca/updir/solidarityen.pdf>.

Lowe, G.S., and G. Schellenberg. 2001. *What's a Good Job?: The Importance of Employment Relationships*. Canadian Policy Research Network Study No. W/05. <http://www.cprn.org/doc.cfm?doc=50&l=en>.

Norman, K. 2008. "What's Right is Right: The Supreme Court Gets It." *Just Labour: A Canadian Journal of Work and Society* 12: 16–22. <http://www.justlabour.yorku.ca>.

OCHU (Ontario Council of Hospital Unions). 2008. "Full-Time Collective Agreement between (Herein after called the "Hospital") and CUPE Local. Expires: September 28, 2009." <http://www.ochu.on.ca/section-10/documents/CUPEFull-Time2006-2009-Final-Signed.pdf>.

Statistics Canada. 2009a. CANSIM. Public Sector Employment, Wages and Salaries (employees). <http://www40.statcan.gc.ca/l01/cst01/govt54a-eng.htm>.

———. 2009b. Guide to the Labour Force Survey. Catalogue no. 71-543. <http://www.statcan.gc.ca/pub/71-543-g/71-543-g2009001-eng.htm>.

———. 2007/2004. Labour Force Historical Review CD-ROM. Catalogue No.71F0004X.

Stinson, J., N. Pollak, and M. Cohen. 2005. *The Pains of Privatization: How Contracting Out Hurts Health Support Workers, Their Families and Health Care*. Vancouver: Canadian Centre for Policy Alternatives B.C. Office.

Vosko, L.F. 2007. *Precarious Employment: Understanding Labour Market Insecurity in Canada*. Montreal and Kingston: McGill-Queen's University Press.

6. Dialling for Service
Transforming the Public-Sector Workplace in Canada

NORENE PUPO AND ANDREA NOACK

Introduction

In 2004 the federal government began to integrate its services into a "one-stop service delivery network," known as "Service Canada" (Service Canada 2006). The goal of this integration is accessibility. Canadians can now easily access many government departments and services via a single telephone number, website, or local office. The Service Canada network, operating through 595 points of service across the country, is widely advertised by the federal government as a handy way for the public to access services, and the new program has received positive support from the public. The Service Canada call centres now handle about 65 million calls each year (Service Canada 2006). Federal public servants working in Service Canada call centres across the country provide information to callers and connect them to other government services.

This new program, however, resulted in substantial workplace changes for many public-service workers in Canada. In some cases, "front-line" office jobs were converted to call-centre jobs, where workers no longer have direct contact with the public, and in other cases, representatives from various government departments have been physically relocated to work in larger "Service Canada" call centres. In many ways, this move parallels transformations in the banking and financial sectors, where front-line tellers have also been transferred into call-centre jobs. As one Service Canada worker notes, he did not like the fact that his "job changed drastically from administrative to 'call centre'" while he had "no input" and "little" or no impact on the process. In this chapter, we begin to develop a profile of this new group of federal government employees and explore some of the issues involved in this major work-place transformation.

In the Canadian federal government, many of the Service Canada call-centre workers are members of the Public Service Alliance of Canada (PSAC), one of Canada's largest unions, representing over 150,000 workers through more than 230 bargaining units, ranging in size from a few employees to over 70,000, and organized through an alliance of 17 different components (PSAC 2006). The PSAC represents a range of federal public-service workers through units such as the Canada Employment and Immigration Union, Government Services Union, Union of Taxation Employees, Union of Veterans' Affairs Employees, and so on. This research was initiated in part because representatives from the PSAC identified an increasing number of call-centre workers among their membership, and they were interested in knowing more about the working conditions and challenges faced by federal call-centre workers. This project is a result of collaboration between the PSAC and York University's Centre for Research on Work and Society.

Characterizing Call-Centre Service Work

The majority of research on call centres is based in the UK, the largest and most established call-centre market in Europe. There is comparatively little research available about call-centre work in North America. Generally, there are two competing characterizations of call-centre work that re-occur in the academic literature: call centres as "high-tech," high-skilled work environments in an information economy; and call centres as highly regulated, de-skilled jobs in a service economy (Belt, Richardson and Webster 2000). While we certainly acknowledge differences in conditions and experiences of work within various types of call centres, many researchers' descriptions of call-centre work as involving difficult and intense working conditions, physical relocations, repetition, and scripted and highly monitored client interchanges, tip the balance toward the negative in general conceptualizations of call-centre work.

Ursula Huws's (2003) extensive work on the impact of technology on labour processes, the structure of telemediated work, and the impact on women's paid and unpaid work both within and outside the domestic domain provide the theoretical underpinnings for analyzing both the significance of work transformations that accompany changes in technology and also the social forces underlying these transformations. To naively suggest that the use of technologies simplifies labour processes, provides solutions to the management of vast amounts of data, and enhances the capacity of work within organizational frameworks overlooks the central features of information and communication technologies (ICTs) and their associated labour processes. These technologically mediated labour processes are dehumanizing when they eliminate face-to face contact and are de-skilling when they limit deviations from scripts or carefully specified activities. Moreover, telework increases the possibility of the relocation of work, thereby escalating workers' insecurities and making the search for meaningful work even more elusive (Huws 2003; Buchanan 2006).

A central feature of call centres is the standardization of service work. Interactions between clients and service providers are regulated, often via scripts, and monitored for efficiency, speed, and accuracy. Many call-centre workers characterize their work as "repetitive, stressful and tiring," in the same way that they would describe working on a factory production line (Belt, Richardson and Webster 2000). This is in direct contrast to the emotional persona that call-centre workers are required to portray, as "smiling" and helpful service providers, with an even-toned voice and manner. Not surprisingly, women tend to be over-represented among call-centre employees (Glucksmann 2004; Belt, Richardson and Webster 2000). In part, this is because many of these service-provision jobs tend to require feminized skills, such as interpersonal communications and "emotional labour," which women are generally seen as more capable of performing (Hochschild 1983; Glucksmann 2004).

While call-centre work is sometimes framed as the quintessential "McJob" of the "new economy," many call-centre workers note that the "complexity and value of their work ... [are] under-appreciated in other parts of the organization of which the call centre ... [is] a part, and also within society in general" (Belt, Richardson and Webster 2000: 376). Multilingual agents in call centres often use a complex set of skills and abilities to interact in one language and interface with a computer program in another (Belt, Richardson and Webster 2000). Call-centre workers in New Delhi, India, for example, are expected to transform their own identities while at work by undertaking cultural training, adopting accents and diction to blend with that of their North American clients, and masking their real location (Mirchandani 2004). Moreover, these workers often find themselves having to think "on their feet" and respond quickly, carefully balancing their need to remain "on script" and the evaluation of their heavily monitored performance, with the need for a courteous and respectful response to the client.

Despite the hidden demands on call-centre workers to multi-task in an increasingly intense and competitive work environment, in their study of call centres Belt, Richardson and Webster (2000) found that there were few opportunities for promotion, due to "flat" organizational structures. Few employees have access to training that would allow them to be promoted to more senior positions. For the most part, workers are expected to "learn on the job." Younger workers hopeful for promotions are forced into an endless cycle of job searches, only to find themselves in similar employment circumstances after several years' experience.

An exception to the general lack of opportunities for call-centre workers is the development of bilingual call centres offering job-advancement opportunities for francophones living outside of Quebec (Budach, Roy and Heller 2003). In some francophone communities, call centres are seen by community members as crucial for the stability of the local economy, and are especially key for providing French-language work for women. In one case study of a bilingual call centre established in a community that had previously relied on manufacturing labour, the researchers found that use of the French language was not related to valuing cultural or social dimensions of the francophone identity; rather, it was about securing customer loyalty (Budach, Roy and Heller 2003). Bilingual call-centre workers are expected to move back and forth easily between French and English whenever called upon to do so. As one Service Canada employee explains:

> The information is there; you just need more time to look for it and integrate it. Because our French clients they have French documentation, but we are a lot faster in English because we are used to it and the English documentation is easier to access. In French or in English, things are termed this or that way.

Being bilingual in a standardized environment like a call centre is effectively "being unilingual twice over, with each [language] being used in a standard, normative form" (Budach, Roy and Heller 2003: 619). This approach creates difficulties for bilingual workers, as noted by a number of federal service workers. As one bilingual worker located outside Quebec explains:

> ... we are trained in English. We are not trained in French. The
> terminology kills us, really. Completely. Because, it's not ... [the
> same] ... see I am Acadian, not Québécoise. Our French is not
> the same ... [as] the one in Quebec. The terms we use are not the
> same. So if I have a client that calls from Quebec, on line, who
> has the proper terms, the right terminology, I am completely
> lost.

Within the structure of the call centre, the worker's language skills are
commodified. The bilingual worker provides a value-added dimension to
client service as she is able to reach within both the francophone and the
anglophone communities to secure a loyal customer base while occupying only one headset and collecting just one paycheque.

Transforming Public-Service Work

Most of the recent literature on work restructuring and, in particular,
on call centres, considers changing conditions and structures of work
within the private sector. There has been relatively little study of the
state as an employer or of the complex of factors that may contribute
to change within public services. Moreover, there is no consensus on
the personal, political, cultural, and social significance of shifting work
relations and the new "culture" of service provision within the public
domain (Pupo 2007).

Indeed, a complex set of factors has been transforming public-sector work. These include mounting economic pressures to maintain a
Canadian presence in the global economy, the rising costs of social reproduction, and fiscal crises, along with technological innovations, new
management structures and flexibility initiatives. In line with these pressures, the transformations in public-sector work have included privatizing some aspects of work, devaluing or deskilling some categories of
work, and eliminating certain forms of work altogether. These changes
are raising questions regarding working conditions and security amongst
public-sector workers and the risks and benefits to the general public.

A number of social analysts (McBride 2001; Evans and Shields 1998)
have examined the restructuring and shrinking of the state and the adoption of a neoliberal agenda to maintain Canada's competitiveness in
response to global economic pressures. Work restructuring within the
public sector entails a complex and detailed consideration of the movement of work from the public domain to the realm of private enterprise,
as well as to the sphere of unpaid work. Panitch and Swartz (2003) have
argued that trade-union rights and freedoms have been eroded over the

past 30 years, as governments at both the provincial and the federal level have adopted neoliberal business practices in the re-making of the "lean" Canadian state. To do so, state officials and governments have imported the practices of corporate processes, including the operation of call centres, into the public domain. While studies have discussed the consequences of the state's decline for public-sector workers with regard to job loss and growing precariousness, few have considered the changing labour processes or the growing reliance on telemediated work arrangements. One of the ways the Canadian state is responding to global economic pressures is by adopting private-sector practices and promoting (real or anticipated) efficiencies by cheapening its services, engaging in fiscal restraint, shifting the costs of social programs onto individual citizens or unions, and finding ways to cut the cost of public-service work and the size of the public-sector labour force.

Focusing primarily on the private sector, social analysts have studied global economic transformations and considered whether they have contributed to greater opportunities for Canadians or whether they have given rise to an increasing number of peripheral, insecure jobs and consequently to the loss of relatively secure, well-compensated, and respected positions. With workplace restructuring, the main concerns are that there has been a measurable decline in the social conditions of work and that the shifts toward insecure, poorly compensated, non-standard work have overshadowed developments toward quality work. Work restructuring within the public sector has transformed the ways in which work is organized, managed, and defined, and this in turn affects workers' sense of well-being and security, as well as their expectations regarding access to work. Changes in the public-sector workplace also force trade unions to re-visit their agendas, as they are faced with changing work arrangements and new levels of insecurity amongst their memberships. Key to the restructuring of public-sector workplaces are processes of privatization, contracting out, commercialization, and the use of temporary work agencies. These new arrangements have a huge impact on workers and their families, collective bargaining and trade unions, social policy and the legal framework, and the meaning of social citizenship.

For Canada to mark its place within a global economic system in which internationalized capital and global organizations dominate, the Canadian state, along with other advanced capitalist states, has been engaged in repositioning itself by adopting a monetarist economic agenda and contracting the welfare state, that intricate web of social programs and services referred to as the social safety net (Teeple 1995). Beginning in the 1970s as the globalization of production expanded, Keynesian policies and liberal welfare-state practices were gradually replaced by a monetarist approach that was required by internationalized capital in a global economy (Teeple 1995: 70). A primary goal of the state, in order to maintain its new status within the global economy, was to lower the costs of production; this eventually led to the dismantling of the welfare state. In turn, this has meant a restructuring of work and a reorganization of the public-sector workplace. During the 1980s and early 1990s, downsizing became the order of the day. It took two forms: the elimination of middle levels of public servants and the conversion of full-time (unionized) positions to part-time or contractually limited positions. Moreover, whenever possible, relatively well-paid, more highly educated and skilled workers were replaced with lower-paid workers who often had fewer years of training and experience and less education.

More recently, public-sector workers have faced new insecurities from freshly implemented work arrangements, such as privatization, contracting out, and various forms of electronic monitoring and electronic work. Restructuring initiatives, including flexibility measures, new management practices, and technological change, have also given rise to alternative work arrangements. Public-sector unions are currently engaged in strategies to oppose such initiatives, arguing that they contravene existing collective agreements by removing guarantees of rights to work, security, and in some cases, seniority. It is within the context of these transformations within the public services that we examine work arrangements and conditions within federal public-service call centres.

Study Methodology

The profile of federal call-centre workers below was developed based on mailed questionnaires and semi-structured interviews. The PSAC asked union representatives in each workplace to identify members in their area who were primarily engaged in call-centre work, and these individuals were invited to participate in the research.

On February 27, 2006, about 2,400 members of PSAC were mailed a package, individually addressed to their homes, containing a bilingual information letter, a four-page questionnaire in both English and French, and a postage-paid envelope for returning the completed survey to the Centre for Research on Work and Society (CRWS).[1] The content of the questionnaire was developed in consultation with union representatives. On March 17, 2006, a reminder postcard was sent to every member who had been sent an initial package, asking them to complete and return their questionnaire if they had not done so already, and thanking them for returning their questionnaire if they had already done so. The postcard also provided directions for downloading a blank questionnaire from the CRWS website, in case the original mailing had been lost or discarded. Three respondents returned questionnaires that they had printed out from the website.

In total, 671 completed questionnaires were returned. Assuming that all of the individuals listed on the PSAC mailing list were eligible to participate in the research, the overall return rate was about 28 per cent. This is an adequate response rate for a mail survey, though it is difficult to know exactly how the perceptions and experiences of members who did not return the questionnaire differ from those of members who did. It is possible, but not certain, that members who participated in this research are less satisfied with their work environments than members who did not. Questionnaire data was entered into SPSS for further analysis.

The final section of the questionnaire asked respondents whether they would be willing to participate in a brief telephone interview with a researcher from York University, and if so, to provide a contact number and first name. Respondents who did not provide this information remained completely anonymous. In total, 38 per cent of respondents indicated that they would be willing to participate in an interview, and a smaller proportion was selected as potential interviewees. Some of these respondents were selected by the research team, based on an attempt to acquire a diversity of perspectives, especially in relation to gender, visible-minority status, Aboriginal status, disability status, and work satisfaction. Twenty-five semi-structured interviews were completed between May and October 2006. Thirteen interviews were conducted in French, and the remaining twelve interviews were conducted in English. Interviews generally took 20 to 40 minutes and were focused around a series of questions developed by members of the research team and PSAC representatives. Interviews were audio-taped, and key ideas from each interview were transcribed. Together the survey and interview data provide a rich source of both qualitative and quantitative information about the work environments and experiences of call-centre workers in the federal government.

The results below focus on the sub-sample of respondents who work in Service Canada or its sub-departments, including Social Development Canada, Citizenship and Immigration, Veterans' Affairs, and the Canada Revenue Agency (about 60 per cent of survey respondents).[2] People who spent less than half their time doing call-centre work, and people who worked in offices where fewer than half of the employees were engaged in call-centre work were excluded from this analysis. The result is a sample of 342 Service Canada "dedicated" call-centre workers. Of this sample, 70 per cent spend all of their time doing call-centre work.

Who are Service Canada Call-Centre Employees?

Given the characterization of call-centre work as a feminized occupation, it is not surprising that about three-quarters of the respondents
(74%) were women. This is substantially higher than in the Canadian
labour force overall, where just less than half are women (Statistics
Canada 2008). This gender division provides an important context for
understanding the characteristics of call-centre work, given that women
tend to have substantially different experiences in and expectations of
employment than men. The proportions of visible-minority respondents (13%) and Aboriginal respondents (4%) were similar to the proportion of these groups in the overall Canadian population (Statistics
Canada 2008). Interestingly, among visible-minority respondents, more
than a third (38%) were men. These results suggest that visible-minority men may be over-represented in this type of employment. The age of
survey respondents ranged from 22–68 years old, with an average age
of 42 (s.d.=9.6). The age distribution of survey respondents also mirrors
those of the Canadian workforce more generally. Notably, more than
half (58%) of these "dedicated" call-centre employees are over age forty,
suggesting that these jobs are not simply entry-level civil-service jobs, nor
are these employees lacking in work experience.

Survey respondents were also more highly educated than the overall Canadian workforce, and this conforms to the long-standing profile
of public-service work as providing opportunities for educated workers.
None reported having less than a high-school diploma, 25 per cent had
a high-school diploma or equivalent, 41 per cent had a college/CEGEP
diploma, and about a third (32%) had at least one university degree. In
contrast, almost a quarter (23%) of the Canadian population of working age does not have a high school diploma, and about the same proportion has a university degree (Statistics Canada 2001). Considering
the educational credentials of workers then, we can see that federal call-
centre work may be perceived as a skilled job.

Among this sample of survey respondents, two-thirds (67%) were permanent (classified as "indeterminate"[3]) workers, and the remaining third
were contract workers. Slightly more than half of the respondents (55%)
were employed full-time. Permanent workers are much more likely to be
employed full-time than contract or casual workers. Almost two-thirds
(63%) of the permanent employees worked full-time, compared to only
37 per cent of the non-permanent employees. Non-permanent employees tended to be younger and better educated than permanent employees.
It is likely that permanent employees have fewer educational credentials but have more seniority and experience working in the federal civil

service. Visible-minority and Aboriginal respondents were also slightly more likely to be non-permanent employees, but more data are needed to discern whether there is any notable trend in these areas.

On average, respondents had worked in their current job for about five years (s.d.=4.0). About half of the respondents (54%) had been in their current position for less than four years. Not surprisingly, non-permanent employees tended to have been in their job for less time. Eighty-seven per cent of non-permanent employees had been employed in their job for less than two years, compared to only 9 per cent of the permanent employees. On average, non-permanent employees had been in their position for 1.4 years (s.d.= 0.9), compared to permanent employees, who had been in their position for an average of 6.8 years (s.d.=3.8).

A "Factory of Voices": Work and Workplace Characteristics in Federal Call-Centre Work

Federal call-centre work is shaped in part by the organizational culture of the federal government, but is also influenced by the expectations for call-centre work more generally. As unionized workers in a structured workplace, most respondents agreed that they can take regular breaks (as specified in their collective agreement) and work the same days and hours each week (see Figure 6.1). There is some evidence that call-centre workers are a contingent labour force. About 80 per cent of respondents reported that they work shifts; of those, about 70 per cent reported that they are asked to work overtime when there is more work. Only about half of shift workers reported that their shifts are reduced when there is less work, though this result is more difficult to interpret: it may be that their shifts are not reduced, or that there is never "less work."

Figure 6.1   Characteristics of Work Organization in Federal Call Centres (n=342)

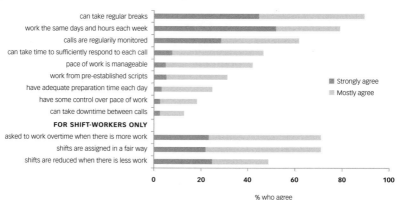

A key area of concern for call-centre employees seems to be the pace of work. Fewer than half of the respondents (42%) reported that the pace of their work is manageable, and employees are generally not able to control the speed of incoming calls. Fewer than one in five respondents (18%) reported that they have some control over the pace of their work. In addition, many respondents noted that they are unable to prepare adequately for their shifts or for the next call. Only a quarter of respondents reported that they have adequate preparation time each day, and only 13 per cent of respondents indicated that they can take down time between calls. One respondent noted that "two seconds between calls is not reasonable. [It's] not possible to take a breath between each call" (translated from French). Another reported that "the calls come in 3 seconds apart. [There's] not enough time to have a drink of water in between calls." Since workers are required to complete the accompanying paperwork by the end of the call, some (right-handed) workers reported that they have rearranged their workstations and trained themselves to operate the mouse with their left hand so that they can write while talking. One worker explicitly compared her conditions in the call centre to the dehumanizing conditions of globalized labour practices: "I like my work a lot, however employees are treated like machines and not humans for those stats. Three seconds between each call is like a 'sweat shop'" (translated from French).

While the pace of work at the phones is heavily monitored and expectations regarding employees' efficiencies are high, there is little time provided for workers to update themselves on new departmental procedures, legislative changes affecting service delivery, or other matters. Workers reported that they are allotted 15 minutes a day "to read up on our information bank, which is national, to update ourselves in our emails, and to read a whole bunch of readings related to work...." Because the work is "too complex and there is too much to read," most find themselves using personal time to maintain both accuracy in the information they will provide to callers and confidence in their performance. For many workers, this seems to reflect a situation where technological control effectively structures the pace of the work environment without attention to the quality of service provided.

For many employees, this high-paced environment conflicts with their idea of public service. As one respondent noted, there is more of a focus on "quantity not quality. Increasingly over the years numbers seem to matter more than the people we serve." Several respondents reported that it is stressful to have to account specifically for all of the minutes that they are on a shift. For many respondents, there was a clear disconnect between liking their job and being able to serve the public, and the conditions under which they perform their job. One respondent summed it up in this way:

> I like my job. I hate the conditions I work under. I have to take a minimum of 12 calls per hour. I must be on the phone 92% of my day or I have to explain why. Calls come in non-stop with no break in between.

Another noted that it is "called 'client services' but it's more about their 'numbers.'" Several respondents reported feeling conflicted that they are not actually able to help people in the time allotted. Others reported situations where they are told to deliberately misrepresent information to the public in order to meet their hourly or daily quotas, and how this leaves them feeling ineffective in serving clients.

The conflict between quotas and the time allotted per call on the one hand, and quality and efficiency on the other, is a constant source of tension:

> Time around calls can get pretty tense. It sometimes feels like you have no breathing room ... There's something like [a] 200 seconds goal to finish calls; but that's not the reality. It just doesn't always work like that. We have some people with real issues and sometimes they need to vent frustrations, ask a lot of questions, or they need a lot of information explained because they're just not familiar with the procedures.

Another worker described resisting the push by management to shorten calls and continues to work at the standard of 12 calls per hour on average. The dilemma, however, is in having to be compared to a "rate-buster" who logs considerably more calls per hour:

> ... there were people, next to me that answered pitifully to clients, but that didn't matter. The person had 15 calls an hour. But the service to the client! But they left him alone because he did 15. Probably, the managers have to answer to quotas, probably at this level they were under pressure too.

Another dimension of the downward pressures on average call times and the close environment of the call centre is that many workers experience a competitive atmosphere amongst co-workers, contributing to the pressures to increase productivity. In the words of one of the workers,

> it's not like there is no solidarity ... but given that we are sur-
> rounded by people [who] take call after call, without stopping,
> non-stop, it's like we are sucked in ... in the system ... it snow-
> balls. I cannot not take a call, when my colleagues right beside
> me are answering non stop ... it's not fair for them.

While they are on the phones, the workers are continually aware of
each call's time score and the way in which it may affect their overall
numbers. This worker described the balancing and time management the
work involves: "statistically they ask us not to take more than 300 seconds per call. That's 5 minutes, 300 seconds ... that's an average for the
week. Not for a day, but for the week. If you have an average of 300 seconds or less, that's a good score." The issue of time pressures and keeping
scores, as if the work were a basketball game, conflicts with the human-
service capacity of the job at hand. One worker presented the dilemma
of taking a "long" call:

> Sometimes, when we have 2 or 3 situations that surface dur-
> ing the call, well the call will end up being 45 minutes. And
> a 45-minute call massacres your stats. And because I am part
> time, it's even worse. One 45 minute call in a week, given that
> I work only 3 days ... it will massacre my stats even if I would
> work 5 days.

Time management and statistical record-keeping (workers' "scores") are
not particular to public-service call-centre work. However, unlike their
counterparts in the private sector, public-sector workers are not simply
selling a product or providing a technical service for the callers. They
understand that in their capacity as "information specialists," they perform a valuable service for Canadians, often providing information and
service that make a considerable difference in people's lives. Subjecting
their work to time monitoring and intensification not only devalues the
service these workers provide, but also erodes the public's confidence in
the public service.

The result of a pace controlled via technology and high levels of time-
accountability is a high-stress work environment. Almost 9 out of 10
respondents (89%) agreed that they work in a stressful environment. As
one respondent noted: "I feel the high stress levels caused by answering
calls with no pause between calls causes my work place to be poisoned."
Another respondent asserted that "the environment we work in could
be related to a 'sweat shop.' The work itself is manageable, it's the envi-

ronment ... that's hard to work with or in." The working conditions are reminiscent of a Fordist assembly line, as one worker suggested:

> I call it a "factory of voices." That's all it is. Instead of assembling parts for cars, you're just processing people or processing calls—"a factory of voices." Everybody is sitting there in their little stalls talking and producing customer service.

According to a significant number of the workers surveyed, the techniques of supervision and micro-management exacerbate the stresses of time pressures and the physical and mental demands of the job. Workers described being "monitored, timed and required to explain every moment of the day outside of breaks to the point ... [of harassment]." Some described management's "system of fear and intimidation," the inability or refusal to communicate with staff, the high expectations, and the lack of positive feedback. "The 'Big Brother' aspect of the call centre," the feeling of "being under a microscope," and the "zero tolerance" for being late by a minute or for any other minor infraction were regarded by some as more stressful than the work itself. One worker clarified that the management system is not simply stressful, but it is in every way "overwhelming." Another described supervision and management as "a dynamic of surveillance." One person explained:

> ... it's the police. And the police is very serious ... It's really like the police; it's surveillance. It's like at school. But there is a lot of policing, in the sense that they imposed things on us, norms toward people, certain sentences we have to say. Extremely ridiculous. Like robotized ... but if we didn't say it, we lost points. And it was a big thing.

In terms of traditional health-and-safety concerns, call-centre environments seem to be relatively responsive. The physical characteristics of workstations were highly rated: more than 80 per cent of the respondents reported that they have adequate lighting and can adjust their chair for their comfort (see Figure 6.2). Most also reported that they can modify their workstation to meet their needs and that the headsets are reasonably comfortable. Despite this, however, the job is associated with some physical discomfort. Two-thirds of respondents (67%) reported that they often experience bodily pain as a result of their work. Workers reported feeling "tied to their desk" and not being able to get up and walk around when they experience discomfort. As one worker noted, the job involves "multi-tasking" with the extensive paperwork required in addition to the telework, and "on a bad day, that means multi-pains, headaches, stiffness." About half of the respondents (46%) also reported that they often lose their voice as a result of their work. These results suggest that despite physical accommodations, the physical implications of this type of service work must be better addressed.

Figure 6.2   Characteristics of Work Environment in Federal Call Centres (n=342)

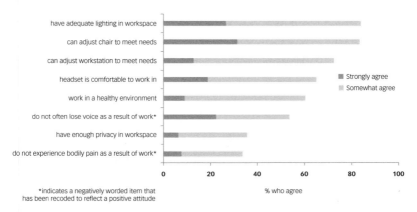

*indicates a negatively worded item that
has been recoded to reflect a positive attitude

% who agree

The relatively good report on physical work space and equipment conforms to a traditional view of white- (or pink-) collar work, particularly in the public sector. Interestingly, however, a few workers characterized their work environment as "dirty" and referred to their work as "dirty work in clean places." Some employees noted that they work in a different station or cubicle each shift. Not only does this give employees a sense of impermanence or instability, but it increases the likelihood of germ transmission, as numerous employees share a single headset or keyboard. Some employees have compensated by purchasing their own equipment, effectively transferring the burden of maintaining a healthy workplace from the employer to employees.

For many teleworkers, work space has been reduced to accommodate the computer screen, with little room left for personal comfort and privacy. With dozens or even hundreds of workers plugged into their headsets within the same room, the noise is often overwhelming. With two-ear headsets on, some workers said that their hearing is blocked and described the experience as "claustrophobic." Moreover, as they are focused on the caller, they do not realize that their conversations are a source of stress and interruption for others. Many said that in addition to the "constant buzzing" of the headsets, the background noise level is "incredible."

The stress of the high noise levels and uncomfortable work spaces is compounded for some by the cramped quarters. In some offices workers complained, "instead of being in an isolated cubicle, there are four agents in each cubicle. It's an open cubicle ... and [we] work back to back, and there are no walls between us." Another worker said, "cubicles resemble veal pens more than work stations." Yet although the work spaces are small, many complained that they are not "closed off enough," that "neighbors are 'too close,'" and that there are not enough "divisions," making the work "feel like a production line" while workers are "shackled to a phone."

Conclusion

It is clear that the implementation of the Service Canada call-centre delivery model has substantially transformed the work experiences and career trajectories of Canadian public-service workers. This workplace transformation can be conceptualized as yet another outcome of the trend toward a globalized economy and the adoption of neoliberal government structures. Despite the characteristics of the civil service as a "helping" and "white-collar" profession, workers in public-service call centres experience many of the same challenges as private-sector call-centre workers: they are treated as contingent labour, subjected to authoritarian management practices, and technological developments control the pace of work. Many workers view the adoption of "efficiency" practices as incompatible with the goals of the public service. Graphic characterizations of federal call centres as "sweat shops" and "veal pens" by some employees reflect the move toward standardized labour practices and their dehumanizing effects.

This new workplace culture is associated with new career trajectories for some public-service workers. An older cohort of workers has been moved out of "front-line" service work and into these call-centre environments. They remain in this work because at this late point in their employment trajectories, they have "nowhere else to go." Another group, those who are bilingual, experience better working conditions and pay levels as compared to their previous positions within the private sector. However, most workers within federal public-service call centres regard their positions as simply "jobs," thereby challenging more entrenched notions of the possibility of a "career" in the civil service. These workplace changes must be understood within the context of a changing notion of the public service more generally.

This first profile of public-service call-centre workers in Canada highlights the need for more research in this area. A direct comparison of the working conditions in public-service call-centres and similar private-sector workplaces would generate a better understanding about what, if anything at all, is unique about the government's implementation of tele-work. In addition, following the concerns voiced by many research participants, it would be worthwhile investigating whether the "service" (and not just the "accessibility") to the public is perceived to have improved or decreased as a result of the move to a call-centre model. Finally, the changing role of union and collective bargaining in these transformed workplaces provides another rich topic for labour researchers.

Discussion Questions

1. How has public-service work in Canada been transformed in the past decade?

2. How have these transformations affected the everyday work experiences of federal employees?

3. What role has the Canadian state played in public-sector restructuring?

Notes

1   Of the first survey mailing, 159 packages and 35 follow-up postcards were returned as "undeliverable" or "return to sender." Some of these PSAC members were likely not notified about the research and therefore were not given the opportunity to participate.

2   Other federal call-centre workers, such as those working for Statistics Canada or Canada Post, as well as those who did not specify what agency they worked for, are excluded from this analysis.

3   In the workplace, so-called "permanent" workers are formally categorized as workers whose job has an "indeterminate" end date. This further adds to feelings of job insecurity.

References

Belt, V., R. Richardson, and J. Webster. 2000. "Women's Work in the Information Economy: The Case of Telephone Call Centres." *Information, Communication & Society* 3 (3): 366–85.

Buchanan, R. 2006. "1-800 New Brunswick: Economic Development Strategies, Firm Restructuring, and the Local Production of 'Global' Services." In Vivian Shalla (ed.), *Working in a Global Era: Canadian Perspectives*. Toronto: Canadian Scholars' Press. 177–97.

Budach, G., S. Roy, and M. Heller. 2003. "Community and Commodity in French Ontario." *Language in Society* 32: 603–27.

Evans, B., and J. Shields. 1998. *Shrinking the State: Globalization and Public Administration Reform*. Halifax: Fernwood.

Glucksmann, M.A. 2004. "Call Configurations: Varieties of Call Centre and Divisions of Labour." *Work, Employment and Society* 18 (4): 795–811.

Hochschild, A.R. 1983. *The Managed Heart: Commercialization of Human Feeling.* Berkeley: University of California Press.

Huws, U. 2003. *The Making of a Cybertariat: Virtual Work in a Real World.* New York: Monthly Review Press.

McBride, S. 2001. *Paradigm Shift: Globalization and the Canadian State.* Halifax: Fernwood.

Mirchandani, K. 2004. "Practices of Global Capital: Gaps, Cracks and Ironies in Transnational Call Centres in India." *Global Networks* 4 (4): 355–73.

Panitch, L., and D. Swartz. 2003. *From Consent to Coercion: The Assault on Trade Union Freedoms.* 3rd ed. Toronto: Garamond Press.

PSAC (Public Service Alliance Canada). 2006. "Negotiations." <http://www.psac.com/ bargaining/index-e.shtml>.

Pupo, N. 2007. "Behind the Screens: Telemediated Work in the Canadian Public Service." *Work Organization, Labour and Globalization* 1 (2): 155–67.

Service Canada. 2006. "Fast Facts." <http://www.servicecanada.gc.ca/en/about/facts/ fastfacts.shtml>.

Statistics Canada. 2008. "Census 2006: Topic Based Tabulations – Labour Force Activity." <http://www12.statcan.ca/english/census06/data/topics/ListProducts.cfm ?Temporal=2006&APATH=3&THEME=74&FREE=0&SUB=741&GRP=1>.

Teeple, G. 1995. *Globalization and the Decline of Social Reform.* Toronto: Garamond Press.

7. Student Workers and the "New Economy" of Mid-Sized Cities
The Cases of Peterborough and Kingston, Ontario

STEVEN TUFTS AND JOHN HOLMES

Introduction

Historically, post-secondary education (PSE) institutions have played a complex and at times contradictory economic role. In the Anglo-American tradition, universities and colleges have served as spaces where ideas can develop free from the pressures of commercialization *and* as powerful economic agents in their own right through the local purchasing power generated by their employees' wages and the purchasing of goods and services (Fallis 2007). The transition to a knowledge-based economy has, however, increased pressure on universities and colleges to commercialize knowledge and build corporate partnerships. Universities increasingly find themselves at the centre of "new economy" development initiatives. For example, they are often perceived to be anchors of innovative "clusters" that drive accumulation and enhance the competitive advantage of specific places in a global economy (Wolfe and Gertler 2004; SSTI, 2006; CREST Expert Group, 2006). Linked to this latter role is the desire to attract and retain highly-skilled knowledge workers, and especially graduates from local universities and colleges.

In mid-sized cities, PSE institutions are expected to foster growth in new economy industries to help stem the tide of deindustrialization and the outflow of young workers to larger metropolitan centres. This chapter investigates the links among post-secondary institutions, student workers, and the development of the new economy in two mid-sized Canadian cities: Peterborough and Kingston, Ontario. While more is known about the role that PSE institutions play in labour-market formation in metropolitan centres and locales dominated by large, historic institutions (see Lafer 2003; Appleseed Inc. 2003), much less is known about the role that such institutions play in smaller urban centres.

Post-secondary institutions do play a complex role in the local economic development of medium-sized centres. Beyond the local economic impact of faculty and staff salaries and local procurement of goods and services by the university or college, other impacts are difficult to quantify. We argue that universities may provide a temporary buffer in medium-sized centres against the loss of younger skilled workers to larger metropolitan labour markets. Specifically, we attempt to link changes in the roles that students play in local labour markets to broader trends in economic development. We conclude with some policy implications with respect to the links between PSE institutions and local economic development initiatives.

Following a brief synopsis of the changing economic role that universities and colleges play in communities, we contextualize the two cities and the university located in each one.[1] While the two locales share several similarities, it is important to note that the institutions are *scaled* quite differently as a result of their different historical legacies. Queen's University is an established major research-intensive institution that draws students from across Canada and beyond and whose graduates enter an increasingly far-flung global labour market. In comparison, Trent University is much more regionally focused, with regard to both the place of origin of its students and the geographical distribution of its graduates. Using alumni data, we attempt to map the shifting geographies of graduates from each institution. These data are complemented by qualitative data drawn from interviews with current full-time university students who work while studying, and with local urban development officers. The interviews were carried out in 2005 and 2006.

PSE Institutions, Student Workers, and the New Knowledge-based Economy

It is false to assume that universities and colleges have only come to play a significant economic role during the era of neoliberalism that has characterized the last quarter-century. There have long been historical tensions over the multiple roles that universities play in society (Fallis 2007; Axelrod 2002). Almost since the inception of publicly funded universities, economic arguments have been used to justify state support for post-secondary education. First and foremost, PSE institutions train future workers for certain higher-level segments of the technical division of labour. Second, the salaries and wages of university employees have a significant local economic impact in smaller communities. When the physical infrastructure of campuses is being expanded through new building projects, jobs are created locally in construction and ancillary services (as in the case of the current multi-million-dollar building program at Queen's). In communities facing prolonged periods of economic restructuring and loss of manufacturing employment (as was the case in both Kingston and Peterborough throughout the 1980s and 1990s), the relatively high wages and secure jobs in universities and colleges provide a degree of economic stability. For Peterborough, the economic impact of Trent University has been calculated by university administrators to be over $200 million per year (Michael 2004). Similarly, a 2003 study (KEDCO 2003) estimated that Queen's University generated a total direct economic impact on Kingston of $567.9 million ($207.3 million from student spending, $186.3 million from faculty and staff spending, $6.4 million from visitors (e.g., parents, guests), $36.5 million in goods and services purchased locally, and $131.4 million by the medical school and teaching hospital). By contrast, in his study of the impact of Yale University on New Haven, Connecticut, Lafer (2003) argued that the economic impacts may be limited in small towns with large private universities that dominate the economic landscape. The tax base of the town may be adversely affected by the tax-free status of the university, other types of industrial development limited, and a pool of low-wage service labour created to support the university.

Third, PSE institutions are increasingly viewed as "incubators of innovation" where private and public capital can be combined for research and development purposes (Rutherford and Holmes 2008; Atkinson-Grosjean 2006; Branscomb, Kodama and Florida 1999). Universities and colleges lie at the heart of specialized "clusters" in new economy industries ranging from biotechnology to information and communication technologies (ICTs) (see Appleseed Inc. 2003 for a report on the impact of such research institutions in the Boston area). At Trent, a platform for a DNA cluster has been established on the campus with physical space (i.e., pods) for start-up companies to network with faculty specializing in biology and forensics. Queen's has recently opened an Innovation Park focusing on advanced materials, alternative energy, and environmental technologies, which "through the co-location of academic and industry researchers, service providers and commercialization experts, ... [helps] researchers and entrepreneurs to create, develop and market their innovations" (Innovation Park 2008).

Related to the development of knowledge-based economic "clusters" is the economic role universities play as the primary drivers of new spaces of consumption that are deemed increasingly important for the attraction of "talent" and creative knowledge workers (Florida 2002, 2008; Martin Prosperity Institute 2009). Faculty and student demand for arts and cultural amenities, recreation facilities, and "cool" bars and cafes leads to the development of consumption spaces that attract "creative" people. In promotional material for Trent University, Peterborough is defined as "a great university town" with "the energy, diversity and resources of a larger centre, plus the welcoming sense of community found in smaller towns" (Trent University 2006: 4).

But students not only drive demand for these amenities and as a result shape place identity; they also increase the supply of labour to deliver these services. Over the past three decades, labour-force participation rates for full-time students aged 20 to 24 years has doubled in Canada (Figure 7.1). In the 1990s, labour-force participation rates increased steadily for 20–24 year olds as the rate for younger students (15–19 years old) decreased, only to recover in the late 1990s. Here the connection can be made between rapidly rising post-secondary tuition fees and the increase in the number of students seeking part-time employment while enrolled as full-time PSE students. There is evidence of such students displacing younger secondary school-aged students from part-time service-sector work in Kingston (Denstedt 2008). The 2002 National Graduate Survey found that for students who graduated in 2000, employment earnings constituted over 50 per cent of the resources used to finance their post-secondary education (Barr-Telford 2005).

Figure 7.1   Participation Rates by Full-time Students during School Months, Canada, 1976–2006

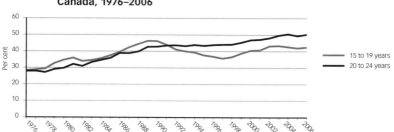

Source: Statistics Canada 2008, Labour Force Survey, CANSIM Table 282-009.

This shift in the paid-employment patterns of full-time students over the last 30 years raises interesting questions regarding school-to-work transition and local labour-market development. Does increased labour-market participation while studying serve to "attach" university students to places in ways that increase their likelihood of remaining in that community after graduation? Do such processes of student labour-market integration have broader implications for communities facing youth out-migration? Will young creative and skilled workers, who are viewed as central to ensuring the viability of the new knowledge economy in medium-sized communities, remain in university towns such as Peterborough and Kingston?

Patterns of Alumni Retention in Peterborough and Kingston

Peterborough and Kingston are both situated in southern Ontario, east of the Greater Toronto Area (see Figure 7.2). The historical geographies of each centre are quite distinct. Kingston is an older settlement with a rich pre-Confederation political and military history (Osborne and Swainson 1988). Peterborough was a later nineteenth-century settlement, and Trent University was not established until 1964, well over a century after the Presbyterian Church founded Queen's University in 1841. Queen's, once known in Canada for the quality of the liberal arts undergraduate education it offered students, has evolved into an internationally recognized research-intensive institution with law, business, and medical schools and an associated teaching hospital. Trent is a relatively young institution established as part of the expansion of PSE in Ontario to meet the demand generated by the "baby boomers" who came of age in the 1960s. The institutions, therefore, are scaled quite differently, with Queen's servicing a national and even international labour market while Trent is a highly rated but primarily undergraduate liberal arts and science institution serving a more regionally based student body. This creates a unique set of challenges for each community as it seeks to embed its university into the local economy. Furthermore, the presence of Queen's University, RMC, St. Lawrence College, and major hospitals in the mid-sized Kingston labour market skews the education level of the population. In 2006, the number of people with PSE diplomas and degrees in Kingston was above the Ontario average, whereas the Peterborough population had a level of educational attainment below the provincial average (see Table 7.1).

Figure 7.2   Canada First Letter Postal Code Designations

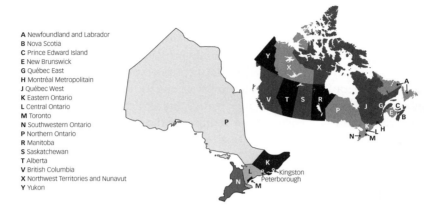

A Newfoundland and Labrador
B Nova Scotia
C Prince Edward Island
E New Brunswick
G Québec East
H Montréal Metropolitain
J Québec West
K Eastern Ontario
L Central Ontario
M Toronto
N Southwestern Ontario
P Northern Ontario
R Manitoba
S Saskatchewan
T Alberta
V British Columbia
X Northwest Territories and Nunavut
Y Yukon

Table 7.1   Kingston and Peterborough Census Metropolitan Areas, 2006 Census

	Kingston CMA	Peterborough CMA	Ontario
Population	152,358	116,570	12,160,282
Population Increase (%), 2001–2006	3.8	5.1	6.6
Unemployment Rate (%)	6.6	7.1	6.4
Immigrant Population (%)	12.5	9.4	28.3
Median age	40.7	43.6	39
Percentage of population 15 years or over with college diploma or university degree	46.1	38.5	43.0
Percentage of population 15–24 with college diploma or university degree	22.4	17.8	19.2
University enrolment, total 2007–2008	Queen's: 21,510 RMC: 1,550	Trent: 7,890	
College enrolment, full-time equivalent 2007–2008	St Lawrence: 5,487	Sir Sandford Fleming: 5,934	

Sources: Statistics Canada, 2006 Community Profiles; AUCC 2009; Colleges of Ontario 2009.

Despite these differences, both mid-sized centres face similar challenges from the continued loss of manufacturing jobs and the flight of younger people to larger urban centres. Throughout the 1980s and 1990s, both cities experienced major reductions in private-sector industrial employment (e.g., General Electric in Peterborough, Alcan and Northern Telecom in Kingston) as the local economies succumbed to global competition. In the recession of the early 1990s, unemployment reached 13 per cent in Peterborough and over 9 per cent in Kingston (Statistics Canada 2008, Labour Force Survey Estimates). If the presence of young people is measured in terms of cohort survival (i.e., the relative size of the cohort as it ages), both Kingston and Peterborough experienced overall shrinkage in the age group 20–34 during this period, while Toronto experienced rapid growth (via in-migration) in these age categories. While the numbers in the younger cohorts stagnated in Peterborough and Kingston, declines were not as severe as those in northern Ontario communities such as Elliot Lake (see Table 7.2).

Table 7.2   **Cohort Survival Ratios* for Selected Census Metropolitan Areas and Census Agglomerations**

CMA/CA	Cohort survival ratio (20–24 to 25–29) 1981–86	Cohort survival ratio (25–29 to 30–34) 1981–86	Cohort survival ratio (20–24 to 25–29) 1986–91	Cohort survival ratio (25–29 to 30–34) 1986–91	Cohort survival ratio (20–24 to 25–29) 1991–96	Cohort survival ratio (25–29 to 30–34) 1991–96	Cohort survival ratio (20–24 to 25–29) 1996–2001	Cohort survival ratio (25–29 to 30–34) 1996–2001
Kingston	0.93	1.02	0.99	1.09	0.94	0.99	0.80	0.92
Peterborough	0.95	0.99	1.05	1.13	0.86	0.96	0.80	0.96
Toronto	1.13	1.07	1.19	1.12	1.12	1.06	1.16	1.11
Elliot Lake	1.03	0.96	0.53	0.58	0.76	0.96	0.53	0.83

*Cohort survival ratios are calculated by dividing the number of persons in a selected age cohort (e.g., 20–24) in period one (e.g., 1981) by the next age cohort (e.g., 25–29) in the subsequent period (e.g., 1986).

Source: Statistics Canada, Custom tabulation of Census Data (selected years) requested by the authors.

The post-secondary institutions in both Kingston and Peterborough potentially act as a buffer to youth out-migration. Much research and policy analysis related to rural–urban migration in the 1990s has focussed on the experience of small towns, often in the Prairie provinces or Atlantic Canada (Bollman and Bryden 1997; Dupuy, Mayer and Morissette 2000; Rothman et al. 2002). Much less is known about the experiences of mid-sized centres which, as Trent University claims, share characteristics of both large cities and small towns.

Methods and Data Limitations

In order to study the migration patterns of students on a finer scale than allowed by published census data, we analyzed data from Trent and Queen's for four graduating classes (1986, 1990, 1995, and 2000). Data were attained from the universities in 2004/05. For each student in the four graduating cohorts we were provided with the gender, degree program, address at time of application to the university, and current address. To protect the privacy of alumni we were not given their names, and the addresses were limited to the forward sorting area (i.e., three-digit) postal code. The quality of the alumni data was uneven. Although universities have become more aggressive in tracking alumni for fundraising purposes, accurately tracking down former students is a formidable task. Given the fundraising pursuits of universities, graduates have a disincentive to report their address, and it may take years to "catch up" with a graduate. Therefore, the current addresses of the most recent graduates are less reliable than the other information.[2]

We compared the addresses of undergraduate- and graduate-degree alumni at the time they applied to enter the university (i.e., their

application address) to their current place of residence. By cross-check-
ing and eliminating current alumni addresses that matched application
addresses (assuming these were mostly inaccurate) and first limiting
the geographical scale of our analysis to the first letter of the Canadian
postal code designation (see Figure 7.2), addresses in the United States,
and another category for addresses outside Canada and the US, we were
able to identify some broad trends.

Alumni Addresses and Shifts in the Canadian Urban System

The first finding, which was expected, is that the students entering the
two universities are increasingly being drawn from regions with growing populations. It is, however, important to recognize some of the differences between the cohorts and the two institutions. For both universities
there is a shift over time toward fewer students being drawn from eastern
Ontario and more from central and southwestern Ontario (Table 7.3).
This is expected, given higher population growth rates for these latter
regions. There is also a slight decline in international and US-based students. Overall, Queen's has a much more geographically diverse student
body (at both the international level and regionally within Canada).

**Table 7.3   Alumni Entry Addresses, by Selected Regions, % of Classes of 1986
and 2000**

	CLASS OF 1986		CLASS OF 2000	
	Queen's n=3771	Trent n=882	Queen's n=4478	Trent n=1026
Eastern Ontario	43.8	44.6	33.4	37.9
Central Ontario	15.5	27.2	22.7	33.1
Toronto	13.4	12.7	13.9	12.8
Southwestern Ontario	5.8	2.8	8.2	7.1
Northern Ontario	4.5	2.9	3.4	3.0
Rest of Canada	11.9	6.1	14.1	5.3
US and International	5.0	3.4	3.9	1.2

Source: Institutional Alumni Data.

There are similar differences with respect to the current locations of
alumni (see Table 7.4). Trent alumni are still primarily concentrated in
eastern and central Ontario, while Queen's alumni are more dispersed
nationally. Both institutions have greater numbers of alumni from the
1986 cohort reporting addresses outside of Canada. There are several
possibilities to consider here. First, as mentioned above, the accuracy
of current addresses is most problematic for the class of 2000. Second,
the findings could reflect the different labour-market location of the
later graduating class. For example, recent graduates may not have yet
advanced far enough in their careers to secure jobs in international locations. Third, as Trent alumni are more geographically concentrated than

Queen's graduates, it could simply be evidence of Trent's greater orientation toward training for the regional southern Ontario labour market.

Table 7.4   Alumni Current Addresses, by Selected Regions, % of Classes of 1986 and 2000

| | CLASS OF 1986 | | CLASS OF 2000 | |
	Queen's n=2757	Trent n=738	Queen's n=2584	Trent n=1022
Eastern Ontario	32.4	29.8	33.4	37.6
Central Ontario	18.3	27.4	17.3	32.0
Toronto	18.0	14.2	21.1	13.2
Southwestern Ontario	5.9	5.7	7.0	6.7
Northern Ontario	2.6	2.0	2.4	3.2
Rest of Canada	14.4	10.0	15.0	5.6
US and International	8.2	10.8	3.7	1.8

Source: Institutional Alumni Data.

This last point is supported by the data when we analyzed entry and alumni addresses at the three-digit postal-code level for Kingston and Peterborough. Striking differences and similarities emerge between the two cities. First, as Trent maintained a steady percentage of new students from Peterborough, the percentage of Queen's students drawn from Kingston declined from 18.6% in the class of 1986 to 12.0% in the class of 2000 (Figure 7.3).[3] However, the number of alumni from these classes reporting current local addresses remained stable, between 10% and 13% of alumni for both locations. It is here where we begin to see evidence of a tendency for some students to remain in the immediate area after graduation. Graduates remaining in the area after their studies act as a partial buffer to the overall trend of out-migration of people in their 20s from these centres. It is important to consider not only how many younger workers are remaining in local labour markets challenged with out-migration, but also who is staying and what skills these workers possess. Here again, findings from the alumni data analysis are relevant. First, we found that a gendered pattern does exist, with higher percentages of women alumni living closer to their former university than men. Higher percentages of female alumni reported addresses in eastern and central Ontario; more men reported addresses in Toronto. We attribute this, in part, to social, gendered, and spatial divisions of labour. Males, still disproportionately trained in the sciences, engineering, and business, are more likely to find employment opportunities outside of the local area and closer to metropolitan centres. Women, however, disproportionately trained in areas such as health services and education, can find stable public-sector employment closer to where they studied.[4] To examine more closely what may influence a student's decision to remain in or leave Peterborough or Kingston after graduation, we now turn to interview data.

Figure 7.3   Local Alumni by Entrance and Current, Selected Forward Sorting Area (FSA)

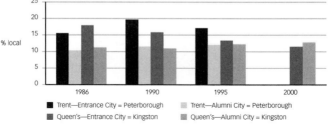

Note: Peterborough FSAs = K9K, K9H, K9L, K9J; Kingston FSAs = K7N, K7P, K7M, K7L, K7K

Trent alumni data for the class of 2000 was considered unreliable at the 3-digit FSAs.

Student Worker Perceptions of Kingston and Peterborough

Research indicates that transition from university or college to full-time work for PSE graduates currently is more difficult than in the past (Betts, Ferrall and Finnie 2000). While some new economy sectors require a range of skills, from high technology to entrepreneurialism, many old and new economy industries demand flexible, low-wage workers (e.g., consumer services). The availability of such precarious jobs and the financial necessity for students to work while studying has had an impact on post-graduation labour-market transition (i.e., finding a "real" job) and also has lengthened the time to degree completion for student workers (Allen, Harris and Butlin 2003).

But does such integration into the local labour market increase the possibility of students remaining in the area following graduation? To examine this question we interviewed 30 full-time undergraduate students who worked part- or full-time during the school year (15 from Queen's and 15 from Trent). Participants were recruited through poster advertisements on campus, and demographically respondents broadly reflected the general university populations. The interviews covered several aspects of their working lives, most of which are beyond the scope of this chapter. Of relevance here are the questions concerning their reasons for working during the school year, their role in the local labour market, and their perceptions of Kingston and Peterborough as attractive, amenable places to live and work after completing their studies.

Student Workers in the New Economy

The economic rationales provided by students for working during the school year ranged from absolute necessity to debt avoidance to merely earning "extra spending" money. But other reasons also came up in the interviews with both Queen's and Trent students. The importance of gaining experience and voluntarism were also mentioned. Particularly valued were jobs that may have paid relatively little but provided experience beyond the consumer service sector. For example, in Peterborough, summer internships (paid and unpaid) with the Ministry of Natural Resources (the provincial headquarters was moved from Toronto to Peterborough in the 1990s) were valued by more than one Trent participant.

There was a significant difference among the types of labour-market participation between the Trent and Queen's students. While the students at Trent held a wider variety of jobs, on- and off-campus, inside and outside of Peterborough, most of the Queen's students interviewed were employed by the university itself. Yet there were several common responses concerning their working lives as students, including conflicts with schoolwork (although campus employment was more accommodating during examination periods) and the relatively low pay. Perhaps most important, most of the participants recognized the role of students in precarious segments of the labour market:

> I think one of the new things that is part of this new economy is the rise of contingent employment and the rise of part-time work, and as far as a pool of part-time workers, I mean students are sort of the epitome of that, and I think that a lot of businesses, I mean the bars and more touristy things and stuff around Kingston, I mean students are a great pool as far as hiring. (Queen's student, interview #4)

> Well, Peterborough is an odd town, I think, because it's close to Toronto but it's still kind of (fairly) isolated; there's no train or GO system that goes to Toronto. I see—like there's a growth in the call-centre culture, what I call the call-centre culture. It's all about those kinds of jobs in Peterborough right now. (Trent student, interview #10)

For students, contingent work is very much part of the new economy they experience daily. When asked to define the "new economy" of Peterborough or Kingston, most students had difficulty providing a definition. The question elicited responses ranging from increased globalization, the emergence of new technologies, to the growth of retail services. For the most part, students also did not make connections to their role in local economic development in terms of becoming high-skilled workers upon graduation, contributors to the vibrant cultural life of the city, or workers in revitalized spaces of consumption. One participant, however, did express the importance of Kingston employers hiring Queen's students:

> ... if they [Kingston downtown employers] hire someone who is like not our age it might backfire on them because like if you ever go into those stores the people usually help you out and tell you...you know choose outfits for you, or be like try this, try this, or this is really trendy, and if they hire people who are like really old or aren't in our like age range, Queen's students might be less likely to be influenced by what they have to say. (Queen's student, interview #2)

In a recent study (Denstedt 2008) of restaurant work in Kingston, a significant number of both employers and employees commented on the important role played by Queen's student workers in local restaurants and bars. A number of employers expressed a hiring preference for PSE students over other local workers, and non-student workers expressed some resentment of the fact that the large student-labour pool had a depressive effect on wages and increased their own levels of labour-market insecurity.

For the most part, student workers occupied lower segments of the labour market, something they were all naturally hoping to escape once they had attained their degrees.

"Staying Behind": Living in Peterborough and Kingston beyond Graduation

Interview participants did not see remaining in Peterborough or Kingston to be a viable option, even though there was a common sentiment that both cities were in some ways ideal. Reference was often made to the natural amenities of the locations (e.g., access to various bodies of water or the lakefront of Lake Ontario); an ideal, safe, inexpensive, "small-town" lifestyle (often expressed in contradistinction to the expensive and "unsafe" Toronto); and in the case of Queen's students, the potential to continue with graduate studies. But remaining in Kingston or Peterborough was at best viewed as a transitional arrangement.

> I find that students choose to stay in Kingston ... because there seems to be like this whole ghetto, weird culture around the school, and so people seem to stay because Queen's is a good university and they're like well, I can stay and do a master's in this ... and so it continues to be a focus around the university. But they stay because it is easier and because of Queen's. Because Queen's is here, and it is a good school and it just seems easier.... Like people just keep staying and staying and never leave this place. (Queen's student, interview #8)

This was, however, a minority perception. Overwhelmingly, remaining in a "small town" after graduation was not considered a likely option, largely due to the limited number of "real jobs" in the community. This was particularly the case for Queen's students majoring in sciences or professional programs (e.g., engineering).

> I think it's a really aesthetically nice city. I think that the crime is low. I think that it is a great place to raise a family. It's really good location wise to major cities that you can travel out of, or, I think in general it's a very attractive city. I just think that the employment really isn't here. (Queen's student, interview #11)

> ... I know a lot of my friends move, you know, go back home because it's cheaper to live back with their parents till they find a good job. So in that respect, I don't know. Peterborough for me, if I could get a job at the MNR [Ministry of Natural Resources], for sure I would stay, you know. Or if I could get a job making decent money working for Peterborough Greenup or something, just because it's a good environmental community compared to Bowmanville or Oshawa [relatively close-by communities] or something like that. (Trent student, interview #11)

> I think any town that has a university tends to be a (kind of) interesting place. Just 'cause university brings a lot of culture and arts stuff and theatre and music. So I think that makes it a good town to live in, like even if you're not a student anymore. Though in terms of (a) long-term career, I'm not sure; (it might be a little) too small for that. (Trent student, interview #3)

> Certainly it is a nice small city, and if you feel ... and this is again something that comes up you hear all the time ... Queen's University isn't connected to the Kingston community in general,

and I think that there is a lot of truth to that. I think that for those students who do feel connected to the extended community, and I feel that I am through my job at —— ... if I graduated and I mean ... right now I'm making basically minimum wage, which isn't much of an incentive for me to stay here because I know that I could get that almost anywhere. If I was making a decent wage in Kingston, given that Kingston is a very appealing city, generally, and I had nothing else planned ... which a lot of students don't ... I mean a lot of students graduate and don't have any idea what they are going to do ... yeah, I think that it would be appealing for me to stay in Kingston. The rent here is relatively affordable. Students know that they can find a place for relatively cheap, even after they graduate. And yeah, I do feel that Kingston would be appealing. (Queen's student, interview #14)

In this last interview excerpt, the connection made to community through labour-market participation is noted, but this realization was not evident in other interviews. What was expressed as lacking by participants was simply the availability of good jobs that were more readily available in larger metropolitan labour markets. Despite the recent popular theory which suggests that capital increasingly follows "talent" (Florida 2002, 2005, 2008), real challenges face non-metropolitan labour markets as they attempt to capture or retain the high-skilled labour necessary for knowledge-based economies. A very recent study titled "Retention of Queen's Graduates in the Greater Kingston Area," undertaken by the Kingston Economic Development Corporation (KEDCO) in collaboration with the Monieson Centre in the School of Business at Queen's University, observed that

> Students come to Kingston to obtain their university education at Queen's; they are not coming to Queen's so they can find employment in Kingston. That said, each year Queen's graduates a potential talent pool of bright, motivated students who offer significant intellectual capital.... [Our] survey results illustrate a challenge in retaining current Queen's graduates, and, indeed, in recruiting knowledge workers to the Kingston area. *While students and alumni both indicate employment prospects are the most important factor in deciding where to live, both groups express strong dissatisfaction with Kingston's employment prospects.* (KEDCO 2008: 4; emphasis in original)

One finding of the KEDCO study that resonates with the comments of one of the students we quoted above is that "those students who feel part of the Kingston community are more likely to seek employment in Kingston. Thus, increasing the number of students who consider themselves part of the community also increases the number willing to consider Kingston as a place to live and work after they graduate" (KEDCO 2008: 28).

Concluding Comments

Our study of student workers and the retention of graduates from universities located in medium-sized cities has perhaps raised as many questions as it has answered. However, we do wish to summarize the main points of our analysis and perhaps identify some policy implications. First, although the alumni data are limited, it does appear that a significant number of university graduates do in fact remain in Peterborough and Kingston after graduation. How long these graduates stay and what activities they engage in remain unclear. PSE institutions can, however, be viewed as playing a role in buffering the kind of net youth out-migration experienced in Peterborough and Kingston in the 1980s and 1990s. But the integration of recent graduates into the local labour market is perhaps fragile and short-term. Young workers, including many students, occupy specific segments of the local labour market (e.g., retail, restaurants and bars) characterized by lower-paying precarious work. Recent graduates are likely to migrate to larger labour markets with better employment opportunities and especially are pressured to do so if they have accumulated significant levels of student debt while studying.

While Peterborough and Kingston may hold some allure for recent graduates, in terms of natural, cultural, and aesthetic amenities, they are clearly limited in their ability to attract and retain young workers seeking more permanent employment. This challenge is especially relevant in the case of mid-sized cities with an aging population and a restructured economic base. In the alumni data we analyzed, large cities still attract high numbers of science and business graduates. Furthermore, students themselves clearly perceive large centres as providing greater job opportunities and an enhanced social life. Small centres continue to be at a disadvantage when developing new economy industries, such as information technology and biotechnology, as larger centres are better able to attract both highly qualified knowledge workers and venture capital.

There has been a great deal of theorization of "re-scaled" economic development policies as national and provincial governments refocus initiatives at the local level and large city-regions, such as the GTA, acquire the status of key centres of innovation and creativity within a global-izing economy (Brenner 2004). If Peterborough and Kingston wish to make serious efforts to retain university graduates, the state needs to be involved. For graduates who do remain in these medium-sized centres, public-sector employment is often the most attractive option. For exam-ple, graduates with education degrees require positions in local school boards, but this is difficult given shrinking elementary-student popula-tions in eastern Ontario. Similarly, the state plays a major role in main-taining administrative centres such as the provincial Ministry of Natural Resources in Peterborough, and the provincial Ministry of Health and the federal penitentiary service in Kingston. Trent University has been able to engage partners such as the MNR and municipal, provincial, and federal government support for the establishment of a DNA research cluster (with a platform for corporate partnership physically located on its campus). It is, however, too early to evaluate the job-generation potential for Trent graduates. Similarly, the Queen's Innovation Park in Kingston with its emphasis on sustainable bioenergy is still in its infancy. Smaller centres may have to build on their existing base of public sectors such as education and health in order to retain and attract young, edu-cated workers, and this will inevitably require multi-level government support and investment in local communities.

At the local level, there are initiatives aimed at facilitating the par-ticipation of students in experiential learning opportunities (e.g., paid and unpaid internships with local employers). The Trent Centre for Community-Based Education (TCCBE) matches students with employ-ers in the private, public, and not-for-profit sectors in order to build links between students and the community with different projects. One of the aims of TCCBE is to create long-term relationships between stu-dents and local employers.[5] While most of the positions are voluntary, students acquire diverse work experience beyond consumer service employment. This is only one model that may help integrate students into higher ends of the labour market from which they are presently excluded. Exposure to "real jobs" through experiential learning opportu-nities may remedy the perception that medium-sized centres fail to offer opportunities to recent graduates. Such local placement programs are not as well developed at Queen's, perhaps again reflecting the broader national and global orientation of the university—Queen's slogan being "Preparing Leaders and Citizens for a Global Society." Without such ini-tiatives, however, local economic development planners will continue to be frustrated at the flight of talent from the community upon gradua-tion (KEDCO 2008).

In this paper we do not mean to reduce universities to a purely instrumental economic role, which has clearly been a desire of the neoliberal project (Axelrod 2002). We do feel, however, that "multiversities" (Fallis 2007)[6] will be expected to play an increasingly central role in local economic development, despite our misgivings. Whether it be by local economic multiplier effects, training a local workforce, or serving as the centre of cultural life to attract talent, universities in non-metropolitan centres will be called upon to aid in the transition toward knowledge-based production. While living up to heightened expectations will be a challenge, it remains to be seen how smaller urban centres without sizeable PSE institutions will develop in the new economy.

Discussion Questions

1. What economic roles have universities played in the new economy?

2. Why are non-metropolitan areas limited in their ability to retain university graduates?

3. What initiatives will the state have to take to assist non-metropolitan areas in retaining university graduates?

Notes

1   For the purposes of this chapter, we focus on Queen's University in Kingston and Trent University in Peterborough. Kingston is also home to St. Lawrence Community College and the degree-granting Royal Military College of Canada (RMC). However, most graduates of the latter make the transition directly into a military career and, hence, have less relevance for the development of the local skilled labour force. Similarly, we have not included data from Sir Sandford Fleming College in Peterborough.

2   Consequently, the most recent cohort for which we requested data was the class of 2000.

3   This trend appears to have continued. A recent study (KEDCO 2008) reported that only 6% of Queen's students in their survey came from the Greater Kingston area and that number was consistent with current enrolment data.

4   A very recent study (KEDCO 2008) of Queen's graduate retention in the Kingston area observed that graduates from the nursing program reported good employment opportunities in Kingston whereas graduates from business, engineering, and science programs reported a notable lack of opportunities.

5   In Ontario, co-op programs at universities such as Waterloo and Guelph are pointed to as having been critical in developing and retaining a highly skilled regional labour force to support the growth of industries based on wireless, photonics, and biotechnologies.

6   Fallis uses the term "multiversity" to describe a university that has numerous constituent and affiliated institutions, such as separate colleges, campuses, and research centres. They are sometimes referred to as "research-intensive" universities. Fallis sees multiversities as a product of the latter half of the twentieth century.

References

Association of University and Colleges of Canada (AUCC). 2009. Fall 2008 preliminary full-time and part-time enrolment at AUCC member institutions. Ottawa: AUCC. <http://www.aucc.ca/policy/research/enrol_e.html>.

Allen, M., S. Harris, and G. Butlin. 2003. *Finding Their Way: A Profile of Young Canadian Graduates.* Catalogue no. 81-595-MIE—No. 003. Ottawa: Statistics Canada.

Appleseed Inc. 2003. *Engines of Economic Growth. The Economic Impact of Boston's Eight Research Universities on the Metropolitan Boston Area.* Report prepared for the Association of Independent Colleges and Universities in Massachusetts, Boston. <http://www.masscolleges.org>.

Atkinson-Grosjean, J. 2006. *Public Science, Private Interests.* Toronto: University of Toronto Press.

Axelrod, P. 2002. *Values in Conflict: The University, the Marketplace, and the Trials of Liberal Education.* Montreal and Kingston: McGill-Queen's University Press.

Barr-Telford, L. 2005. "Postsecondary Financing. Making Ends Meet—with a Focus on Ontario." Presentation for OCUFA, Toronto, 21 January.

Betts, J., C. Ferrall, and R. Finnie. 2000. *The Transition to Work for Canadian University Graduates: Time to First Job, 1982–1990.* Catalogue No. 11F0019MPE No. 141. Ottawa: Statistics Canada.

Bollman, R.D., and J.M. Bryden (eds.). 1997. *Rural Employment: An International Perspective.* Wallingford, UK: CAB International.

Branscomb, L.M., F. Kodama, and R. Florida (eds.). 1999. *Industrializing Knowledge: University—Industry Linkages in the United States and Japan.* Cambridge, MA: MIT Press.

Brenner, N. 2004. *New State Spaces—Urban Governance and the Rescaling of Statehood.* London: Oxford University Press.

Colleges of Ontario. 2009. "The 2009 Environmental Scan." Toronto: Colleges of Ontario. <http://www.collegesontario.org>.

CREST Expert Group. 2006. *Report of the CREST Expert Group on: Encouraging the Reform of Public Research Centres and Universities, in Particular to Promote Knowledge Transfer to Society and Industry.* Brussels: European Council.

Denstedt, M. 2008. "Precariousness on the Menu": Restaurant Work and Labour Mobility within the Low-wage Service Industry in Kingston, Ontario. Unpublished M.A. Thesis, Queen's University.

Dupuy, R., F. Mayer, and R. Morissette. 2000. *Rural Youth: Stayers, Leavers and Return Migrants.* Catalogue No. A21-46/1-2000E. Ottawa: Statistics Canada.

Fallis, G. 2007. *Multiversities, Ideas and Democracy.* Toronto: University of Toronto Press.

Florida, R. 2002. *The Rise of the Creative Class and How It's Transforming Work, Life, Community And Everyday Life.* New York: Basic Books.

———. 2005. *Flight of the Creative Class: The New Global Competition for Talent.* New York: Harper Collins.

———. 2008. *Who's Your City?: How the Creative Economy Is Making Where to Live the Most Important Decision of Your Life.* Toronto: Random House of Canada.

Innovation Park, Queen's University. 2008. "Who we are." <http://www.innovationpark.ca/content/who-we-are>.

KEDCO (Kingston Economic Development Corporation). 2003. *Queen's University and the Kingston Area: An Economic Partnership Report.* Kingston: Kingston Economic Development Corporation.

——. 2008. *Retention of Queen's Graduates in the Greater Kingston Area*. A Study undertaken by the Kingston Economic Development Corporation in collaboration with the Monieson Centre in the School of Business at Queen's University. Kingston: Kingston Economic Development Corporation.

Lafer, G. 2003. "Land and Labor in the Post-industrial University Town: Remaking Social Geography." *Political Geography* 22: 89–117.

Martin Prosperity Institute. 2009. *Ontario in the Creative Age*. Toronto: Martin Prosperity Institute, University of Toronto.

Michael, C. 2004. "Economic Impact of Trent University on Local Economy." Report Presented to the Trent University Board of Governors, 30 April, Peterborough.

Osborne, B., and D. Swainson. 1988. *Kingston: Building on the Past*. Westport, CT: Butternut Press.

Rothman, N., R. Bollman, J. Tremblay, and J. Marshal. 2002. *Migration to and from Rural Small Town Canada*. Rural and Small Town Canada Analysis Bulletin 3 (6). Catalogue no. 21-006-XIE. Ottawa: Statistics Canada.

Rutherford, T., and J. Holmes. 2008. "Engineering Networks: University–Industry Networks in Southern Ontario Automotive Industry Clusters." *Cambridge Journal of Regions, Economy and Society* 1 (2): 247–64.

SSTI (State Science and Technology Institute). 2006. *A Resource Guide for Technology-based Economic Development: Positioning Universities as Drivers Fostering Entrepreneurship Increasing Access to Capital*. Prepared for the Economic Development Administration. Washington DC: U.S. Department of Commerce.

Statistics Canada. 2008. Labour Force Survey Estimates; Labour Force Survey, CANSIM Table 282-0095; 2006 Community Profiles. <http://www.statcan.ca>.

Trent University. 2006. Trent University Promotional Calendar. Trent University Office of the Registrar and Communications Office, Peterborough.

Wolfe, D., and M. Gertler. 2004. "Clusters from the Inside and Out: Local Dynamics and Global Linkages." *Urban Studies* 41 (5/6): 1071–93.

8. Labour Migration and Temporary Work
Canada's Foreign-Worker Programs in the "New Economy"

MARK THOMAS

Migrant labour plays a key role within many "new economy" labour markets of contemporary global capitalism.[1] Often employed in low-wage and insecure jobs, whether in agricultural harvesting, domestic service, manufacturing, or cleaning services, migrant workers are an unseen engine behind the economic growth of capitalist economies in the late 1990s and early twenty-first century (Bacon 2007). The significance of migrant labour to contemporary labour markets raises pressing questions about the connections between labour mobility, labour rights, and immigration policy in the new economy.

Growing labour migration is at the centre of contentious social-policy debates within both nation-states and international institutions (Hollifield 2004). Rising levels of international migration increase state–market tensions characterized on the one hand by the economic need for labour migration, and on the other by political movements that seek to regulate national boundaries and restrict access to citizenship (Martinello 2002). Migration processes have also fuelled debates over the nature of citizenship rights and have produced calls for strategies to improve the economic and political rights of migrants in host societies

(Schuster and Solomos 2002). The goal of combining an open labour market with social protection for the growing numbers of migrant workers has emerged as a key political challenge in the new economy (Engelen 2003). Simultaneously, employers in many sectors have sought to employ migrant workers as a means to secure low-wage and "flexible" workforces.

In this context, temporary migrant-labour programs have become increasingly common as nation-states attempt to address labour-market demand for both high- and low-skill workers, as well as employer prerogatives for labour "flexibility." Temporary labour programs facilitate the entry of workers into a host country's labour market for a specified period of time, often with restrictions on the economic and social rights of the migrant workers. These programs may be regulated through regional agreements such as the North American Free Trade Agreement, national immigration policies, or industry-specific arrangements like Canada's Seasonal Agricultural Workers Program (Aleinikoff and Chetail 2003). The expansion of avenues for temporary labour migration is being promoted by international organizations such as the International Organization for Migration (IOM) as a strategy for economic development for both sending and receiving countries (IOM 2006; Valiani 2007a). As such, these programs are increasingly viewed as a key policy measure for managing both labour forces and migration patterns in the new economy.

Taking temporary migrant labour as a focal point, in this chapter I examine contemporary foreign-worker programs in Canada as a means to explore processes of labour mobility, labour-market incorporation, and the labour rights of migrant workers in the new economy. The chapter is organized into three sections. In the first section I briefly review migration and labour-market data from North America and Western Europe to outline contemporary labour-migration patterns. The second section raises the key analytic questions that guide the chapter and develops a political economy framework to analyse processes of labour migration in contemporary capitalism. Using this political economy framework, in the third section of the chapter I construct an overview of several temporary-migration programs in Canada, highlighting the intersection of processes of migration, labour-market incorporation, and labour-market inequality. While focusing on the Canadian case, I conclude the chapter by suggesting that the study of these programs has broader implications. Specifically, the case study demonstrates how national and transnational policy frameworks regulate global migration patterns in ways that contribute to the production and reproduction of patterns of labour-market segmentation and the marginalization of particular groups of migrant workers. In particular, the chapter connects patterns of segmentation (and differential access to social rights) to the capacities for labour-market mobility, residency status, and family unification of those entering temporary foreign-worker programs.

Globalization and Labour Migration

International migration has been increasing since the end of World War II. With over 190 million people living outside their country of origin, approximately 95 million are economically active migrant and immigrant workers (IOM 2006). Contemporary migration patterns are shaped by what the International Labour Organization terms a "global jobs crisis," whereby the ILO estimates that over one billion people are un/underemployed (ILO 2005). As Burrow (2005: 275) notes, "the greatest structural deficit of globalization is the failure to create jobs where people live." In this context, South-to-North migration is the fastest growing migration path, with approximately 60 per cent of migrants living in advanced industrialized countries (Castles 2004a). From the 1970s through the 1990s, the ten countries with the highest levels of emigration were in the global South (IOM 2003).

Labour migrations to Northern economies are also driven by demand for low-wage labour created by the "downgrading" of a broad range of manufacturing sectors and the "informalization" of a wide range of economic activities (Sassen 2002). Growing numbers of immigrant and migrant workers perform many important but often invisible forms of labour in the major cities of the global economy, in both private service sectors and manufacturing. With the development of new information and communications technologies (ICTs), there is also growing demand for high-skill, high-tech workers for the service economies of the North (IOM 2002).

OECD countries with the highest proportions of foreign workers include the United States, Germany, France, Switzerland, Austria, the United Kingdom, and Canada. In Canada, it is estimated that immigration will likely account for all net labour-force growth by 2011, and for total population growth by 2031. In the European Union-15, between 1997 and 2002, third-country nationals—those whose nationality is of a country outside the EU—contributed to 22 per cent of employment growth, accounting for 3.6 per cent of total employment by 2002.[2] As stated in the Commission of the European Communities' First Annual Report on Migration and Integration (CEC 2004: 3), "third countries' labour is increasingly appearing as a major potential, which can be tapped to respond to both the continuing demand for low skilled as well as the growing demand for skilled labour." Foreign workers are employed in a wide range of occupations in the OECD, with employment in the service sector accounting for the largest share (OECD 2008). Foreign workers are generally over-represented in construction, hotel, and restaurant sectors, as well as some social service areas. Table 8.1 illustrates the employment of foreign-born labour in selected OECD countries in 2005–06.

In this context, many Northern states have begun to place greater emphasis on increasing the number of workers entering on non-permanent work visas for both "high-skill" and "low-skill" occupational categories (Burrow 2005; IOM 2002).[3] Unlike other categories of immigrants, these migrant workers often do not have access to permanent residency rights (Satzewich 1991). In the EU, over 20 per cent of third-country nationals held fixed-term contracts in 2001, compared to 13 per cent of EU nationals (EIRO 2003). In some countries, including Denmark, the Netherlands, and Sweden, the rate of non-EU nationals holding temporary employment contracts as compared to EU nationals is more than double.[4] In Canada, the number of foreign workers entering on temporary work permits grew by 71 per cent between 2004 and 2008, from 112,719 to 193,061 (Alboim 2009). Table 8.2 indicates the numbers of temporary workers entering selected OECD countries in recent years (2003–06). As the table indicates, the number of workers

Table 8.1 **Employment of Foreign-born by Sector, 2005–06 Average (percentage of total foreign-born employment)**

	Agriculture and Fishing	Mining, Manufacturing, and Energy	Construction	Wholesale and Retail Trade	Hotels and Restaurants	Education	Health and other Community Services	Households	Admin. and ETO*	Other Services
Austria	1.3	21.8	10.0	14.1	12.6	3.8	9.4	0.4	3.4	23.9
Belgium	1.1	16.7	7.2	13.0	8.2	6.4	10.4	0.6	11.6	24.7
Denmark	1.7	17.0	4.4	12.0	7.2	7.8	20.2	-	3.4	26.2
France	1.9	13.7	10.8	12.8	6.1	5.8	9.8	5.6	6.4	27.1
Germany	1.1	29.0	6.3	14.7	7.6	4.5	9.9	0.8	2.9	23.1
Greece	6.2	15.4	29.1	10.6	10.2	1.7	2.3	13.9	1.4	9.2
Ireland	2.3	16.0	14.2	11.8	12.3	5.5	10.8	1.1	2.5	23.6
Italy	3.5	23.6	14.2	11.3	8.7	2.4	4.7	10.4	1.8	19.6
Japan	0.5	52.0	1.0	9.2	7.4	8.2	-	-	-	21.3
Luxembourg	0.9	9.1	13.1	10.9	6.5	2.9	7.4	3.3	13.0	32.9
Netherlands	1.5	17.3	4.0	12.9	7.1	5.5	14.6	-	6.9	30.1
Norway	1.1	12.3	4.9	12.0	8.2	8.6	25.4	-	3.9	23.5
Portugal	2.0	13.8	14.8	14.6	8.2	8.0	8.0	4.9	7.3	18.5
Spain	5.6	13.0	19.7	11.2	14.2	2.9	2.8	13.3	1.1	16.1
Sweden	0.8	16.9	3.1	10.8	7.3	11.4	19.1	-	3.9	26.8
Switzerland	1.1	18.4	8.6	14.2	7.7	6.4	13.2	1.5	3.5	25.3
United Kingdom	0.5	11.9	4.9	13.0	8.5	8.1	15.7	0.7	5.3	31.4
United States	2.3	23.7	11.8	13.3	11.9	15.6	-	-	2.5	28.9
EU25	2.3	19.3	9.9	12.7	8.6	5.3	9.6	4.5	4.1	23.8

* ETO refers to "extra-territorial organizations."

Source: OECD (2008).

entering on temporary work permits is clearly increasing in key OECD economies.

Table 8.2 Inflows of Temporary Migrant Workers, 2003–06 (thousands)

	2003	2004	2005	2006
Australia	152	159	183	219
Austria	30	27	15	4
Belgium	2	31	33	42
Canada	118	124	133	146
Denmark	5	5	5	6
France	26	26	27	28
Germany	446	440	415	379
Italy	69	70	85	98
Japan	217	231	202	164
Korea	75	65	73	86
Mexico	45	42	46	40
Netherlands	43	52	56	83
New Zealand	65	70	78	87
Norway	21	28	22	38
Portugal	3	13	8	7
Sweden	8	9	7	7
Switzerland	142	116	104	117
United Kingdom	137	239	275	266
United States	577	612	635	678
All Above	2180	2360	2401	2498
Annual Change (%)	-	8.3	1.7	4.0

Source: OECD (2008).

While temporary migrant labour ranges in occupational categories, workers in low-skill occupational streams continue to be the majority (United Nations 2004). Without access to permanent residency or citizenship rights, these workers are viewed by employers and governments as a key source of flexible labour in the new economy.

The Political Economy of Migration

To understand issues surrounding labour migration, this chapter builds upon research that studies "the political economy of migration," a theoretical approach developed to explain why and how migrations happen by focusing on the economic, political, and cultural factors that produce inequality related to patterns of migration (Stasiulis 1997). Key to this perspective is the recognition that the migration decisions and actions of individuals and families are rooted in contemporary manifestations of histories of economic and political inequalities between sending and receiving countries (Bacon 2007). This approach places primary emphasis on the importance of structural factors in explaining both the determinants of migration and the processes by which migrants are incorporated into a destination society. Furthermore, this perspective draws attention to the ways in which labour mobility is constrained by economic and political institutions, thereby creating conditions for the production of low-wage labour forces.

A second theoretical perspective that guides the chapter is labour-market segmentation theory, a framework developed both to analyze the structural divisions that exist within labour markets and to identify the sources of these divisions (Peck 1996). With respect to the experiences of migrant workers, labour-market segmentation is directly connected to the role of the state in constructing and regulating migrant-worker programs and policies. A key concept advanced to explain this relationship is "incorporation," a term used to refer to the manner in which migrants are integrated into the dominant relations of production of the society they are entering. With reference to the use of foreign-born labour, Satzewich (1991) identifies four primary forms of incorporation of foreign-born labourers: free immigrant labour, unfree immigrant labour, free migrant labour, and unfree migrant labour. The immigrant/migrant distinction is defined by access to formal citizenship rights, while the free/unfree distinction is determined by formal rights to labour-market mobility. Migrant workers in temporary labour programs constitute a form of unfree labour in the global economy: their labour-market mobility is limited by a labour contract that ties them to a specific occupation, and their political rights are circumscribed due to lack of access to political citizenship in the nation-state within which they live and work.

Citizenship is thus a key variable in the existence of forms of social exclusion and marginalization. Citizenship denotes the formal entitlement to political rights within a national community and constitutes a central means through which migrants are excluded from full participation in the receiving society (Baines and Sharma 2002). Key to that process is the ideological assertion that "foreigners" should not have the same social rights as nationals. By controlling access to citizenship rights, the state plays a key role in determining the nature of incorporation experienced by newly arriving migrants. Citizenship is thus connected to the creation of groups of "highly exploitable and socially excluded workers" (Baines and Sharma 2002: 76).

Building from these theoretical frameworks, research on labour migration has identified factors that shape patterns of employment of migrant workers. Contemporary patterns of labour migration take place in the context of economic globalization, processes defined by the extension of markets, the increased mobility of capital, and the restructuring of production. Several overarching international trends define this context in relation to increased levels of international migration: a demand for low- and high-skill migrant workers from receiving countries; increased "push" factors, including growing inequality between the North and South; and intensified competition in global markets (Martin 2002; Stephen 2001; Taran 2000). These processes have been accompanied by increased levels of marginalization of migrant-worker populations due to racism, discrimination in employment, and restrictive migrant-labour policies.

In many areas of the world, globalization has led to increased poverty and precariousness, the "push" factors that stimulate migration (Pellerin 1992). The development of free-trade areas (the EU, North America, and ASEAN countries) has promoted regionally based migrations, including the movement of low-wage labour from the periphery to the "centres" of these economic regions. The promotion of emigration as a development strategy (to secure remittance income from migrant workers) is also significant, as is the related labour-market demand in industrialized economies for workers for low-wage, insecure employment. Migration is often considered "one of the few avenues of hope for material survival" in the highly polarized international economy (Rosewarne 2001: 72). The North–South divide—defined as "growing disparities in income, social conditions, human rights and security linked to globalization"— is a key factor in producing South-to-North migration flows (Castles 2004a: 211).

In relation to contemporary migration patterns, the data presented above illustrate the emergence of two general tiers of migrants: skilled, educated professionals with few barriers to restrict their mobility; and lower-skilled workers admitted for limited periods of time, primarily for seasonal work, domestic caregiving work, or lower-tier service-sector occupations (Rosewarne 2001). In general, the entry of low-skilled workers has been highly controlled, as states have increased regulations that restrict border crossing for those who do not meet specific labour-market requirements. These contemporary patterns of employment of migrant workers replicate long-standing patterns of labour-market segmentation, with immigrants channelled into either skilled professional, technical, and managerial positions, or labour-intensive, insecure forms of employment (Richmond 1991; Wong 1984).

Temporary labour programs are a key example of the intersection of increased labour migration, labour-market segmentation, and state regulation of migrant workers. These programs provide states with the means to address the need both to promote economic openness and to resolve political concerns over the permanent settlement of immigrants (Hollifield 2004). Temporary migrant workers hold highly vulnerable positions within European labour markets, characterized by limited legal rights in their country of employment. Migrant labourers generally hold jobs that are characterized by low status and employment insecurity, that are difficult to fill, and that are highly subject to demand fluctuations. These types of programs have the effect of creating a form of "differentiated exclusion," whereby migrants are granted access to the labour market, but not to other aspects of society, for example political citizenship rights (Castles, cited in Engelen 2003: 517). This process of exclusion creates a form of labour-force stratification based on legal status, whereby migrant workers are marginalized through the intersection of the need to address labour demands with concerns over the need to protect national resources and culture from "outsiders" (Castles 2004b; Morris 1994).

These policies are constructed in relation to patterns of racism. Contemporary foreign-worker programs in Canada build on a history of racial discrimination in the Canadian labour market that includes the employment of temporary foreign workers in jobs that Canadian citizens deem "undesirable." Racist discourses and ideologies continue to play a central role in the construction of Canada's migrant-labour policies, with migrant workers constructed by policymakers as "problems" for Canadian society (Sharma 2001). In the late nineteenth and early twentieth centuries, male Asian workers who immigrated to Canada were employed in a range of low-wage, labour-intensive occupations but were denied access to permanent residency and citizenship (Creese 2006). Canada's migrant agricultural labour program (discussed below), which prohibits migrants from Mexico and the Caribbean from applying for citizenship, emerged, in part, through race-based concerns over the construction of the "national community" (Satzewich 1991). This discursive and ideological construction contributes to a differentiation of migrants from Canadian citizens within the Canadian labour force and legitimizes substandard rights for those workers. This long-standing trend is perpetuated through several foreign-worker programs outlined below.

Migration processes are also highly gendered (Pessar and Mahler 2003). Domestic-worker programs, which facilitate the mobility of women from the South to work in households in North America and Western Europe as caregivers, are a prime example (Chang 2000). A key component to the gendered character of temporary-worker programs is the tendency to privatize the costs of, and responsibilities for, social reproduction. As non-citizens, migrant workers are often unable to access basic social services entitled to the citizens of the host national community. Further, in some cases, migrant workers are prohibited from bringing family members to the host country. This ensures that social reproduction is managed in the home country, minimizing or eliminating the social obligation of the host nation-state and further intensifying gendered care-giving norms.

In the current context, temporary-worker programs have been restructured through increased restrictions on the residency of migrant workers (Martin 1997). For example, new programs in Germany have made it more difficult for migrant workers to become permanent residents in order to promote a system of temporary but returning migrants. Similarly, rather than weakened state powers, the overall state regulation of migration "has once again become a key instrument in state endeavours to facilitate particular accumulation paths within the national economy," in particular through temporary-labour programs (Rosewarne 2001: 79). Through these policies, capital gains access to "global reserves" of labour, and nation states are able to relinquish responsibility for long-term investment in the social reproduction of the labour force.

The remainder of the chapter focuses on temporary foreign-labour programs in Canada. It identifies the ways in which different forms of labour market incorporation created by these programs contribute both to differential access to social rights for particular groups of migrant workers and to patterns of segmentation within Canada's labour market.

Immigration Policy and Canada's Labour Market

Recent policy on immigration to Canada has increasingly emphasized the need for economic priorities in determining eligibility for immigration. A 1994 report, *Into the 21st Century*, outlined the federal government's strategy for immigration reform (CIC 1994). Selection criteria were to place greater emphasis on immigrant labour-market credentials and labour-market demand. This approach would expedite applications of immigrants needed to fill specific labour-market shortages. As well, there would be streamlined processing of temporary foreign workers in occupations listed as "high-skill" in Canada's National Occupational Classification system (NOC)[5] and expedited processing of limited numbers of independent and business immigrants to meet the economic or market-development objectives of the provinces (IOM 2002).

In 2002, the *Immigration and Refugee Protection Act* (IRPA) replaced the *Immigration Act*, which had been implemented in 1976. Under the IRPA, applicants can be admitted to Canada as permanent residents through the Family Class, Protected Persons Class, or Economic Class. This latter class of immigrants is the largest, comprising the majority of permanent residents, and includes skilled workers, business immigrants, and the self-employed.[6] In 2008, 247,202 permanent residents landed in Canada. Sixty per cent (149,047) came through the Economic Class, while 27 per cent came through the Family Class, nine per cent as Protected Persons, and four per cent accepted for exceptional humanitarian, compassionate, or public policy reasons (Alboin 2009).[7]

Canada also maintains a number of temporary foreign-worker programs. To be eligible to work temporarily in Canada, a foreign national must have a job offer and (generally) a work permit, which is valid for a specific job and for a limited time period.[8] There are a number of restrictions placed upon temporary workers, limiting their mobility while employed in Canada. For example, they may not undertake full-time studies and may not change jobs or employers unless authorized. Employers who wish to hire temporary foreign workers must have job offers approved by Human Resources and Skills Development Canada (HRSDC).

The Philippines, the United States, and Mexico are the leading source countries for temporary foreign workers. While the United States provides workers for predominantly higher-skill occupational categories, Mexico's primary contribution is to the Seasonal Agricultural Workers Program and that of the Philippines is to the Live-In Caregivers Program.[9] Demonstrating an increasing emphasis on temporary foreign work permits, between 1997 and 2006 the numbers of workers entering Canada as temporary foreign workers on an annual basis has been close to double the numbers entering as permanent residents under the skilled worker or self-employed categories (Valiani 2007b). Table 8.3 outlines the numbers of temporary workers in Canada between 2003 and 2007, indicating the top ten source countries.

Table 8.3   Temporary Foreign Workers in Canada: Top Ten Source Countries, 2003–07

	2003	2004	2005	2006	2007
Philippines	12,526	15,330	17,723	21,595	33,926
United States	21,152	22,069	23,794	25,328	26,737
Mexico	11,643	11,949	13,312	15,178	18,138
United Kingdom	7,530	9,492	10,757	11,148	12,600
France	4,410	5,982	7,485	9,080	9,994
Australia	6,914	8,289	8,625	9,077	9,845
India	2,716	3,736	5,118	6,374	8,706
Japan	8,284	8,612	8,844	8,429	7,867
Germany	2,276	3,138	3,657	5,441	6,885
Jamaica	5,859	5,918	6,117	6,413	6,732
Top 10	83,310	94,515	105,432	118,063	141,430
Other countries	27,166	31,516	36,311	43,983	59,627
Total	110,476	126,031	141,743	162,046	201,057

Source: CIC (2008).

Temporary Foreign-Worker Programs in the New Economy

As discussed in other chapters in this book, the new economy is most often associated with growth in occupations in knowledge-intensive sectors and communications, information technology, and financial services, for example. In recent years, temporary-labour programs have been developed both to fill specific labour needs in these areas and to facilitate the labour mobility of "high-skill" knowledge professionals.

Information Technology–related (IT) occupations are a key area for high-skill foreign workers entering Canada. In the late 1990s, the Canadian federal government expanded the opportunities for foreign workers with IT training and work experience to obtain work permits in Canada, specifically by identifying these workers as a priority and establishing expedited procedures for their application and permit-approval processes. This facilitated a large inflow of workers during the years of the high-technology boom period that lasted until 2001–02 (Habtu 2003). Following a downturn in that sector, the numbers of foreign workers entering through this stream declined: in 1993, for example, 3,199 workers in this occupational group were admitted; by 2000, this number had risen to 9,500, but then it dropped to 5,689 in 2004. Under the expedited procedures for IT professionals, it is not necessary for an employer to obtain HRSDC approval for each individual employee in designated IT occupations. In 2004, there were approximately 2,000 workers employed through this program, the majority of whom came from India (CIC 2005a). Workers who obtain work permits through this stream are not prohibited from applying for permanent residency status (unlike the "low-skill" temporary-labour programs discussed below). In addition, because they are high-skill workers, their spouses and common-law partners are themselves eligible for work permits.

The provinces also maintain Provincial Nominee Programs (PNPs) for temporary foreign workers. These programs are designed to fill specific labour-market needs, primarily in high-skill occupational areas. As a general condition attached to work permits issued through the PNPs, and like the federal IT program, these programs offer greater potential for family reunification, as spouses or common-law partners may themselves receive authorization to work in Canada, without first having a confirmed job offer (CIC 2005b). In 2004, for instance, 2,553 partners of skilled workers were given work permits (CIC 2005a).[10]

Entry to the Canadian labour market for high-skill occupations is also regulated by the North American Free Trade Agreement (NAFTA), which was implemented in 1994 to create a free-trade region between Canada, the United States, and Mexico. Specifically, through NAFTA's Chapter 16, citizens of Canada, the United States, and Mexico can gain temporary entry into each of the three countries to conduct business-related activities. While Chapter 16 purports to apply equally to citizens of the three countries, it actually applies to only four specific categories of businesspeople: business visitors, professionals, intra-company trans-ferees, and persons engaged in trade or investment activities. Chapter 16 enables each of these categories of businesspeople to enter Canada with-out a labour-market test being applied.

While these high-skill occupations in knowledge-intensive sectors are most often associated with the new economy, since the mid-1990s there has been significant growth in the numbers of workers at the NOC lower skill level categories (C and D), in large part due to the recently estab-lished Low Skill Pilot Project (discussed below) (Alboim 2009). The most common occupational group of foreign workers was the NOC level C grouping of "intermediate occupations in primary industries." The key program within this stream is the Seasonal Agricultural Workers Program (SAWP), which operates in nine provinces[11] and facilitates the incorpora-tion of migrant workers from the Caribbean and Mexico into seasonal agricultural production (Preibisch and Binford 2007; Sharma 2006). This program employs predominantly male workers (97 per cent), with the two leading source countries being Mexico and Jamaica (CIC 2005a). The pro-gram now brings in over 18,000 workers annually (Gibb 2006). Because of its proven record of ensuring a permanent flow of temporary foreign workers, Canada's SAWP is often considered by employers and policy-makers as a "model" program for the new economy (Basok 2007).

The workers in the SAWP are incorporated into agricultural pro-duction in Canada as "unfree migrant labour" (Basok 2002; Satzewich 1991). Their period of employment in Canada ranges from 6 to 40 weeks, with a minimum of 40—but often exceeding 60—hours of work per week. The workers are paid at an hourly wage that is set through employment agreements negotiated by the countries participating in the program and that slightly exceeds provincial minimum wages. Employers participating in the program must provide accommodation for the dura-tion of the employment contract and cover transportation costs for their employees.

These workers are "unfree migrant labourers" in that they are not permitted to seek employment outside their specified contract and they are not permitted to apply for permanent residence in Canada. Through these restrictions, the Canadian state is able to continually secure a labour force that is both seasonal in nature and static in terms of upward mobility. This illustrates the contradictory nature of the use of temporary foreign workers. Migrant workers are needed in agriculture production to fill persistent labour shortages. But it is because they are foreign work-ers, and not recognized as deserving of the political rights of Canadian citizens, that makes the workers so desirable. Thus, the SAWP is shaped not only by the class dimensions of labour migration, but also by the racial/ethnic and gender relations that shape access to Canadian citizenship rights, with denial of access to such rights constituting a central feature of the program. The workers' position as unfree migrant labour ensures their temporary status in the country and provides Canadian agricultural producers with a seasonal labour force.

Despite the existence of some formal standards that cover basic rights, the social rights of workers in the program are severely compromised, since "serious absences exist even on the surface of the SAWP agreements, and further problems exist in the gaps between theory and practice" (Suen 2000: 203).[12] For example, those who are employed through the SAWP as either "farm workers" or "harvesters" are exempt from minimum employment standards regulating maximum hours of work, daily and weekly rest periods, eating periods, and overtime pay (Thomas 2009; Verma 2003).[13] They are also not permitted to engage in collective bargaining under provincial labour-relations legislation. Moreover, workers employed in the program are not permitted to seek alternative employment, nor are they able to bring family members to Canada. Workers' vulnerability is increased due to linguistic and cultural barriers and a lack of access to legal authorities and social services. Liaison services do not have sufficient support staff to address worker complaints. Moreover, the threat of premature repatriation, the possibility of "blacklisting," and a lack of alternative employment constitute further disincentives to registering complaints. The race-based discrimination that was present in the construction of the original program continues to be present in a "systematic fashion," as it creates what Suen (2000: 208) terms a "transnational dark-skinned underclass welcome to do menial work but not welcome as immigrants."

A second major occupational group in the low-skill temporary foreign-worker stream is intermediate sales and service. These workers are primarily employed in child care and domestic service through the Live-In Caregivers Program (LICP) (CIC 2005a). Workers in this program perform child and elder care, as well as domestic work. In 2006, 7,915 workers were admitted through the LICP, the majority of whom are from the Philippines (Valiani 2009). Unlike workers in the SAWP, these workers may apply for permanent residence in Canada after completing 24 months of employment over a period of three years. So while not tied to a cycle of temporary, seasonal employment like agricultural workers, they nonetheless hold a temporary attachment to the Canadian labour market through their employment contract in the program.

This program is situated in the broader context of what Glenn (2001) describes as a "re-privatization" of domestic work through the employment of economic migrants from the South who work as private domestic workers—housekeepers, nannies, and maids—in the homes of professionals in the North. While historically workers from these jobs have been drawn from racialized groups already present in the domestic labour market, they are increasingly being filled by migrant workers. For some countries such as the Philippines, the export of workers is a major industry, as the remittances provide needed income in the home country. Thus, programs like the LICP contribute to the construction of a transnational race–gender division of labour in the contemporary global economy (Chang 2000).

Live-in caregivers in Canada have historically been exempted from minimum employment standards (Thomas 2009). Reasons presented by government ministries to explain this exemption include the need to recognize the "special relationship" that arises because the workers are employed in the employer's home, the need to avoid increasing the cost of domestic labour (through the minimum wage), and the perceived difficulty in measuring and enforcing hours of work and overtime. For example, the "lack of a sharp distinction between personal time and working hours" was a common rationale provided for exemption from hours of work and overtime provisions (Archives of Ontario 1985: 6). In part, these rationales for the exemptions stem from an assumption that "state intervention in the private sphere is inappropriate" (Macklin 1994: 14).

There is clearly a gendered element to this determination. The labour performed by domestic workers is undervalued due to its characterization as work that is "naturally" done by women, and because it is hidden from public view. As most live-in domestic workers enter into this form of employment as temporary workers from either the Caribbean or the Philippines, these gendered determinations are also subject to processes of racialization. Specifically, women of these national origins have been attributed with a "natural" affinity for domestic labour (Brand 1999; Calliste 2000). Exemptions from legislated standards were constructed (whether explicitly or implicitly) in relation to these gendered and racialized ideological constructions. During the 1980s, domestic workers in Canada were extended coverage under the minimum wage, weekly rest period, vacation pay, and public holidays and overtime provisions of employment standards. However, the (gendered) privatized and individualized character of their employment continues to limit their capacity to enforce these legislated rights (Arat-Koç 2001).

Overall, the Live-In Caregivers Program constructs a highly marginalized workforce in several manners. First, those employed in the program are unable to search for other forms of employment for the duration of their contract, which is a minimum of two years. As stated above, unlike those in the SAWP, they are eventually able to apply for Canadian citizenship, thereby creating the potential for labour market mobility, as well as improving access to political and economic rights. Nonetheless, while employed as live-in caregivers, they are subject to a highly deregulated and invisible work environment. Regular violations of applicable labour standards, including vacation pay, minimum wages, termination pay, overtime pay, and public holidays, have been widely documented (INTERCEDE 1993; Arat-Koç 2001). While their employment is not temporary in the same manner as seasonal agricultural work, they nonetheless have no permanent status in the country until they complete their work contract in the program. Moreover, estimates regarding the transition from temporary employment in the program to permanent residency in Canada indicate that the majority of workers in the LICP do not make this transition (Valiani 2009). The temporary status of these workers with respect to their residency rights thus places them in a highly vulnerable employment context, severely compromising their capacity to enforce their legal rights, and indicates a direct relationship between citizenship rights and labour rights.

These two long-standing programs provided a model for the Canadian federal government's recent expansion of the Temporary Foreign Worker Program. In July 2002, the federal government developed a "Low-Skilled Pilot Project" for occupations requiring at most a high-school diploma or a maximum of two years of job-specific training. These occupations are classified under the National Occupational Classification (NOC) system under skill levels C and D and include occupations in intermediate skills categories in clerical, sales and service, health services, and transportation-related occupations, as well as low-skill labourers in primary resource, construction, and manufacturing sectors. As with other temporary foreign-worker programs, employers seeking to hire foreign workers through this pilot project must first demonstrate efforts to recruit Canadian youth, Aboriginal peoples, recent immigrants, and unemployed Canadians, though reforms to the program in 2006 eased the requirements employers were obliged to fulfill in searching for Canadian applicants before hiring foreign workers (Valiani 2007c). Employers are also expected to assist the foreign workers in finding accommodation, and are required to pay full airfare to and from the home country and to provide medical coverage until the worker is eligible for provincial health insurance. The Low-Skilled Pilot Project initially placed a 12-month time limit on employment contracts for foreign workers, with the requirement that the worker must return home for a minimum period of four months before applying for another work permit. Through recent reforms, it is now possible to get work permits for periods of up to 24 months (HRSDC 2007).[14] In 2006, 37,500 workers were admitted through the program—34,000 in occupational category C (intermediate and clerical) and 3,500 in occupational category D (elemental and labourers) (OECD 2008).

This expanded program holds the potential to extend the principles established by the SAWP and the LICP to a wide range of low-skill occupational categories, as it is a model of employment sought by employer associations in a wide range of sectors. Like the SAWP, workers are prohibited from applying for permanent residency through the program. Moreover, while a spouse may accompany a worker entering through the program, the spouse is not legally entitled to work in Canada, unlike the spouse of a worker who enters on a high-skill temporary work permit (CBA 2006). Foreign workers in the program become effectively tied to and marginalized within a stratum of lower-tier employment and lack effective regulatory mechanisms to enforce basic labour rights (Alboin 2009; Valiani 2007b). Furthermore, due to the temporary nature of both the employment contract and their status in the country, they are placed in an employment context characterized by high levels of precariousness due to the lack of both labour-market mobility and capacity for permanent residency. Moreover, the expansion of this program creates a high level of labour flexibility for employers, as it is based solely on short-term labour demands. The expansion of the Temporary Foreign Worker Program constitutes another growing example of the ways in which racialized migrant workers are constructed as a highly exploited labour force in the new economy.

Conclusion

As I have argued throughout this chapter, labour migration is a key structural feature of contemporary labour markets. This case study of temporary foreign-worker programs in Canada has illustrated that these programs play a key role in filling labour-market demands for both high- and low-skill occupational categories in the new economy. Moreover, these programs may contribute to high degrees of marginalization and labour exploitation for some categories of migrant workers, for example due to temporary employment contracts, formal barriers to labour-market mobility, and restrictions on access to citizenship and permanent residency. With Canada's programs serving as a "model," there is great reason to be concerned about the labour rights of migrant workers in the global economy.

Occupational status plays a key role in this process, as workers entering low-skill occupational categories experience many restrictions on their mobility. Through reforms to its immigration policies in 2002, and through its participation in NAFTA, Canada's approach has been to reduce the formal regulations that govern the entry of high-skill workers into the labour market.[15] Conversely, workers in low-skill occupational categories are not included within the NAFTA framework, and are instead regulated through bilateral agreements such as the Seasonal Agricultural Workers Program, which restricts workers' mobility within the labour market and prevents their permanent settlement. Thus, the high skill/low skill distinction manifests itself not only in income levels and job security, as within traditional accounts of labour-market segmentation, but also in forms of labour-market mobility, residency rights, and possibilities for family unification. Temporary foreign-worker programs that create segmented approaches to labour-market incorporation produce heightened relations of commodification, exploitation, and marginalization for specific groups of migrant workers.

Temporary migrant workers in low-skill occupational categories experience extreme exposure to market forces. These workers exist within a highly commodified state, with few labour laws to regulate their conditions of work, and limited access to social benefits. Further, the state has privatized the relations of social reproduction by prohibiting family reunification, by repatriating workers upon completion of their employment contracts, and by minimizing access to social benefits in between employment contracts. Limited access to benefits and over-representation in forms of low-wage, insecure employment contribute to social stratification not only between migrants and nationals, but also within the overall temporary foreign-labour force.

In the contemporary era of globalization, migration policies are situated within a transnational social policy context, as supranational arrangements like NAFTA have significant impact within nation-states. While individual nation-states retain primary control over migration policies, the development of NAFTA has promoted the increased mobility of specific groups of workers. Further, these arrangements contribute to the entrenchment of regional migration patterns, in this case flows of professionals between the US and Canada. Canada's migration policies are thus shaped by this regional, transnational context. The NAFTA provisions also reinforce the class-based dynamics of migration, as its Chapter 16 supports the mobility of those in primarily high-status and often high-income occupations. NAFTA does not create a situation of free movement for workers across the three countries, as it offers no opportunity for the many workers outside these occupational categories.

These conditions are not simply fuel for further academic debate. The marginalization of many groups of migrant workers presents a key political challenge in the new economy (Burrow 2005). The Commission on

European Communities has called for a "level playing field" for economic migrants across the EU, as well as stronger efforts at promoting social integration (CEC 2004). Proposed strategies for the latter include language training, involvement in political decision-making processes, increased access to affordable housing, greater dialogue with migrant organizations, and efforts to combat both unemployment and discrimination and racism.

Central to this challenge is the need to address marginalization and social exclusion in a transnational context. While many nations have adopted international human-rights standards, they have often applied them only to nationals, and have excluded migrants. And while there are a number of international instruments designed to protect the human rights of migrants, there are also many political, social, and economic obstacles that prevent their application (Mattila 2000). The 1990 UN Convention on the Protection of the Rights of All Migrant Workers and Members of their Families was developed to address this gap, as were Conventions 97 and 143 of the International Labour Organization. But these conventions still have not been ratified by many states, including Canada. Overall, current models of international standards have been ineffective in protecting the rights of migrants, often because individual nation-states have failed to implement them effectively (Taran 2000).

For migrant workers in North America, the North American Agreement on Labour Cooperation (NAALC, NAFTA's labour standards side accord) includes a provision to require the signatories to ensure that migrant workers are treated on equal standing to citizens in a "host" labour market. While the NAALC includes this commitment, its capacities to protect migrant workers in the NAFTA region are extremely limited (Thomas 2008). The NAALC's Commission for Labour Cooperation has very little power to ensure compliance, as it lacks an effective enforcement mechanism. Instead, it defers to the legislative bodies in each country to regulate working conditions. In cases where complaints are raised through the NAALC dispute-resolution process, resolutions are focused on educative and information-related activities, rather than on employer sanctions. In effect, this reduces the NAALC to a normative rather than regulatory role, offering little in terms of effective labour standards protections for those migrant workers who work in the NAFTA region outside their country of origin.

As temporary foreign-worker programs continue to expand, there is a need for stronger labour-rights protections for migrant workers.[16] As a starting point, immediate action is needed to ensure that migrant workers have access to information about basic labour rights, including information about legislated standards (minimum wages, maximum hours of work, etc.), freedom-of-association rights, and how to file complaints regarding employer non-compliance. Beyond educative measures, action needs to be taken to ensure that minimum labour standards are both applied and enforced, that migrant workers are covered by minimum standards and freedom-of-association legislation, and that employers respect such standards. Such action must also include strengthening the enforcement capacities of transnational regulatory bodies such as the NAALC so that labour rights are effectively regulated in a transnational context. Beyond basic labour standards, migrant workers need access to work visas that permit labour-market mobility, ending provisions in programs that tie migrants to a specific employer and/or sector. The lack of labour-market mobility reinforces conditions of marginalization because, without access to employment alternatives, migrants are placed in a heightened condition of vulnerability. In addition to labour-market mobility, processes to enable settlement rights should be made part of labour-migration programs. Lacking settlement rights, migrant workers face the constant threat of deportation, a condition that perpetuates mechanisms of exploitation in the workplace. Without these kinds of transformations as a basic starting point, temporary foreign-worker programs will continue to serve as mechanisms of labour exploitation in the new economy.

Discussion Questions

1. What role do migrant workers play in new economy labour markets?

2. How are experiences of migrant workers shaped by patterns of labour-market segmentation?

3. What is meant by the "political economy" of migration?

4. How are temporary foreign-worker programs constructed through intersecting relations of race, class, gender, and citizenship?

5. What types of strategies could protect and advance the labour rights of migrant workers?

Notes

1   The terms "migrant labour" and "foreign labour" are used interchangeably throughout the chapter as neither is used consistently or universally within available data sources. The terms are generally used to refer to people who are employed in a country of which they are not citizens, though there are limitations to this conceptualization.

2   Third-country nationals living in the EU-15 in 2001 were estimated at 14.3 million, or 3.8 per cent of the total population (CEC 2004).

3   The IOM (2002) notes that the US currently maintains a quota for temporary workers that is higher than their quota for permanent immigrants.

4   The rates of temporary employment contracts held by third-country nationals as compared to EU nationals in 2001 were as follows: Denmark—18.6%, 9.3%; the Netherlands—32.4%, 13.8%; Sweden—35.3%, 13.9%.

5   The NOC system groups occupations by four general "skill" levels (A, B, C, D), where "skill" is associated with formal credentials and/or training requirements. Skill level A refers to occupations that generally require university education. Skill level B occupations generally require college education or apprenticeship training. Skill level C occupations require secondary school or occupation-specific training. Skill level D occupations require on-the-job training. The NOC is developed in partnership between Statistics Canada and Human Resources and Social Development Canada. (See HRSDC 2006.)

6   Skilled workers are foreign nationals who are chosen based on their labour-market skills, whereas business immigrants are investors and entrepreneurs with a net worth of at least $800,000 or $300,000 respectively.

7   The Protected Persons Class includes refugees and their dependents.

8   These jobs include some commercial speakers, seminar leaders, and guest speakers; some performing artists, students, athletes, sports officials, journalists, and providers of emergency services; business visitors; and diplomats, consular officers, and other representatives or officials of other countries.

9   In recent years there has been a noticeable decline in migrants from countries that tend to supply workers for higher-skill categories. However, some of this decline (particularly from the US and the UK) is explained by changes in 2002 to the IRPA that removed the requirement for temporary work permits from some of the higher-skill categories of workers from these countries, including some performing artists, seminar and commercial speakers visiting for less than five days, and service repair people.

10 While the PNPs include a range of occupational categories, they are employer-driven in that employers must apply to the respective provincial government for permission to employ foreign workers. Thus, provincial governments issue permits to individual employers. In some cases, sectoral agreements have been negotiated to facilitate an approval process for a specific sector or industry where high demand for skilled foreign workers is anticipated. For example, Alberta maintains a program for Oil Sands Construction Projects for foreign workers in skilled construction trades.

11 The SAWP operates in British Columbia, Alberta, Saskatchewan, Manitoba, Ontario, Quebec, New Brunswick, Nova Scotia, and Prince Edward Island.

12 See also Thomas (2006), UFCW (2007), and "Canada's Guest Workers: Not Such a Warm Welcome" (2007).

13 Under the *Employment Standards Act*, there are two primary categories of employees relevant to the SAWP: "farm workers" and "harvesters" (Ontario 2007: 2). A "farm worker" is "a person employed on a farm whose work is directly related to the primary production of certain agricultural products," which could include planting, cultivating, pruning, and caring for livestock. A "harvester" is someone who is employed to harvest crops of fruit, vegetables or tobacco for marketing or storage.

14 The requirement that the worker return home for a minimum of four months between contracts remains in effect.

15 Foreign trained professionals in high-skill occupational categories also face many forms of formal and informal discrimination in the Canadian labour

market, a topic that is beyond the scope of this chapter. See Galabuzi (2006) and Teelucksingh and Galabuzi (2005) for detailed discussions.

16 For detailed discussions of proposals to improve the labour rights of migrant workers see Thomas (2008), Valiani (2007a), and Verma (2003).

References

Alboin, Naomi. 2009. *Adjusting the Balance: Fixing Canada's Economic Immigration Policies*. Toronto: Maytree Foundation.

Aleinikoff, T.A., and V. Chetail (eds.). 2003. *Migration and International Legal Norms*. The Hague and Washington, DC: T.M.C. Asser.

Arat-Koç, S. 2001. *Caregivers Break the Silence: A Participatory Action Research on the Abuse and Violence, including the Impact of Family Separation, Experienced by Women in the Live-In Caregiver Program*. Toronto: INTERCEDE.

Archives of Ontario. 1985. Record Group 7-168, Policy Subject Files, Memorandum, Employment Standards Branch, 17 May.

Bacon, D. 2007. "The Political Economy of International Migration." *New Labor Forum* 16 (3–4): 57–69.

Baines, D., and N. Sharma. 2002 "Migrant Workers as Non-Citizens: The Case Against Citizenship as a Social Policy Concept." *Studies in Political Economy* 69: 75–107.

Basok, T. 2002. *Tortillas and Tomatoes: Transmigrant Mexican Harvesters in Canada*. Kingston and Montreal: McGill-Queen's University Press.

———. 2007. *Canada's Temporary Migration Program: A Model Despite Flaws*. Washington, DC: Migration Policy Institute.

Brand, D. 1999. "Black Women and Work: The Impact of Racially Constructed Gender Roles on the Sexual Division of Labour." In E. Dua and A. Robertson (eds.), *Scratching the Surface: Canadian Anti-Racist Feminist Thought*. Toronto: Women's Press. 83–96.

Burrow, S. 2005. "The Economic Case for Migration and the Protection of Mobile Workers: Challenges for the International Labour Movement." *Global Social Policy* 5 (3): 275–79.

Calliste, A. 2000. "Nurses and Porters: Racism, Sexism and Resistance in Segmented Labour Markets." In A. Calliste and G. Sefa Dei (eds.), *Anti-Racist Feminism: Critical Race and Gender Studies*. Halifax: Fernwood. 143–64.

"Canada's Guest Workers: Not Such a Warm Welcome." 2007. *The Economist* 22 November. <http://www.justicia4migrantworkers.org/bc/pdf/The_Economist_Canada_guest_workers.pdf>.

Castles, S. 2004a. "Why Migration Policies Fail." *Ethnic and Racial Studies* 27 (2): 205–27.

———. 2004b. "The Factors that Make and Unmake Migration Policies." *International Migration Review* XXXVIII (3): 852–84.

CBA (Canadian Bar Association). 2006. *Low Skilled Worker Pilot Project*. Ottawa: CBA.

CEC (Commission of the European Communities). 2004. *First Annual Report on Migration and Integration*. Brussels: CEC.

Chang, G. 2000. *Disposable Domestics: Immigrant Women Workers in the Global Economy*. Cambridge, MA: South End Press.

CIC (Citizenship and Immigration Canada). 1994. *Into the 21st Century: A Strategy for Immigration and Citizenship*. Hull, QC: Minister of Supply and Services Canada.

——. 2005a. *The Monitor*. First Quarter, Summer. Ottawa: CIC.

——. 2005b. *Immigration Canada: Applying to Change Conditions or Extend Your Stay in Canada*. Ottawa: CIC.

——. 2008. *Facts and Figures 2007*. Ottawa: CIC.

Creese, G. 2006. "Exclusion or Solidarity? Vancouver Workers Confront the 'Oriental Problem.'" In L. Sefton Macdowell and I. Radforth (eds.), *Canadian Working Class History, Selected Readings*. 3rd ed. Toronto: Canadian Scholars' Press. 199–216.

EIRO (European Industrial Relations Observatory). 2003. *Migration and Industrial Relations*. Dublin: European Foundation for the Improvement of Living and Working Conditions. <http://www.eiro.eurofound.eu.int/2003/03/study/tn0303105s.html>.

Engelen, E. 2003. "How to Combine Openness and Protection? Citizenship, Migration, and Welfare Regimes." *Politics and Society* 31 (4): 503–36.

Galabuzi, G.-E. 2006. *Canada's Economic Apartheid: The Social Exclusion of Racialized Groups in the New Century*. Toronto: Canadian Scholars' Press.

Glenn, E.N. 2001. "Gender, Race, and the Organization of Reproductive Labor." In R. Baldoz, C. Koeber, and P. Kraft (eds.), *The Critical Study of Work: Labor, Technology, and Global Production*. Philadelphia: Temple University Press. 71–82.

Gibb, Heather. 2006. *Farmworkers from Afar: Results from an International Study of Seasonal Farmworkers from Mexico and the Caribbean Working on Ontario Farms*. Ottawa: North-South Institute.

Habtu, R. 2003. "Information Technology Workers." *Canadian Economic Observer*, September. Ottawa: Statistics Canada.

Hollifield, J. 2004. "The Emerging Migration State." *International Migration Review* XXXVIII (3): 885–912.

Human Resources and Social Development Canada (HRSDC). 2006. *National Occupational Matrix*. Ottawa: HRSDC.

——. 2007. *Pilot Project for Occupations Requiring Lower Levels of Formal Training (NOC C and D): Changes to the Pilot Project as of February 23, 2007*. Ottawa: HRSDC.

ILO (International Labour Organization). 2005. "ILO Director-General Says Global Jobs Crisis Puts Democracy, Freedom At Risk." 6 June. <http://www.ilo.org/global/About_the_ILO/Media_and_public_information/Press_releases/lang--en/WCMS_005166/index.htm>.

INTERCEDE. 1993. *Meeting the Needs of Vulnerable Workers: Proposals for Improved Employment Legislation and Access to Collective Bargaining for Domestic Workers and Industrial Homeworkers*. Toronto: INTERCEDE.

IOM (International Organization for Migration). 2002. *International Comparative Study of Migration Legislation and Practice*. Geneva: IOM.

——. 2003. "Facts and Figures on International Migration." *Migration Policy Issues* 2 (March). <http://publications.iom.int/bookstore/free/MPI_series_No_2_EN.pdf>.

——. 2006. *Making Global Labour Mobility a Catalyst for Development*. Geneva: IOM.

Macklin, A. 1994. "On the Inside Looking In: Foreign Domestic Workers in Canada." In W. Giles and S. Arat-Koç (eds.), *Maid In The Market: Women's Paid Domestic Labour*. Halifax: Fernwood. 13–39.

Martin, P. 1997. "Guest Worker Policies for the Twenty-First Century." *New Community* 23 (4): 483–94.

——. 2002. "Mexican Workers and U.S. Agriculture: The Revolving Door." *International Migration Review* 36 (4): 1124–42.

Martinello, M. 2002. "Protections of Migrants—Human Rights: Principles and Practice." *International Migration Review* 38 (6): 53–69.

Mattila, H.S. 2000. "Protection of Migrants' Human Rights: Principles and Practice." *International Migration* 38 (6): 53–69.

Morris, L. 1994. *Dangerous Classes: The Underclass and Social Citizenship.* London and New York: Routledge.

OECD (Organization for Economic Cooperation and Development). 2008. *International Migration Outlook.* 2008 Edition. Paris: OECD.

Ontario. 2007. *Agricultural Workers: Employment Standards Fact Sheet.* Toronto: Ministry of Labour.

Peck, J. 1996. *Work-Place: The Social Regulation of Labor Markets.* New York and London: The Guilford Press.

Pellerin, H. 1992. "Global Restructuring in the World Economy and Migration: The Globalization of Migration Dynamics." In M. Oliver (ed.), *The Movement of Peoples: A View from the South.* Ottawa: The Group of 78. 90–99.

Pessar, P.R., and S.J. Mahler. 2003. "Transnational Migration: Bringing Gender In." *International Migration Review* 37 (3): 812–46.

Preibisch, K., and L. Binford. 2007. "Interrogating Racialized Global Labour Supply: An Exploration of the Racial/National Replacement of Foreign Agricultural Workers in Canada." *Canadian Review of Sociology and Anthropology* 44 (1): 5–36.

Richmond, A.H. 1991. "Foreign-Born Labour in Canada: Past Patterns, Emerging Trends, and Implications." *Regional Development Dialogue* 12 (3): 145–61.

Rosewarne, S. 2001. "Globalization, Migration, and Labor Market Formation—Labor's Challenge?" *Capital, Nature, Socialism* 12 (3): 71–84.

Sassen, S. 2002. "Deconstructing Labor Demand in Today's Advanced Economies: Implications for Low-Wage Employment." In F. Munger (ed.), *Laboring Below the Line: The New Ethnography of Poverty, Low-Wage Work, and Survival in the Global Economy.* New York: Russell Sage. 73–94.

Satzewich, V. 1991. *Racism and the Incorporation of Foreign Labour: Farm Labour Migration to Canada Since 1945.* London and New York: Routledge.

Schuster, L., and J. Solomos. 2002. "Rights and Wrongs across European Borders: Migrants, Minorities, and Citizenship." *Citizenship Studies* 6 (1): 37–54.

Sharma, N. 2001. "On Being Not Canadian: The Social Organization of 'Migrant Workers' in Canada." *Canadian Review of Sociology and Anthropology* 38 (4): 415–39.

——. 2006. *Home Economics: Nationalism and the Making of "Migrant Workers" in Canada.* Toronto: University of Toronto Press.

Stasiulis, D. 1997. "The Political Economy of Race, Ethnicity, and Migration." In W. Clement (ed.), *Understanding Canada: Building on the New Canadian Political Economy.* Kingston and Montreal: McGill-Queen's University Press. 141–71.

Stephen, L. 2001. "Globalization, the State, and the Creation of Flexible Indigenous Workers: Mixtec Farmworkers in Oregon." *Urban Anthropology* 30 (2–3): 189–214.

Suen, R.L.W. 2000. "You Sure Know How to Pick 'Em: Human Rights and Migrant Farm Workers in Canada." *Georgetown Immigration Law Journal* 15 (1): 199–227.

Taran, P.A. 2000. "Human Rights of Migrants: Challenges of the New Decade." *International Migration Review* 38 (6): 7–47.

Teelucksingh, C., and G.-E. Galabuzi. 2005. *Working Precariously: The Impact of Race and Immigrants Status on Employment Opportunities and Outcomes in Canada*. Toronto: Canadian Race Relations Foundation.

Thomas, M. 2006. "Precarious Status, Precarious Rights." In KAIROS (ed.) *Building Solidarity, Taking Action: National Migrant Justice Gathering*. Toronto: KAIROS. 7–8.

——. 2008. "Labor Rights and Social Justice for Migrant Workers." In R. Perrucci, K. Ferraro, J. Miller, and G.W. Muschert (eds.), *Agenda for Social Justice: Solutions 2008*. Knoxville, TN: Society for the Study of Social Problems. 8–15.

——. 2009. *Regulating Flexibility: The Political Economy of Employment Standards*. Montreal and Kingston: McGill-Queen's University Press.

UFCW (United Food and Commercial Workers Canada). 2007. *The Status of Migrant Farmworkers in Canada, 2006–07*. Toronto: UFCW.

United Nations. 2004. *World Economic and Social Survey 2004, International Migration*. New York: United Nations.

Valiani, S. 2007a. *Analysis, Solidarity, Action—A Workers' Perspective on the Increasing Use of Migrant Labour in Canada*. Ottawa: Canadian Labour Congress.

——. 2007b. *Briefing Note—The Temporary Foreign Worker Program and its Intersection with Canadian Immigration Policy*. Ottawa: Canadian Labour Congress.

——. 2007c. *Labour and Migration Update: Policy and Research News—June 2007*. Ottawa: Canadian Labour Congress.

——. 2009. "The Shift in Canadian Immigration Policy and Unheeded Lessons of the Live-in Caregiver Program." Unpublished Paper.

Verma, V. 2003. *The Mexican and Caribbean Seasonal Agricultural Workers Program: Regulatory and Policy Framework, Farm Industry Level Employment Practices, and the Future of the Program Under Unionization*. Ottawa: North-South Institute.

Wong, L.T. 1984. "Canada's Guestworkers: Some Comparisons of Temporary Workers in Europe and North America." *International Migration Review* XVIII (1): 85–98.

9. Scripting Taste, Marking Distinction
Wine Tourism and Post-Fordist Restructuring in the Okanagan Valley, British Columbia[1]

LUIS L.M. AGUIAR AND TINA MARTEN

Introduction

Traditionally the Okanagan Valley has been a ranching, agricultural, fruit-growing, and manufacturing region with a scattering of forestry mills and plants. And while the presence of organized labour has been spotty in the region, many occupations supported a family wage as a result of some union presence and the extension of the Fordist mode of regulation in the industrial-relations regime governing work in the Okanagan Valley. This economic landscape is, however, changing as a result of globalization, neoliberalism, and the increasing competition that local industry and sectors, such as wine, real estate and development, and technology, are experiencing in the global marketplace. It is also changing as a result of the interests of the regional power bloc (Whiteley, Aguiar and Marten 2008). Whereas in the past the Okanagan Valley marketed its goods to the national and regional market of the Pacific Northwest (Sparke 2000), it now increasingly faces global competition in the fruit, forest and wood products, and manufacturing markets. Many jobs in these industries have been lost or are being threatened, and

many workers, particularly white male workers, have suffered the consequences. For example, in September 2002, Kelowna's Western Star truck-
ing manufacturing company closed its doors, putting some 800 workers
out of a job and leaving an economic shortfall in the area of at least $400
million per annum. The loss was even greater considering that 77 companies, employing over 3,000 workers, were suppliers to Western Star and
were thus also affected by the shutdown (MacNaull 2001). This event,
along with the restructuring of employment at the local saw mill, signals
to us both the death knell of Fordism and the tenuous existence of the
industrial male working class in the hinterland of BC (Behrisch, Hayter
and Barnes 2002/03; Dunk 2003). After all, Western Star and Riverside
Forest Products (later TOLKO Industries and now in permanent partial
shutdown) employed mostly men earning well above $20 per hour and
protected by a collective agreement. In its stead the birthing of the new
economy is taking shape, but not without significant growing pains. For
example, recently two call centres, Marusa Marketing and Sitel, themselves shut down, putting almost 400 mostly female workers out of a
job (Michaels 2008c; Plant 2008). And the fact that the provincial tourism industry pays the lowest wage of all BC industries at $395 per week,
combined with the high cost of housing in the Okanagan and poor public transport, puts the predominantly female workforce in the Valley in a
very tenuous economic position indeed (Okanagan Partnership 2008).[2]

In this chapter we outline the changing socio-economic landscape of
the Okanagan Valley in British Columbia, and of Kelowna in particular. We also provide a brief profile of one of the "clean" industries of the
new economy that is replacing the Fordist economy of the region: wine
tourism. In a global tourism marketplace, the Okanagan Valley is inch-
ing its way onto the tourism map by developing its wine industry and
by arguing that—contrary to the analysis presented in the documentary film *Mondovino* (2004)—Okanagan wine has its own unique terroir pregnant with characteristics for local wine making and taste that
can only be made in the Valley. In the final section we discuss the workers in this industry and their role in selling wine in the scripted space of
the wine shop.

Post-Fordist Region, Post-Fordist Industries

As the demise of the Fordist economy in Kelowna continues, a concerted
and aggressive campaign to shift the local economy permanently to a
post-Fordist regime is taking shape (Aguiar, Tomic and Trumper 2005).
Concomitant with this economic and ideological shift—some would
say leading it—is a regional power bloc pushing a neoliberal agenda of

restructuring by agglomerating industrial interests into sectoral partnerships to improve their position in the global marketplace. Here, often old-time alliances between factions of the bourgeoisie and government (but without organized labour) play an instrumental role in this change via the creation of the Okanagan Partnership Strategy. This partnership maps the Okanagan landscape into seven economic clusters (tourism; wine and beverage; knowledge services; value-added agriculture; aviation; life sciences; and value-added wood products)[3] as it re-imagines and re-engineers the regional economy and culture, utilizing new and existing work relationships and practices. These sectors are then supported by regional and provincial initiatives and policies such as labour recruitment (Squire 2008). Tourism—and wine tourism in particular—has taken centre stage in this shift to a post-industrial economy in the Okanagan. Furthermore, a promotional unleashing of Kelowna, and of the Valley more generally, is afoot, describing the area as especially entrepreneurial to the degree that Kelowna has been officially heralded as the number-one low-waged jurisdiction in the Pacific Northwest. Herein resides a cheap, passive, and docile workforce that speaks English "without accent" (Aguiar, Tomic and Trumper 2005).

But this strategy is backfiring, as many employers now argue that they cannot afford to pay high enough wages to keep and attract a reliable workforce (Field 2008). And while the income gap continues to grow in Kelowna and an acute class polarization takes shape (*Okanagan Life Magazine* 2008), the new (mostly white and female) working class of the service economy must find ways to survive in the world's thirteenth most expensive city (Parletich Properties Limited 2008).[4] This comes at a time when employment remains insecure and a general state of "precarity" reigns.[5] In February 2008 the Teamsters and Sun-Rype signed a memorandum of settlement after a strike, lasting almost four months, during which the union sought to prevent the company from generalizing precarity by contracting out work and jeopardizing job protections, which would potentially have put workers out on the street (Michaels 2008a, 2008b). At the same time, the call centre Marusa Marketing announced its closure, followed closely by the other call centre in Kelowna—Sitel (Michaels 2008c).

The regional power bloc persists in re-engineering the economy and culture of Kelowna and the Okanagan.[6] The repositioning of the region in the global economy points out its competitive economic advantage (low wages; a docile workforce; low union density and a lacklustre labour movement), but is also accompanied by an ideological "localism" built around the inherent attributes of place in order to entice business, investors, and tourists into the region (Couper 2004; MacNaull 2002).[7]

For instance, the BC Wine Institute[8] has published short pamphlets fantasying about the uniqueness of the land and soil and how it produces wine unique to the province. During this process the entire Okanagan Valley is fragmented, re-branded, and commodified. Today, there are five acknowledged wine sub-regions: Kelowna, Naramata, Okanagan Falls, the Golden Mile, and Black Sage/Osoyoos. And while the topography of the Okanagan may indeed be different from wine regions elsewhere, there are too many homogenizing labour processes in the industry for suspicion not to be raised about these marketing campaigns of a unique localism.[9]

In these times neoliberalism is both a culprit in the decline of well-paying jobs and responsible for the rise in service work with its low-paying jobs, insecure employment relations, and general precarity (Bourdieu 2003; *Fibreculture Journal* 2005). And while tourism has been mass produced and consumed since World War II (Dawson 2004; Dubinsky 1999; Urry 2002), there are increasing attempts to develop niche tourist sites and attractions in the new economy of global service industries (Dicken 1998; Gabriel 1999; Harvey 1989; Lichtenstein 2006; MacDonald and Sirianni 1996). This includes attempts at re-branding a region to correspond with shifting economic and political interests (Klein 2000). In the Okanagan specifically, this re-branding seeks to distance the Valley from its former campaign to nose into the high-tech boom of the late 1990s. For instance, the "silicon vineyard" branding idea is now being displaced by more recent campaigns marketing the Okanagan Valley as a playground for the white middle classes, with slogans such as "reds, whites and greens" (Draycott 2007), "grapes and greens" (Kendall 2007) or "Napa North" (Noll 2007). The purpose of differentiating the local in a fragmented market is to appeal to the changing tastes of the middle classes and to distinguish their tastes from those of the general population.

The consumption of wine is a ritual activity, and engagement in wine tourism re-draws lines of social relationship and carries social meanings. It is no coincidence that the large majority of wine tourists are white and middle class (Carmichael 2005; Kochlan 2004). It was Bourdieu (1984) who argued convincingly that taste and class were very much connected, developing into cultural capital (Bourdieu 2001) for the beholder, where "the judgment of taste is the supreme manifestation of the discernment which [...] defines the accomplished individual" (1984: 11). This "accomplished individual" develops in various spaces. Today, however, an increasing number of white middle-class women are seeking wine tours and tastings and are affectionately referred to as "wine divas" (Nowak and Wichman 2004), dispensing, among other things, wine knowledge.

In their efforts to insert the Okanagan wine industry into the global wine-tourism circuit, wine boosters increasingly offer a market of choices in specifying features of each winery as a means of disguising the uniformity of the winespace, while also providing a total experience for the tourist. Wine is often marketed in tandem with golf, as in the grapes and greens slogan (Kendall 2007). A potential wine tourist can even begin to engage in wine tourism from home, choosing and downloading from the "sixteen preplanned itineraries that break British Columbia's wine regions down into bite-sized chunks. Each itinerary provides you with a brief regional overview, highlights of the wineries you'll visit, exact driving directions and recommended tour times" (BC Wine Institute 2008). This is facilitated by a GyPSy Guide to a self-directed tour of 17 Okanagan wineries, pointing out the unique aspects of each and providing tips on "what to taste and look for at each location." This hand-held technology does more: "If you are a first time winery tourer, GyPSy will give you the confidence to go in and taste new wines while experienced wine appreciators will enjoy the tips and specialties to look out for" (GyPSy Guide 2009). According to its marketing, then, wine tourism is safe, clean, discerning, easily accessible, and ready for consumption.

In the Okanagan wine industry it is difficult to separate the "economy" from the "culture," since the discourse of wine is embedded in both. Amin and Thrift (2004) write that separating culture and economy has been a perspective imposed in the past, though many important writers have made a point of saying that the boundaries separating the two are fuzzy and often arbitrary. Further, Amin and Thrift argue that "the [contemporary] pursuit of prosperity is a hybrid process of aggregation and ordering that cannot be reduced to either of these terms and as such, require use of a unitary term such as culture economy" (2004: xii). That is, "the pursuit of prosperity must be seen as the pursuit of many goals at once, from meeting material need and accumulating riches to seeking symbolic satisfaction and satisfying fleeting pleasures" (xiv). It is this symbolic satisfaction and fleeting pleasures that the Okanagan wine-tourism industry is organized to achieve. This is necessary, as Amin and Thrift write above, because people seek their pleasures in a variety of ways, some unconnected to the production processes proper. The new global middle class, with increasing sums of disposable income—but suffering work intensification (Sennett 1998), traffic jams, poor air quality, etc.—are craving "experience." The crises, insecurity, precariousness—in a word, precarity[10]—of the "neoliberal everyday," as well as discourses around personal choice, suggest that tourists are changing their approach to engaging in leisure activity. Because many people have to work more and longer hours in the new economy of post-Fordism (Conley 2009; Schor 1991), people are taking shorter trips rather than long holidays. The short-term wine getaway, with prepackaged tours, tastings, and other leisure pursuits, presents a safe break from which even the occasional forest fire will not deter the Canadian vacationer (Armstrong 2009).[11] Thus the Okanagan leisure experience itself becomes increasingly short-term, a quick, spontaneous consumption of scripted wine experiences. Niche wine tours and tasting rooms help to fulfill these new desires. The "emotional proletariat,"[12] as we show below, plays a key role in creating this experience in the spaces of the wine shop. Therefore, the consumers of wine tourism and the emotional proletariat engage in a dialectical relationship wherein wine plays a supporting role in defining taste and marking distinction.

The BC Wine Industry

Popular history of the Okanagan maintains that it was Father Pandosy, an early colonizer and religious missionary, who brought vines to the region in the 1860s to make wine primarily for sacramental rituals. Some of the early settlers in the Okanagan were Italians, so bringing grape vines to the region made sense since wine is a daily staple of the Italian diet (Schreiner 2004). As wine critic Julianna Hayes stated in an article on the BC Wine Institute website in 2004, it was not until 1926 that "the first commercial vineyards [were] planted and a winery began offering products for sale to the general public. It was not a memorable coming-out party. BC's early foray into the industry was synonymous with jug wines. To serious wine consumers, the products were a joke." By 1978 there were still only 3,000 acres of vineyards in the Okanagan and Similkameen Valleys (Legislative Assembly, Province of British Columbia 1978). But in 1978 and 1979 an unusually severe winter by Okanagan standards destroyed many of the vines (Schreiner 2003, 2004). This, and the fact that many people believed the vines growing in the Okanagan were of inferior quality, led to the first pull-out program where the government subsidized grape growers to uproot unproductive grape stock and replace it with other grape varietals. As a result, 650 acres of Labrusca grapes were removed and replaced with hybrids. A second pull-out occurred in 1984, when 580 acres were uprooted and replaced by vinifera wine grapes (Schreiner 2003).[13] A final pull-out took place in 1988–89, when another 2,400 acres were removed, an area representing about two-thirds of Okanagan vineyards. Today, Chardonnay, Merlot, Cabernet Sauvignon, Pinot Gris, and Pinot Noir grow primarily in the south, and Pinot Gris, Pinot Blanc, Pinot Noir, Gewürztraminer, and Riesling in the mid- and north Okanagan. Some have argued that this final re-planting of new varietals was due to the Free Trade Agreement and the Canadian government's initiative to make wine growers in Canada competitive with their counterparts south of the border (Hackett 1996).

Today 33 per cent of Canada's grapes are grown in BC. There are 157 wineries located in five designated viticultural regions: Vancouver Island, the Fraser Valley, the Okanagan Valley, the Similkameen Valley, and the Gulf Islands.[14] Remarkably, in 1988 there were only 14 wineries in BC, but by 2009 there were 710 vineyards, with 70.4 per cent of wine-grape acreage being controlled or owned by wineries, and the remainder being owned by independent grape growers. The Okanagan Valley is the most important wine region in the province, producing 85 per cent of the province's grapes and containing 75 per cent of the wineries. In 2007, the overall grape harvest in the Okanagan was 19,777 tons, with a value of $36,856,597.

According to the British Columbia Wine Institute (BCWI), about half of the wineries offer tours. Tours range from informal, drop-in tastings at smaller, established wineries, to formal scheduled visits and other events (music concerts and plays, for example) at larger wineries. Some wineries also offer on-site accommodations and gourmet restaurants. In 2000, the number of winery visits by locals and visitors was estimated to be between 550,000 and 650,000; revenue was estimated at $72 million. The number of tourists and their stay in the region would likely increase if the region, especially in the southern part of the Valley, offered more accommodations and better transport lines between towns and wineries (Kochlan 2004). Some wineries have already added to their restaurants expensive guesthouses and outdoor amenities. The impact of building accommodations on winery property on surrounding small business (e.g., motel operators) is not yet known, but the traffic to and from wineries is a growing concern for nearby residents worried about the traffic noise and pollution on their adjacent properties and communities (Kochlan 2004).

The brief history of the Okanagan wine industry summarized above shows that for a long time the land has been treated as a commodity. Its purpose and use have been determined according to economic interest, market readings, and fluctuations. The role of the pull-out programs is a good example, with the government and local capital determining that orchards were in decline while wine production was expected to rise. This led to the removal of vast quantities of farmland and orchards for real-estate development, infrastructure, and grape growing (*Capital*

News 2008b). However, in an attempt to obfuscate this history of neo-liberal market determination and to mythologize the land and its inextricable connection to wine, the BCWI developed the discourse of "land revealed." This implies that BC land is fertile wine land and makes BC wine unique. In fact, it is suggested that one can taste the land as one smells and savours BC wines:

> Our land, revealed.
> Great wine comes from places where winemakers make a conscious choice to craft the kind of wine only they can. And that's how BC wines grew up and went from good to great.
> BC wineries embraced the fact that the truly great wines in the world are as unique as the place they're made. So tasting a BC wine means tasting something that can't be duplicated anywhere else. Something to be cherished. Uniquely BC. (BC Wine Institute 2005: 3)

This discourse is tied to the regionalizing of winespaces in BC within the global division of tourism. That is, BC wine is "uniquely BC" because it can only be produced in that place. It is also an implicit response to critics who say that wine can be made only in specific places (for example, old Europe) or conversely any place in the world (see both of these views discussed in the film *Mondovino* [2004]). It is as if the local land has now finally found its calling—that is, until the next market niche is identified.

Branding Regions, Branding Wines: Creating Tastespaces

The production of wine is not the only economic activity that takes place in wineries. Naomi Klein (2000) has shown us that in the new economy there is as much value in branding companies as there is in their actual economic operations. Perhaps as a result of this knowledge of how companies brand themselves and the increasing competition in the global tourism industry, regions are also re-branding themselves (Saxenian 2006). The Okanagan Valley is no different in this regard. The City of Oliver, in the south of the Okanagan Valley, has branded itself as the "Wine Capital of Canada."[15] Another example is the way in which wineries endorse the creation of uniform tastespaces while at the same time ensuring that their own wineries are made distinct and unique. Mission Hill, one of the largest wineries in the province, distinguishes itself by highlighting its architectural aesthetic: a seventeenth-century bell-tower and winery architecture resembling a monastery,[16] closed off from the surrounding neighbourhood by a four-metre iron gate.[17] Here what is ancient and oppressive-looking is made new and aesthetically pleasing. And, as in the industry generally, wine regions and wineries are reconstructed as having instant histories.[18] But perhaps concerned about its size and how this may not appeal to tourists interested in the romantic gaze (Urry 2003), Mission Hill assures the tourist that it has not lost its personal touch. In addition, Mission Hill promotes itself as a haven for the tourists from the hustle and bustle of their daily lives and city environments: "We hope you'll think of our winery as a refuge from the hurried pace of daily life. We invite you to experience the nature and art of winemaking by walking our lush on-site vineyards and visiting our underground cellars." The same refuge does not seem to apply to its own workforce, however, as all places but washrooms at Mission Hill are armed with hidden cameras.[19] The tranquility alluded to above is difficult to imagine in a place mimicking the imposing and oppressive architecture of a medieval fortress!

Summerhill Pyramid Winery is another, perhaps even more eccentric construction of distinctiveness. Here the wine is almost secondary (though there is a comment on its organic grapes), displaced by the unusual structure of a pyramid on site.[20] This pyramid not only stores wines and gives the wine substance, according to the tour guide, but serves as a key tourist attraction in the winescapes of the valley. Supposedly the pyramid enables liquids to be "placed in sacred geometry," thereby texturing the wine uniquely.

The eccentricity of those involved in the wine industry is a recurring discourse. One example is the owner of Sandhill Wines, who walks barefoot through his vineyard. As an advertisement in the *Globe and Mail* states,

> Maybe it's the heat. Or maybe it's a certain reverence for the soil. But Robert Goltz always goes barefoot when he's working in the vineyard. Of course, being one of the most successful growers in the valley, he's earned the privilege of this little eccentricity. Which is even more intriguing when you consider the property is home to a sizable population of rattlesnakes. (*Globe and Mail* 2005: R5)

However, Julianna Hayes, wine critic for the local Okanagan newspaper *The Daily Courier*, writes that the glamorous wine owners are a fiction. In her view, most winery owners are "farmers, salespeople, bookkeepers and custodians. You'll find them on the bottling line, working the till in the wine shop, driving the tractor during harvest, disinfecting the tanks, pruning the vines and schlepping cases onto trucks. [...] It's backbreaking, and often heart-breaking, work" (Hayes 2004b: C1). In our research, the involved owner is more prevalent in farm-gate wineries[21] where they are actually "sold" as another tourist attraction in the same vein as their wines. Whereas the large wineries are impersonal, farm-gates often promote themselves as spaces where tourists can rub shoulders with the owners, who often are also the winemakers. Hayes confirms this indirectly when she writes that today one has to be "independently wealthy to purchase or start a winery if you're not willing to wager you're [sic] first born" (2004b: C1). In the Northern Okanagan, where winemaking is more demanding as a result of a less than "perfect terroir" and a cooler climate, the buying price for a winery is over $1 million. In the south in 2004, vineyard acreage—excluding production facilities and equipment—cost $1–$2 million (Hayes 2004b: C1). However, prices have increased: a sample of local real-estate listings in early 2008 showed that an established 10-acre vineyard with winery was priced at $4.2 million, while another 18-acre property with 15 acres of wine grapes was listed at $6.8 million.[22] Clearly one must have deep pockets and strong financial backing to become a wine entrepreneur in the Okanagan Valley.

A final distinction in wineries is Nk'mip, located in the Southern Okanagan Valley in Osoyoos—the first Aboriginal-owned winery in North America. According to sources, this isn't completely accurate, as Vincor International (now owned by Australian based Constellation Brands) has a joint business venture with Nk'mip.[23] But the winery's claims to fame are its Aboriginal themes, preservation and understanding of the landscape, and ties to winemaking. The former is readily accessible for the gawking tourist, while preserving the land seems less credible, since a golf course, hotel, spa, and desert research centre occupy the landscape. The climate here is dry, dusty, and desert-like. Nk'mip (like other wineries in similar locations) draws on water resources to irrigate its multiple attractions, which is a growing concern for environmentalists and some city officials in the Valley (Wood 2006), who are worried about depleting water tables. Today, vineyards are heralded as economically sustainable and environmentally worthy of resources—a discourse we question. How vineyards situate themselves in the recent discussions on the Okanagan's current water shortage and depletion crisis is a pressing social and environmental issue that warrants further examination (Wood 2006; *Canadian Geographic* 2008). The fact that there are over 100 vineyards in the Okanagan Valley also raises questions about the economic sustainability of such an activity in the long haul in a stretch of land that is no more than 200 kilometres in length.

Marking Distinction

> If this wine were human, it would always dim the lights at din-
> ner. (And dinner would only be served once the stars were out.)
> In the days, it would take refreshing walks through the hills. In
> the evenings, it would strut. It would believe that all candles
> deserve to be lit.
>
> This wine isn't human. But you are. So enjoy it with grilled
> chicken and roasted vegetables, or a warm squash soup. And
> if you have candles in the house, light them. (Tinhorn Creek's
> Chardonnay wine bottle label)

The role of the wine critic is essential in the process of developing taste
and providing a language to speak of the different "textures" of wine.[24]
Julianna Hayes, who defines wine taste for the Okanagan through her
Sunday newspaper columns, claimed in an interview that this is only partially true. She prefers to say that what she does is consult readers on
how to "experience wine for themselves" and to "trust your own palate" (Hayes 2004a). But leaving it up to the consumer—trusting him
or her to make the right choice—has never been part of the interactive service-industry labour process, as various authors have shown
(Hochschild 1983; Leidner 1993; MacDonald and Sirianni 1996). This
is due to the presence of the customer in the labour process and management's goal to make the behaviour of customers predictable and controllable. Managerial scripts train the customer to interact proscriptively
and thus enable the labour process to run smoothly. In a Foucaultian
sense, the customer needs to be disciplined and spatialized (cf. Foucault
1979). Therefore, the wine tourist has to be socialized and habituated
with the ability of taste and smell in order to "smell, swirl, sip, and
spit," all while understanding where to do this and in what manner.[25]
This managerial pre-emptive move on customers' choice in the business
space is coordinated with employees in operationalizing the labour process (Leidner 1993).

Training the palate to discern wine taste takes place in the wine shop
found in most wineries. It is here that the emotional proletariat plays a
leading role (Leidner 1993). The role of the emotional proletariat is to
encourage tourists to develop a disciplined and discerning nostril and palate by highlighting the various segments of the tongue, and by inferring a
language of wine snobbery in dissecting the aromas of wine. Wacquant
(2000) has argued that social order can be inscribed on the body, inter-
nalized and habituated in learning experiences that happen *in situ*, in the
body of the person learning. The process of learning wine is also visceral,

meaning that the wine experience is practised and understood through the internal organs of a learner's body. The wine pupil (the uneducated wine taster) must embody the wine taste and wine knowledge by seeing, feeling, and smelling with her own body, or in other words developing a cultural capital (Bourdieu 2001) of, in this case, Okanagan wine. The emotional proletariat's performance enhances the confidence of the winery visitors, who often bring limited knowledge of speaking about wine and appreciating taste.[26] This is not easy to do, given the routinization that customers experience in other consumption spaces (for a literature summary on this topic, see Noon and Blyton [2007]). As Leidner (1993) and others (MacDonald and Sirianni 1996) have shown, the service workplace is predictable and controllable thanks to managerial routinization of customers' behaviour and expectations in workspaces. In the wine shop, too, customers have been instructed on how and where to act. But unlike typical service workspaces, the wine shop is where the emotional proletariat attempts to interrupt routinization by surprising the customers with unfamiliar tastes and scents and the qualities of their own palates. The success of the emotional proletariat is, in a sense, measured in her (almost always "her" in the Okanagan) ability to deliver a script that mystifies wine and its ingredients and textures in order then to invoke a language (another script?) to inscribe taste on the expectant wine connoisseurs' taste buds. In other words, the emotional proletariat's goals are to transfer her script onto the lips of the guests. Once pupils/guests adopt the script, they not only become connoisseurs but are more likely to return to the wine shop for repeated purchases of their favourite wine.

In fast-food restaurants, managerial scripts are used to regiment and constrain the behaviour, movements, and choices of customers in the service labour process. Because the customer is the element in the workplace that management does not dominate, scripts are created to compensate for this. It was Foucault (1979: 211) who explained that discipline "functions to create useful individuals." That is, scripts regulate and routinize, as well as attempt to discipline the behaviour of clients. In the wine industry tourists are also organized according to management's ideas of how best to get them moving in and out of the winery. And in the wine shop, too, people are instructed on where to go, how to stand, and how to drink. In this sense they are routinized. However, it is in the instruction of palate discipline that the standardization of taste and smell is scripted and dispensed by winery workers, primarily in the wine shop. It is in this space that the emotional proletariat induces wine snobbery by encouraging guests to recognize the distinct scents and tastes of the various wines. The role of the emotional proletariat is rather ironic, since it is working-class wine-shop workers who are seemingly defining tastes and aromas for middle-class tourists and instructing them on how to properly recognize and appreciate good wine. And while the discourse on wine taste may be scripted by wine critics or winery management, it must still be skillfully performed by members of the new working class in the new economy (Noon and Blyton 2007).

In the wine shop, the emotional proletariat continues the discourse of the wine critic but adds to it in the wine critic's absence. For example, one is instructed on how to hold the wine glass and how to examine for colour, which tells one about the consistency and age of the wine. The educating of the wine tourist and her palate continues, and the tourist is invited to concur with the wine-shop pourer's script on the textures, layers, structure, and complexities in the wine. There is little room here for the wine tourist herself to articulate an interpretation of the smell and taste of the wine. This is because the wine pourer rarely gives the wine taster that opportunity, and because the wine-tasting experience is quite intimidating, especially for the uneducated wine tourist. In the entire experience, little, if anything at all, is said about the conditions under which this wine is produced, who picks the grapes, and under what labour conditions this is done. It is also true, however, that some tourists are very much interested in being occasional volunteer pickers during harvest time. This conforms to what MacCannell (1976) calls "alienated leisure."[27]

Leidner (1993) has argued that scripting is the "routinization" of the social behaviour and movements of customers, concomitant with the control of employees' appearance and performance. In wineries, scripting is less about "working on people" (Leidner 1993) and more about invoking and dispensing a discourse of "taste"—as a social marker rather than a consumable good. In the space of the wine shop, it is the tongue and the nose that are highlighted for the purpose of inducing in the tourist the ability to discern taste, a necessary skill in the enhancement of the social status of wine tourists. Much of the analysis and language about the interactive worker was developed in the fast-food sector; it was also in this sector that the emotional proletariat most prominently came to the fore (Leidner 1993). But unlike fast food, wine tourism deals with a different clientele, one that expects not the consumption of food or drink, but a discourse of taste. In fact, there is very little wine consumed in a winery; the true "consumption" lies in the acquisition of social markers. Yet social markers are meaningless unless they are performed or mimicked. Therefore, learning how to taste wine is an important social marker in that guests can later mimic their abilities to discern wine quality, perhaps while entertaining their house guests. The task of the emotional proletariat, therefore, is to de-routinize drink and substitute it with a discourse of a disciplined, sharpened, trained, and educated palate capable of exercising the judgment of taste. In so doing, discourses of wine express superhuman characteristics that blur true social relations in the production of this commodity (Marx 1976). Wines, as well as their experiences, are attributed values based on social objectivity rather than social relations of exploitation. In other words, commodity fetishism works to substitute relations between classes of people (workers and winery owners) that are exploited by the values of a wine aesthetic that speaks to taste and experience rather than to the experience of those who produce it from the land up (Marx 1976).

Workers in Wine

Hidden from all open discourse are the wine-production workers themselves. This is a result of the dearth of academic and popular sources on wine workers. There is little known about who labours where, under what conditions, and what their labour rights and protections are. And although some grapes are "harvested mechanically, much still has to be picked by hand. That's the job of hundreds of workers who head into the vineyards each September and October, as well as in January for the ice-wine harvest" (Statistics Canada 2006). According to Roy Graham of the Brewery, Winery and Distillery Workers Union (BWDW), there is little unionization in the industry (Graham 2004).[28] The few unionized workers are represented by the BWDW and comprise a very small proportion of the 10,000 union members in the North and Central Okanagan (*Capital News* 2008a). Some feel that unionization in the wine industry is unlikely to take place since the industry cannot support it (Hayes 2004a). Others argue that even though they wish to organize wineries, there is neither the strategy nor the local union resources to do so (Hotel Employees and Restaurant Employees [HERE] representative 2004). To us, there seems to be an interesting opportunity to develop an organizing strategy for a growing number of workers in the service and tourism industry sectors in Kelowna and the Okanagan Valley. Unionization of the vineyard workforces would force many difficult questions upon wine entrepreneurs, who thrive from the continued deregulation of the industry. Oddly enough, unions seem silent on this issue. It appears that this deregulated and fragmented industry (owing to the involvement of several levels of government, the seasonal nature of work, the partially migratory workforce, and few protections for agricultural workers) is also successful at keeping unions at bay by stifling any attempt at unionizing.

The wine-industry workforce is stratified by occupational status and gender. Barely 5 per cent of the winemakers are women, while over 90 per cent of workers in the wine shops are women (Graham 2004). Wineries keep few fieldworkers hired year round. With the exception of the winemaker, his assistant, and the vineyard manager, most other workers are seasonal and contingent workers. Grape pickers are low-end workers in the vineyard whose only job is to pick, though some are also kept on for the purpose of bottling the wine. Hayes has stressed that fruit pickers are not the same workers as wine-grape pickers: the latter are thought to be more experienced and reliable than the younger work-force in the fruit industry in the Okanagan (Hayes 2004a). This is not entirely accurate, however, as married male migrant Mexican agricul-tural workers, initially brought to Okanagan farms under the Seasonal Agricultural Workers Program (SAWP) to prune, pick, and harvest orchards, are increasingly staying on to pick grapes at various wineries (Tomic, Trumper and Aguiar, forthcoming). Whereas in 2004 only a handful of Mexican workers came to the Okanagan to work in farms, they now number close to 1,000. To participate in the SAWP they must be married and preferably have children. They endure a rigorous screen-ing process in Mexico before they are eligible to join the program. Once here, they work long hours, earn approximately $10 per hour, and often reside in sub-par housing accommodations on the farms or close by. They lack representation, since only the Mexican Consulate in Vancouver looks after them—albeit irregularly—and may be more interested in con-tinuing the program than in dealing with the workers' grievances. On the labour front, the United Food and Commercial Workers Union's (UFCW) office in Kelowna had two organizers under contract who were responsi-ble for these workers. In 2008 these two workers left the union and have not been replaced. Now any issue arising for migrant Mexican workers can only be addressed from the UFCW's Abbotsford office, at least three hours away by car. The group Justicia for Migrant Workers has no pres-ence in the Okanagan Valley, though our research into migrant work-ers has enabled them to begin to establish relationships with workers in the region. The only resort for these workers seems to be one or two churches in the Valley, which, in addition to spiritual assistance, provide workers with social functions to enable them to meet Mexican compatri-ots unknown to them prior to working side-by-side on Okanagan farms (Tomic, Trumper and Aguiar, forthcoming).

Developing a wine palate in Canada is not easy, given the dominance of beer and its status in the country (Heron 2005). Therefore, inserting a national discourse about wine into the imagination of the nation is dif-ficult, though a regional identity linked with wine is more feasible and perhaps attractive in the carving up of spaces for tourist dollars. This regional identity seems to be emerging in both the Niagara wine region in Ontario and the Okanagan Valley. In the latter location, there is a network of businesspeople, the Okanagan Partnership, whose purpose includes the development of the wine cluster in the Valley. Interestingly, the labour movement has not participated in this partnership (Jatel 2004), nor is it likely to do so in the future. This demonstrates both the strength of regional capital and the weakness of the local labour movement. Until the latter mounts a strategy to organize workers in the tourism industry, capital will continue to have the upper hand.

Conclusion

Wine tourism is symbolic both of the changes taking place in Kelowna (and the Okanagan generally) and of the shift to a new economy of service work. This shift has resulted in a post-industrial working class that is remarkably precarious in its employment situation. Yet winery owners and managers increasingly use workers in their wine shops in particular to sell their brand of uniqueness. A scripting of wine taste is invoked and delivered by the emotional proletariat of the wine industry. These are interactive workers, employed by the winery, who relay managerial scripts onto guests to induce positive wine experiences during winery visits. In this transformation of the Okanagan hinterland into a post-Fordist economy, wine tourism is marking out a niche in the global division of tourism sites. In so doing, Okanagan wineries are marketing a total experience for tourists along with creating a winespace focusing on the education of a discerning palate, particularly among white middle-class tourists. On the other hand, unions, and the labour movement more generally, remain outside of the restructuring and reengineering of the Valley, unable to secure provisions against the growing prevalence of precarity in Kelowna. And yet there is increasing need for unions to play a significant role in the industry and the Valley as new and migrant workers enter the industry with little organizational support. In the wine industry in the Okanagan Valley, employers are well organized but workers are not. This may be a typical characteristic of the new workforce in the new economy of the twenty-first century.

Discussion Questions

1. Describe the shift in the socio-economic landscape of the Okanagan Valley as it changes from a Fordist to a post-Fordist economy. Why is the Okanagan economy changing and what are the characteristics of the

changes? What economic engines are important in the new Okanagan Valley economy? What role does neoliberalism play in these changes?

2. Does the absence of unions in the Okanagan Valley play a role in enticing entrepreneurs to enter or stay in this market? What is the relationship between unions and the new economy?

3. Discuss how organized labour can play a more significant role in the restructuring of the economy in the Okanagan valley.

4. In what ways does your own work experience relate to the concept of emotional proletariat and the routinization process described in this chapter?

Notes

1   We would like to thank all the research participants who gave their time so that we could better understand wine tourism. Patricia Tomic and Ricardo Trumper's influence in this chapter is significant, since they were part of a research team examining the rise of the new economy in the Okanagan Valley. For various reasons they could not commit to joining us in this writing assignment. We thank them nonetheless.

2   At the same time, "Kelowna has been identified as one of Canada's 26 wealth pockets, so it qualifies for a stand-alone BMO Harris Private Banking branch" (MacNaull 2008: C9).

3   See the Okanagan Partnership website: <http://www.okanaganpartnership.ca/clusters/tourism.htm>.

4   In the 2009 survey, Kelowna dropped to 19th on the list of "severely unaffordable housing markets," with only the Canadian cities of Vancouver (no. 3) and Victoria (no. 7) ahead. Kelowna remains more expensive than world cities such as Brisbane, Dublin, San Diego, Miami-West Palm Beach, Boston, and Seattle (Parletich Properties Limited 2009: 6, Table ES-3).

5   For a discussion of "precarity" see the special issue (#5) of *Fibreculture Journal* (2005).

6   For a discussion of the power bloc in the Okanagan see Whitely et al. (2008), especially as it pertains to their coalescing around land and higher education.

7   Consider this anecdote from a family that moved from the Niagara region of Ontario to a house on 6.5 acres of property in the hills of Kelowna: "We took up skiing—a sport we had abandoned because of high costs, long lift lines and short runs. We found that tennis nets remained up in winter and we could often play in December and January. We tried snowshoeing, sailing, orienteering and mountain climbing and also rediscovered fishing, hiking and mountain biking. The array of outdoor activities so amazed us that we started a magazine about health, ecology and participation sports and then had a new experience—business failure" (Couper 2004: 12–13).

8   For information on the BC Wine Institute and BC wines in general, see the website: <http://www.winebc.com>.

9   For a good discussion of these processes, see the documentary *Mondovino* (2004).

10 It is generally understood that precariousness means either a marginal connection to the labour market or a temporary state of dislocation from the said market.

Precarity refers to the more general phenomenon, under neoliberalism, of permanent vulnerability and precariousness in the everyday reality of neoliberalism.

11   See also the special Tourism Kelowna advertising supplement that appeared in the *Globe and Mail* on 10 June 2006: <http://www.tourismkelowna.com/media/articles/PDF/Globe-Feature-3.pdf>.

12   By this term we mean the "front-line service workers and paraprofessionals engaged in service work" (MacDonald and Sirianni 1996: 3), whose job it is to display emotions, with "the aim of engendering a particular response: the response of a 'satisfied customer'; and thus a customer more likely to return with repeat business in the future" (Blyton and Jenkins 2007: 65). See also Leidner (1993).

13   See also <http://winesnw.com>.

14   Unless otherwise stated, the information on the wine industry in the province and the Okanagan Valley in particular is drawn from BC Wine Institute (n.d.) and the Institute's website: <http://www.winebc.com/>.

15   Wine Capital of Canada. Oliver, BC, < http://www.winecapitalofcanada.com/>, accessed 23 February 2008. The city of Oliver has a new site (http://www.go2oliver.com), which does not include this self-designation. However, if you drive south on highway 97 to Oliver, you can find a large billboard, as you enter the city, announcing its status as the Canadian capital of wine.

16   See the Mission Hill website: <http://www.missionhillwinery.com>.

17   It is interesting that in the virtual online tour of the winery, the gates are absent in the presentation. See <http://www.missionhillwinery.com/default.asp>.

18   See, for example, Cedar Creek Winery: <http://www.cedarcreek.bc.ca/1_about_us/our_heritage.htm>.

19   Personal communication with a former Mission Hill employee.

20   The Pyramid at Summerhill Pyramid Winery, <http://www.summerhill.bc.ca/winery/pyramid.cfm>.

21   A farm-gate winery is smaller than an estate winery and usually isn't part of the VQA standards system.

22   These are examples from February 2008 listings from Penticton realtor Mr. Jakes and Kelowna realtor Jane Hoffman.

23   See <http://www.nkmipcellars.com/winery/default.asp>, <http://www.vincorinternational.com>.

24   However, consider the following: "Ever bought a bottle of wine just because it had won a gold medal? Dumb move. You might as well have based your choice on the label design or sound of the name, because wine judges are inept. It's a scientific fact" (Crosariol 2009: L1).

25   Adapted by Tina Marten from the BC Wine Institute website: <http://www.winebc.com/touringtips.php>.

26   The wine knowledge and expertise displayed by "Miles" in the film *Sideways* (2004) does not reflect the large majority of wine visitors encountered in our research.

27   Urry (2002: 10), paraphrasing MacCannell, writes, "work has become a mere attribute of society and not its central feature. MacCannell characterizes such an interest in work displays as 'alienated leisure.' It is a perversion of the aim of leisure since it involves a paradoxical return to the workplace."

28   It is extremely difficult to collect accurate numbers from wineries about their employees and levels of unionization. The wine-production process is hidden from view, and so are the workers. In addition, due to the seasonal nature of the job, as well as different grape-picking and production times, part of the workforce is very transient, travelling from the south to the north of the Valley during picking

season. These factors also make it difficult for unions to organize the workers. All of this is compounded by the fact that there is no government body responsible for the wine industry. We understand this fragmentation of industry as intentional to keep the wine workforce unorganized and seasonal, with little worker protection.

References

Aguiar, L.L.M., P. Tomic, and R. Trumper. 2005. "Work Hard, Play Hard: Selling Kelowna as Year-round Playground." *The Canadian Geographer* 49 (2): 123–39.

Amin, A., and N. Thrift. 2004. "Introduction." *The Blackwell Cultural Economy Reader*. Malden, MA: Blackwell. x–xxx.

Armstrong, J. 2009. "Can't Smoke them out of Kelowna." *Globe and Mail* 25 July: S3.

BC Wine Institute. 2005. 2004/2005 Annual Report. <http://www.winebc.com/library/reports/2005_Annual_Report.pdf>.

——. 2008. Tour BC Wineries: Wine Tour Itineraries. <http://www.winebc.com/winetouritinerary.php>.

——. (n.d.) "Vision 2006 ... and the Beyond." Draft Strategic Plan for the British Columbia Wine Institute 2002–2006.

Behrisch, T., R. Hayter, and T. Barnes. 2002/03. "I don't really like the mill; In fact, I hate the mill: Changing Youth Vocationalism, under Fordism and Post-Fordism in Powell River, BC." *BC Studies* 136: 73–101.

Blyton, P., and J. Jenkins. 2007. *Key Concepts in Work*. Los Angeles: Sage.

Bourdieu, P. 2001. "The Forms of Capital." In M.S. Granovetter and R. Swedberg (eds.), *The Sociology of Economic Life*. Boulder, CO: Westview Press. 96–111.

——. 2003. *Firing Back: Against the Tyranny of the Market 2*. Verso: New York.

——. 1984. *Distinction: A Social Critique of the Judgement of Taste*. Cambridge, MA: Harvard University Press.

Canadian Geographic. 2008. "The Big Thirst. Beaches, Orchards, Vineyards: the Okanagan's Got it All ... except Enough Water." July/August: 11–56.

Capital News. 2008a. "Sun-Rype Dispute Called 'Historic Battle.'" 10 February: A30.

——. 2008b. "Farmers Left Behind." 13 August: A3.

Carmichael, B. 2005. "Understanding the Wine Tourism Experience for Winery Visitors in the Niagara Region, Ontario." *Tourism Geographies* 7 (2): 185–204.

Conley, D. 2009. *Elsewhere, USA*. New York: Pantheon Books.

Couper, J. 2004. *Discovering the Okanagan: The Ultimate Guide*. Vancouver: Whitecap Books.

Crosariol, B. 2009. "Taste Test: Inept Wine Judges Exposed." *Globe and Mail* 4 February: L1.

Dawson, M. 2004. *Selling British Columbia*. Vancouver: UBC Press.

Dicken, P. 1998. *Global Shift*. New York: Guilford.

Draycott, A. 2007. "Red, Whites and Greens." *Doctor's Review*. October: 60–65, 127.

Dubinsky, K. 1999. *The Second Greatest Disappointment*. Toronto: Between the Lines.

Dunk, T. 2003. *It's a Working Man's Town*. Montreal and Kingston: McGill-Queen's University Press.

Fibreculture Journal. 2005. Special issue no. 5: "Precarious Labour."

Field, B. 2008. Interview. CBC Kelowna Morning Show. 4 February.

Foucault, M. 1979. *Discipline and Punish*. New York: Vintage Books.

Gabriel, C. 1999. "Restructuring at the Margins: Women of Colour and the Changing Economy." In E. Dua and A. Robertson (eds.), *Scratching the Surface*. Toronto: Women's Press. 127–64.

Globe and Mail. 2005. Advertisement. 22 July: R5.

Graham, R. 2004. Interview. 16 August.

GyPSy Guide. 2009. "Okanagan Wine Tour." <http://www.gpstourscanada.com/where/OkanaganWineTour.html>.

Hackett, N. 1996. "Surprise Success: Wine, Tourists and the Woes of Free Trade." Centre for Tourism and Policy Research, Simon Fraser University. December.

Harvey, D. 1989. *The Condition of Postmodernity*. Malden, MA: Blackwell.

Hayes, J. 2004a. Interview. 9 August.

——. 2004b. "Winery Ownership not for the Faint of Heart." *The Daily Courier*. 15 August: C1.

HERE (Hotel Employees and Restaurant Employees) representative. 2004. Interview. 15 July.

Heron, C. 2003. *Booze*. Toronto: Between the Lines.

Hochschild, A.R. 1983. *The Managed Heart: Commercialization of Human Feeling*. Berkeley: University of California Press.

Jatel, N. 2004. Interview. 9 August.

Kendall, B. 2007. "Grapes and Greens." *Globe and Mail* 1 August: R10.

Klein, N. 2000. *No Logo*. New York: Picador.

Kochlan, S. 2004. Interview. 13 August.

Legislative Assembly, Province of British Columbia, Select Committee on Agriculture. 1978. *The Grape and Wine Industries of British Columbia. A Commodity Report*. Richmond, BC.

Leidner, R. 1993. *Fast Food, Fast Talk*. Berkeley: University of California Press.

Lichtenstein, N. (ed.) 2006. *Wal-Mart: The Face of Twenty-First-Century Capitalism*. New York: New Press.

MacCannell, D. 1976. *The Tourist*. New York: Schocken Books.

MacDonald, C., and C. Sirianni (eds.). 1996. *Working in the Service Society*. Philadelphia: Temple University Press.

MacNaull, S. 2008. "There's a lot of Wealth in Kelowna." *The Daily Courier* 20 June: C9.

——. 2002. "We're Still No. 1." *The Daily Courier* 18 September: A3.

——. 2001. "$400-Million Void." *The Daily Courier* 12 October: A1.

Marx, K. 1976. *The Fetishism of the Commodity and its Secret*. In M.J. Lee (ed.), *The Consumer Society Reader*. Oxford: Blackwell. 10–18.

Michaels, K. 2008a. "Tentative Deal Reached in Long-Running Sun-Rype Strike." *Capital News* 22 February: A3.

——. 2008b. "Labour Strife Rears its Head at Sun-Rype Once Again." *Capital News* 9 April 9: A6.

——. 2008c. "Another Call Center Hangs Up on Kelowna Operations." *Capital News* 7 May: A22.

Mondovino. 2004. Paris: Diaphana Films.

Noll, R.M. 2007. "Napa North: The Okanagan Valley in Canada's British Columbia is Spectacular Golf and Extraordinary Wine." <http://www.golftipsmag.com>.

Noon, M., and P. Blyton 2007. "Emotion Work." *The Realities of Work*. New York: Palgrave. 177–209.

Nowak, B., and B. Wichman 2004. *Saucy Sisters*. New York: NAL Trade.

Okanagan Life Magazine. 2008. "A Jolt from the Blue: The Future of Our Valley: A Round Table Discussion." <http://www.okanaganlife.com/okanagan-life-feature-story/archive/2008-JanFeb-feature.php>.

Okanagan Partnership. [2008.] Okanagan Tourism Labour Study 2008. [Kelowna]: Okanagan Partnership/Service Canada.

Parletich Properties Limited. 2009. *Demographia: 5th Annual Demographia International Housing Affordability Survey: 2009*.

——. 2008. *Demographia: 4th Annual Demographia International Housing Affordability Survey: 2008*.

Plant, D. 2008. "Marusa Closing Its Doors." *Kelowna Daily Courier* 21 February. <http://www.kelownadailycourier.ca/stories.php?id=93274>.

Saxenian, A. 2006. *The New Argonauts: Regional Advantage in a Global Economy*. Cambridge: Cambridge University Press.

Schor, Juliet. 1991. *The Overworked American: The Unexpected Decline of Leisure*. New York: Basic Books.

Schreiner, J. 2003. *British Columbia Wine Country*. Vancouver: Whitecap Books.

——. 2004. *The Wineries of British Columbia*. Vancouver: Whitecap Books.

Sennett, R. 1998. *The Corrosion of Character: The Personal Consequences of Work in the New Capitalism*. Norton: New York.

Sideways. 2004. Fox Searchlight.

Sparke, M. 2000. "Excavating the Future in Cascadia: Geoeconomics and the Imagined Geographies of a Cross-Border Region." *BC Studies* 127: 5–45.

Squire, J.P. 2008. "Labour Shortage Bruising Industry." *Okanagan Sunday* 27 January: A1.

Statistics Canada. 2006. "From the Vine to the Glass: Canada's Grape and Wine Industry." <http://www.statcan.ca/english/research/11-621-MIE/11-621-MIE2006049.htm>.

Tomic, P., R. Trumper, and L.L.M. Aguiar. 2009. "Housing Regulations and the Disciplining of Mexican Migrant Workers in the Okanagan Valley, British Columbia." *Canadian Social Issues* (forthcoming).

Urry, J. 2002. *The Tourist Gaze*. Thousand Oaks, CA: Sage.

Wacquant, L. 2000. *Body and Soul: Notebooks of an Apprentice Boxer*. Oxford: University Press.

Whiteley, R., L.L.M. Aguiar, and T. Marten. 2008. "Neo-Liberal Transnational University: The Case of UBC Okanagan." *Capital & Class* 96: 115–42.

Wood, C. 2006. "Drying up the Okanagan." *The Tyee* 17 August.

10. Regeneration among Coal-Mining Communities in Canada and the UK
The Role of Culture

LARRY HAIVEN

Introduction

In many parts of the world, industrial communities have been left bereft by the loss of heavy industry. "Good" jobs are lost, as are the services that came with them. What is to stop the out-drainage of formerly blue-collar families and the dereliction in its wake? Worldwide, regions left dispossessed by industry are falling over each other to declare themselves cultural centres. Many countries have national committees supporting the "creative cities" concept. Cities and regions once powered by industry now seek a renaissance through creative industries and the arts. Close to 90 Canadian locations are members of the "Creative Cities Network."[1] But can they all be creative cities?

In this chapter I discuss two communities that have a fighting chance to do so. And I use the word "fighting" purposely, since both of the regions have a long history of labour militancy and solidarity. They also share a legacy of two of the most storied industries, which in their hey-day generated more than their share of cultural originality: coal mining and steelmaking. Today those cultural legacies are contributing to regeneration and different kinds of work—this time cultural.

The Cultural Economy

Much of the discussion of the role of culture and creativity in the economic renaissance revolves around the work of Richard Florida, who has approached superstardom with the idea of a "new creative class" (Florida 2002). Florida's basic premise is straightforward: "There is a creative class in Western societies, which wants to live in diverse, tolerant, cool cities; The creative class shapes the economy of many cities. Increasingly, jobs move where the skilled people are, and cities which attract and retain the creative classes do better. Creativity is driving their development" (Nathan 2005: 3). But Florida has been savaged by several scholarly critics (see Peck 2005; Scott 2006; Pratt 2008). The problem with Florida, or with the cult that has risen up around him, is not with the idea that cities must be inviting places to which creative people would want to come, or that economic prosperity is good. Instead, the problem is in raising the issue to the level of a system or an ideology, trying to present one true answer to the problems of urban economic development.

Yet, outside academe, Florida's fame and success continue seemingly unabated. As Nathan (2005) suggests, Florida appears to be "wrong in the right way," or makes intuitive sense. Human capital is increasingly at the heart of economic development, those with high amounts of knowledge and creativity are the engines of such development, and creative people like to live in and will flock to "funky" places. We know that traditional manufacturing and extraction are declining as a proportion of GDP in most advanced "industrial" economies, that knowledge goods and services are produced by clever and highly educated people, and, while they work, those people like to play and enjoy life and will prefer places that give them that opportunity more than places that do not.

Another thinker who tackles, in a more unassuming way, the transition from the unsustainable old to the more sustainable new economy is Thomas Michael Power. In his *Lost Landscape and Failed Economies: The Search for a Value of Place* (1996) and *Post-Cowboy Economics: Pay and Prosperity in the New American West* (with Richard Barrett, 2001), the author suggests that traditional economic thinkers have been totally wrong-headed about what makes a place liveable and what contributes to a sustainable economy. In traditional or "folk" economics, the "extractive view" of a local economy dominated. Extraction and industrial activity were the prime motivating force of the economy. In the new or "environmental" view, it is the quality of a place and its people that determines development potential. Power bases his ideas on communities abandoned by mining and heavy extraction processing in the American mountain West.

Power discusses the difficulties in dichotomizing the creative class and everyone else, challenging the conventional wisdom on service jobs.

> When one looks closely at service jobs, the suggestion that there is something categorically inferior about those jobs is simply false. There are lousy service jobs, but there are also lousy manufacturing jobs.... (2005: 4)

He points to contemporary examples of terrible and low-paid manufacturing jobs in settings such as enormous meat-packing plants and textile sweatshops (mostly employing immigrant labour—both legal and illegal). But then he turns to service jobs:

> ... services include business services, medical services, educational services, and computer services ... [and] an expanding service employment that certainly has attractive characteristics.... The pay in the service industries in the United States is as high or higher than it is in goods-producing or manufacturing jobs. This is partly tied to the deunionization of manufacturing jobs and the shift of manufacturing jobs from highly paid areas of the United States to rural low paying areas in the south. Services jobs are not dead-end jobs. Once the pay profiles over a lifetime of employment are considered, the opportunities for improvement are as great or greater in services than in manufacturing or goods production. Services are significantly more skill intensive. There is a larger technical and managerial component associated with services than with goods production in general. (4)

We now think of manufacturing historically as a locus of high wages, but Power insists that that is quite erroneous.[2] Before the second half of the twentieth century, the majority of those jobs were brutal and low paid. The minefields of Cape Breton Island are a good example. Power stresses that manufacturing became a relatively high-wage area in the second half of the twentieth century, not because of any natural tendencies but because a combination of public policy and unionization together made it so.[3] Likewise, there is nothing inherent in service jobs that makes them low-paid. We could make them as highly paid as high-end manufacturing if only we decided to do so. Thus, concludes Power, the loss of heavy industry is not a tragedy but rather an opportunity. The emerging alternative is clear:

> While the extraction of materials from the earth and their return to the biosphere as waste are always disruptive, improving quality of life does not have to be. Because "qualities" are not primary material, they can be limitlessly improved without burdening the natural world. *A more beautiful song, a more graceful athletic performance, a better designed home, greater knowledge, or honed professional skills do not necessarily require expanded material flows out of and into the natural world. A dynamic and efficient economy could increase access to valuable qualities while decreasing the material throughput of resources and goods.* (Power 1996: 25; emphasis added)

Some may question whether this post-industrial economy is a viable alternative to the old industrial economy. How can one compare a miner's or a steelworker's wage and their multiplier effect across the local economy to those coming out of a cultural and touristic economy? We can begin by examining some of the limitations of the industrial economy:

- Miners, steelworkers, and fishers were always a minority of the labour force, a kind of aristocracy of labour with many others coping as they could in poorer jobs.
- Their earnings were, by and large, men's earnings. In a highly sex-divided labour market, women were excluded from the benefits unless they happened to be married to, or young daughters of, those workers.
- As we will see below, historically the "good" earnings were a relatively temporary phenomenon, lasting for really no more than a single generation. This was preceded by a long period of rank exploitation and followed by a period of industrial closure.
- Even in the period of prosperity, the profits extracted were not shared equitably with the workers and the larger community. Dufour and Haiven (2008) show that although real productivity in Nova Scotia rose prodigiously in the quarter-century after 1980, average real earnings fell. Moreover, over the same period, the share of productivity gains going to labour declined, while capital's share rose and much escaped from the local economy entirely.
- The extractive economy demands export-led development, which local politicians and business and community leaders tout as the

solution in a vicious circle, distorting their activities in horrible ways to please the outside capital. Mine disasters, both physical and economic, are commonplace. In 1991, the Westray mine in Plymouth, Nova Scotia, exploded, killing 26 miners. The desperation that drove the workers and the community to endorse the doom-laden project, which was not even economically viable (see Glasbeek and Tucker 1999), emerged from the historical cycles of coal boom and bust.

• Even where the risk of physical disaster can be lessened, it is difficult to avoid economic disaster. As soon as the outside investors grow weary or impatient or politically dissatisfied with the local economy, they exit, leaving the local economy devastated with unemployment and disillusionment. Therefore communities must find means of economic development that are not totally dependent on outside investment.

Perhaps even more acute than the loss of earning power may be the emotional or spiritual devastation of communities. If the bereft communities are to survive outmigration and other forms of social dislocation, then the communities must have something that holds them together, comforts them in their loss, gives them hope for the future, and builds the confidence to rebuild. It is in this area that the cultural economy has its first great success, as we will see.

As the examples from Cape Breton Island and County Durham will show, many cultural enterprises emerge from strong communities, nourished within family, neighbour, cooperative, and communal networks, given exposure through locally based institutions and generating a devoted following among the wider regional community. The role of federal and provincial governmental institutions, public cultural agencies, and regional development agencies in fostering cultural production is also integral in the development of cultural resources.

The Rise and Fall of Heavy Industry in Cape Breton and County Durham

Cape Breton Island, Canada
Cape Breton Island, off the northeast tip of Nova Scotia, is about the size of Jamaica, but with a population of a small city (126,000). Heavy industry was concentrated in only a small portion (about 20 per cent) of the island, while the rest of the island (and even parts of its industrial core) has a bucolic, often breathtaking, setting. With the Atlantic Ocean no more than about 40 kilometres from any interior point, a long and

indented coastline, mountains plummeting to the sea, and a huge internal saltwater lake, it is no wonder that it has been selected as a prime tourist location, acknowledged as one of the most beautiful islands in the world.[4]

At the end of the nineteenth century, full-scale coalmining began in the northeast, around Sydney. A smaller coalfield, on the western side of the island, also operated until 1958. Soon coal's availability led to the largest integrated steel mill in the British Empire. The population of the region grew rapidly in the first two decades of the twentieth century. Employment in coal and steel peaked in 1913 and then fell gradually as technology grew and demand shrank. By the end of World War II, the days of both the coal mines and the steel mill were numbered. By the early 1960s, the global demand for steel and coal had dropped drastically, and the jobs of thousands of workers were at stake. The Canadian federal government stepped in to purchase the mines in 1968, and the steel plant was bought by the provincial government. The energy crisis of the 1970s and early 1980s provided a slight upswing in the fortunes of the coal mines, but the writing was on the wall. The 1990s and the turn of the century provided a perfect economic storm: not only did the coal mines and the steel mill finally shut down, but one of the island's other great economic engines faltered. The once bountiful groundfish[5] harvest crashed, and employment in fishing plummeted.

At its height, in the 1920s, coal mining employed 12,000 people. By 1961, 24 per cent of the island's workforce was employed in either coal or steel. Today, that number has been reduced to zero. Over the past three decades, approximately 7,000 jobs have been lost in the coal and steel industries, and an estimated 2,300 people have been impacted by the collapse of the groundfish harvest (ECBC 2003). In 1971, the population of the Island was 170,000; by 2001, it was down to 147,500—a drop of 14 per cent, compared to a rise of 10 per cent for the province of Nova Scotia—and it is still dropping. Unemployment between 1976 and 2002 hovered between 14 and 26 per cent, consistently around twice the Canadian rate and 1.5 times the Nova Scotia rate. Average income in 2000 was $20,766, 16 per cent below that of Nova Scotia and 30 per cent below that of Canada (Locke and Tomblin 2003; ECBC 2003). The impact of these events upon the health and social dislocation of residents has been powerful. Rates of illness, drug addiction, teen pregnancy, life expectancy, and other indicators are considerably higher than the rest of the province and the country (Veugelers and Hornibrook 2002).

The trade-union and political history of the Cape Breton miners is legendary. In the 1920s, the coal bosses cut wages by one third, launching a bitter struggle. The region virtually came to resemble an armed occupation, as fully one half of Canadian soldiers were deployed in Cape Breton coalfields.[6] The red flag flew over the coalfields as well (see below), and the miners' leader, J.B. McLachlan, was an unabashed Communist. The dispute was suppressed by collusion among the employer, governments, and the US-based union. Yet the miners eventually won their struggle (see Frank 1999).

County Durham, England

Similarities between the industrial rise and fall of County Durham, England, and that of Cape Breton Island are striking. In a country renowned for the abundance of its coal, County Durham in the English northeast was the largest coalfield, and perhaps the largest in the world (Beynon and Austrin 1994). First dug in the 1200s, coal became the engine of the local economy. The lands surrounding the rivers Tyne and Wear produced 40 per cent of the national output in 1700, 25 per cent in 1830, and 20 per cent in 1913 (Levine 1989). Some of the original industrial developers of the Cape Breton coalfield were companies from County Durham. While coal extraction was a rural activity, it gave rise to associated industries like steelmaking and shipbuilding in the muscular urban centres like Newcastle upon Tyne, Sunderland, Gateshead, and North and South Shields. With locally sourced limestone and iron imported from Sweden, steelmaking was also performed in smaller, inland communities, which dominated the British steel industry until the mid-1800s.

The slow decline in the mid-twentieth century and the sudden death of these industries has much in common with the Canadian example above, for many of the same reasons. The coal and steel industries were taken over by governmental agencies in mid-century, a decade earlier than in Canada. A unique but powerful punctuation for the decline came with the tumultuous British miners' strike of 1984–85, as much about culture as about economics. The National Union of Mineworkers was arguably one of the strongest in the country, particularly because of the cohesion of communities of miners and their families. When British Coal and the Thatcher government threatened these communities with rationalizing, downsizing, and pit closures, and the attendant rule changes and job losses, the union fought back (Milne 1994). The union was ultimately defeated, and the government proceeded with the almost complete closure of British coal mines, including the vast majority of County Durham pits, but the defeat was both ignominious and glorious. Far from fading away, as we shall see, County Durham mining culture has been resurrected and has persisted, and community solidarity has benefited from pride in a shared industrial past.

The last fifty years of the twentieth century saw coal employment in the UK fall from 700,000 to 13,000. From the start of the miners' strike to the present alone, 200,000 jobs vanished (Waddington et al. 2001). In County Durham, the impact was even more devastating. A 2005 report showed the lowest levels of employment in the UK, with nearly one in five of the working population claiming unemployment benefits. Between 1982 and 2002, the region lost 100,000 jobs in manufacturing, and predicted a further 25,000 jobs lost by 2012 and 39,000 jobs lost in mining over two decades (*Northern Echo* 2005). As can be expected, "high levels of long-term unemployment, poverty, social exclusion and a decline in community resources have left the now post-industrial mining communities devastated. Both voluntary and government agencies have long recognized a significant increase both in youth crime and in the abuse of drugs and alcohol generally" (Stephenson and Wray 2005).

Cultural Regeneration

Cape Breton Island and County Durham share a response to industrial devastation through a prodigious outburst of culture, especially related to coal mining. These cultural manifestations were present before the demise of coal, but they have taken on a new significance since then. They are manifestations of "mining culture"[7] in both senses of the phrase: the culture arising out of mining communities, and the mining of value from it.

Cape Breton Island

The following is a sampling of the cultural activities, events, and venues associated with coal mining in Cape Breton Island.

MUSEUMS

There is a major museum devoted to the history of mining on both sides of the island. The history of the western one is shrouded in mystery, as many of the ex-miners have moved away or died. Initiated by a local high-school teacher and municipal councillor and based in a small railway station dating back to 1901, the Inverness museum carries a trove of items relating to the coalfield. A particularly arresting photo shows a miner holding a hammer-and-sickle flag sometime around 1919.

The larger museum, in Glace Bay, founded in Canada's centennial year, 1967, celebrates the history of the northeastern coalfield. Despite the island's renowned Scottish and English roots, industrial Cape Breton has always had strong ethnic communities from outside the British Isles. The driving force behind the Glace Bay museum, Nina Cohen, was a doctor's wife and community activist whose mother, as part of the Jewish community, helped the miners in the 1920s' strikes. Like the Inverness museum, the Glace Bay museum is unabashedly pro-union. Prominent among the displays are pictures and documents relating to the "labour wars," and the 1979 National Film Board film "12,000 Men" is shown in the theatre, a film in which the interviewees make no attempt to hide their commitment to the union and contempt for their employer. The highlight of the museum is an underground tour of the Ocean Deeps Colliery, a coal mine located beneath the Museum building; ex-coal miners act as guides. The website of the Glace Bay museum is quite extensive,[8] including sections on history and materials to assist schoolchildren.

MUSIC

Cape Breton Island is famous for the quantity and quality of its singers and songwriters. Many have composed original coal-mining songs. Among these, "Coal Town Road" and "No. 26 Mine Disaster" by Allister MacGillivray, "Now That the Work is Done" by J.P. Cormier, "In the Pit" by Leon Dubinsky, and "Working Man" by Rita MacNeil have become classics, sung around the world. By far the most celebrated of music-makers is the choir Men of the Deeps, another centennial project. Made up exclusively of working (now former working) miners, it has toured extensively and has become a Canadian cultural icon. It is difficult to overemphasize the affection for the choir in Cape Breton, Nova Scotia, and across Canada.

FILM AND VIDEO

John Walker's award-winning *Men of the Deeps*, produced by the National Film Board of Canada (2003) is a paean to both the Cape Breton miners and the choir. Walker obtained permission to film in the mines even as the final shutdown was announced. He weaves the story of the mines' demise with the story of the choir and punctuates the film with the choir's songs.

Several fictional films and television shows about Cape Breton mining have received international acclaim. Perhaps the best known is *Margaret's Museum* (1995), starring British actors Helena Bonham-Carter and Clive Russell as well as Canadians Kate Nelligan and Kenneth Welsh, an adaptation of novelist Sheldon Currie's *The Glace Bay Miner's Museum* (1981). Both the novel and the movie are dark and bawdy satires about the safety hazards of mine work and the stalwart mining communities of the island.

Another film, later a television series, is *Pit Pony* (1997), directed by Eric Till and starring Richard Donat and a young Ellen Page (later the star of *Juno*). Taken from the children's novel by Joyce Barkhouse (1990), it tells of an early twentieth-century boy's love of a mining dray-horse and of the physical hazards of mine work, especially for children.

BOOKS

The two novels above may have been made into movies, but the most celebrated of contemporary authors is short-story master and novelist Alistair Macleod, winner of the International IMPAC Dublin Literary Award. Many of his short stories and his novel *No Great Mischief* (1999) involve Cape Breton coal miners. An earlier master was Hugh MacLennan, born in Glace Bay, whose first novel *Each Man's Son* (1951), is about a doctor in a Cape Breton mining town. Non-fiction books abound, including historian David Frank's biography of miners' union leader J.B. McLachlan (1999) and Rennie Mackenzie's several books about his adventures underground.

VISUAL ART

Visual art of the coalfield is not as prevalent in Cape Breton as in its British counterpart, but throughout the coal-mining town of New Waterford are murals by local artist Terry MacDonald, depicting historical scenes, some of the mines that used to employ the local people, and some of the town itself.

SPECTACLES

Every June 11, businesses and government offices shut down in industrial Cape Breton as ex-miners, trade-union leaders, local dignitaries, and community members join to commemorate the killing of William Davis. As one local newspaper columnist writes,

> June 11 is a sacred, defining day, for labour in Cape Breton. It calls up within the hearts of miners, active and retired, the deprivation and the exploitation experienced by their brothers in the first days of the 20th century.
>
> Indeed, it is a day to recall the infamy that led to the death of William Davis in 1925—a day to remember, as well, those miners who, over the years, died in the deeps. (Peach 2008)

County Durham

People from County Durham and Newcastle upon Tyne are known as "Geordies" and, like those in many English districts, have a distinct accent and culture. Despite striking similarities with Cape Breton, County Durham has its own cultural manifestations, unique either to

British mining areas or to itself. As in Canada, the pit closures have given them more resonance.

MUSEUMS

Each of England, Scotland, and Wales has its own national mining museum. England's is in Netherton in Yorkshire, 150 kilometres south of the city of Durham. The North East of England Mining Archives and Resource Centre (NEEMARC), based in Sunderland, houses the heritage of not only County Durham but also of several other northeast regions. However, a County Durham mining museum of note is at Beamish,[9] fifteen kilometres from Newcastle. It is an open-air museum that tells the story of northeast England at two historic points: 1825 and 1913. Its main features include a simulation of a historic drift mine that takes visitors underground, a manor house, pit village, school and church, and historic trams and trains, brought from around the region and restored.

MUSIC

English pit communities, especially in Yorkshire, have become famous for their brass bands. County Durham has several mining brass bands, including those associated with the Easington, Trimdon, and Craghead Collieries and the resurrected Washington Colliery Band (Hands 2008). But the greatest showcase for the bands occurs annually on the second Saturday in July at the Durham Miners' Gala (see below). The Gala marchers at the 'Cotia Pit[10] at Harraton have bucked the brass-band tradition to celebrate the folk music composed by two local miner singer/songwriter/poets, Jock Purdon (1925–98) and Jack Elliott (1907–66). Purdon acted as a troubadour during the 1984–85 miners' strike. Several other County Durham musicians, such as Jez Lowe, also composed and sang about miners.

FILM AND VIDEO

There is no shortage of films about mining in County Durham. Probably the most famous internationally is *Billy Elliot* (2000) by Newcastle-born playwright Lee Hall. The play (and the subsequent movie and stage show) is about an eleven-year-old boy whose father and brother are involved in the miners' strike, who goes to the gym to take boxing lessons and decides to take up ballet instead, much to the consternation of his family. Set in a fictional County Durham town, it was shot mainly in Easington.

Amber is a film-and-photography collective in Newcastle, which has made a series of well-received documentaries and dramas about mining in the region.[11] *The Coalfield Trilogy*, a series of dramas, includes

The Scar (1997), about how women deal with the failure of the miners' strike; *Like Father* (1999), about generations of a pit family torn
apart by industrial decline; and *Shooting Magpies* (2005), about substance abuse in post-industrial Durham colliery villages. *Seacoal* (1985)
shows the hard lives of those who collect washed-up coal on the beaches
of the county. Amber's documentaries include *It's the Pits* (1995), about
youth organizing in pit communities, and *Can't Beat It Alone* (1985),
which combines the pit closure with the anti-nuclear and the peace
campaigns.

BOOKS

As in Cape Breton, Country Durham has produced a rich supply of novels about mining and its people, of which the following are only a few.
Sid Chaplin (1916–86) was a writer of novels, television scripts, poems,
and short stories, many set in County Durham of the 1940s and 1950s,
especially the finely observed stories about coal-mining life, including
The Leaping Lad (1946), *The Thin Seam* (1950), and *The Day of the
Sardine* (1961). Almost all of historical romance writer Janet MacLeod
Trotter's books occur in local communities. *The Hungry Hills* (1993) is
set in a County Durham pit village during the 1926 General Strike. *Blink*
(2001) by Andrea Badenoch is set in a depressed contemporary County
Durham mining community.

VISUAL ART

Not only is there a robust body of visual art inspired by the northeast
coalfield, but many of the artists were themselves miners—the so-called
"pitmen painters." Emerging from the Ashington pit in Northumbria,
just north of Durham, several of its members were from Durham. The
most famous are Norman Cornish, a miner for 33 years, and Tom
McGuinness. Both emerged from the Spennymoor Settlement movement,
an arts collective started in the Depression for the unemployed and for
mining families. It included future writer Sid Chaplin (see above). In
2002, Robert McManners and Gillian Wales published a collection of
the pitmen painters entitled *Shafts of Light*, as well as earlier and later
books concentrating on McGuiness. Playwright Lee Hall (see above) has
written *The Pitmen Painters*, which is playing at the time of this writing
to audiences across the UK.

Another important form of indigenous coalfield visual art is cloth
(usually silk) banners of the miners' union branches. As old as the trade-
union movement, and true icons of the British working class, they bear
the name of the branch as well as paintings of various types. Some have
religious themes related to human labour, but most carry portraits of

famous mining-union leaders, historical Labour Party politicians (such as Keir Hardie) and occasionally revolutionary leaders such as Karl Marx and Friedrich Engels. The banners, which are professionally painted and can be very costly, are stunning and distinctive: "There are no union banners in the world which are the equal of those of the Durham miners. In their number, their colours, their design and their complexity of motif they are an astonishing testament of a vibrant political tradition" (Beynon and Austrin 1994: xvi; quoted in Mellor and Stephenson 2005).

THE CLUB SCENE

For a city that was a leader in the derelict league only a quarter-century ago, Newcastle has led the way in "cool Britannia." Light years from the grimy coal boats, industrial wharfs, and sooty slums of yesteryear, the downtown area is packed with restaurants, bars, and clubs, thronged by snappily dressed youth. Indeed, the 2006 Edition of *The Rough Guide to Great Britain* classified "a night out" in Newcastle as the top of 35 attractions in the entire country (Katz 2006). While this development is not directly related to the coal culture of yesteryear, Geordies (those from Newcastle) seem to take perhaps a perverse pride in the contrast between the hipness of the present and the griminess of the past.

SPECTACLES

Above all others, one spectacle in County Durham epitomizes the cultural renaissance, although ironically the Durham Miners' Gala is 136 years old. Known also as the "Big Meeting," it almost faded away in the 1990s in the wake of the mine closures, but it has returned with a vengeance. County Durham university instructors Carol Stephenson and David Wray[12] have written of its significance to the emotional regeneration of mining communities (Mellor and Stephenson 2005; Stephenson and Wray 2005) and, although I myself have attended two Galas, the following description owes much to them.

Early in the morning of the second Saturday in July almost every year since 1872,[13] groups of miners and ex-miners and their families and friends from pit villages all across County Durham descend on historic Durham Town. Each group is usually accompanied by a brass band (either their own or one hired), and each group carries a banner (see above). Bands playing and banners fluttering, the groups march through Durham Town, stopping for a few minutes under a reviewing party on the balcony of the County Hotel. The reviewers, traditionally chosen by the miners themselves, are union officials and local political leaders friendly to labour. National politicians appear only if they are deemed friendly to labour. Therefore Tony Blair, Gordon Brown, and their cabinet members have not been chosen (nor, it is presumed, would want to be chosen) while Tony Benn, the former Labour MP and radical leftist leader, appears almost every year. The groups proceed to the local fairground, to partake in food, entertainment, amusements, fairground rides, and exhibits in tents. On a stage, more dignitaries preside and a more formal set of speeches is given, often radical in their condemnation of injustice around the world and of the policies of the presiding national government. The day's events are marked with an emotional sense of history.

Once drawing up to 150,000 participants, the Gala reached a low point after the defeat of the miners' strike and the subsequent pit closures, with only 8,000 people at its lowest point in 1993. Much to the amazement of everyone concerned, the participation rebounded and has reached up to 70,000 people in recent years. In its low years, many pit communities stopped coming to the Gala. When they decided to return, one of the activities that galvanized them involved their banner. Many old banners were too fragile, so new ones were commissioned. Every Gala Day, communities with new banners attend a religious service where community members, complete with bands and banners, march into the 900-year-old Durham Cathedral and the priest blesses the banners. This too is a highly moving experience, rich in historical import. Raising funds for new banners, communities across the county have found a new mission and zeal to preserve their heritage. Many of those involved are schoolchildren, for whom the experience of coal mining is at least one and sometimes two generations removed. Stephenson and Wray (2005: 193) contemplate the motivating factors behind communities returning to the Gala and re-commissioning banners:

> For these communities, regeneration, economic or otherwise, is not about moving on and forgetting the past. On the contrary, memory is the source of succour and inspiration for activists, as they see the continuance of occupational identity as crucial to the well-being of their communities. Mining culture, as symbolized by iconic banners and by involvement in the festival of the Gala, is deeply-rooted in the consciousness ...

Conclusion

Cape Breton and County Durham are not the only locations in the world where a cultural upsurge has followed the demise of coal mining, but they are uncanny in their similarity and their vitality. While one cannot be too sanguine about the possibilities for this cultural revival to bring back the same level of prosperity as that spawned by heavy industry, one must also not be dismissive of its potential for the future development of these communities.

But how long can the echo of mining culture continue to resonate loudly? The participation in the Durham Miners' Gala has grown dramatically since the dark days of the 1990s, but how long will aging miners and their families continue stubbornly to remake their banners and carry them to the "Big Meeting"? With its insistence on ex-miners as choristers and no major new supply in sight, how long until the Men of the Deeps no longer serenades its fond audiences? It is possible that in a world increasingly hungry for ever-diminishing energy, both regions will see a limited coalfield revival.[14] Have governments and communities learned their lesson? Do they see the folly of the purely extractive view so that they do not go coal crazy again? Will they instead use the resource with an eye to maximum good for the community? The Westray mine explosion in Nova Scotia is only a decade and a half old, and the memory of its political opportunism still makes Nova Scotians shudder. But it is not remotely likely that heavy industry will return on the scale of yesteryear.

Therefore, we must see cultural revival as a transitional phase, a way of providing comfort, cohesion, and stability for communities looking for long-term solutions. The skills and traditions developed in the cultural economy will, it is hoped, have a greater staying power than those of its industrial predecessor. While the memory of coal may spawn books, movies, paintings, and songs, those cultural forms may turn to other subjects as time passes. Hence, cultural regeneration may not be about just dollars and cents or pounds and pence. They are fundamentally about communities and collective self-confidence. Indeed, Robert Hughes has commented,

> My own blunt evaluation of regeneration programmes that don't have a culture component is they won't work. Communities have to be energised, they have to be given some hope, they have to have the creative spirit released. (quoted in Evans 2005)

I have said elsewhere (Haiven 2008) that culture—the songs, stories, and rituals of communities tied together with bonds of common occupation—can act in two directions: as a soporific, inducing retreat from painful reality, and as a prod to action.

Graeme Evans puts it thus:

> Culture is a critical aspect of mediating and articulating commu-
> nity need, as development is planned and takes shape, through
> culture's potential to empower and animate. This should in
> turn lead to participation in, and ownership of, regeneration
> by the residents and other beneficiaries in an area. Alternatively,
> culture-led regeneration can be used as a 'sop' to distract atten-
> tion from the underlying power over place that finally mani-
> fests itself in the type of projects and landscapes created and
> imposed on communities and sites undergoing regeneration.
> (2005: 971–72)

Of Evans's three dimensions of regeneration—physical, economic, and
cultural—I would suggest that cultural generation must take precedence
before the other two can be achieved.

Discussion Questions

1. Can every geographic locality in a country be a "creative" centre? If
not, what will determine who succeeds and who does not? Do former
mining communities have an advantage in this competition?

2. Is the new cultural economy less gender-exclusive or just as gender-
exclusive as the old industrial economy?

3. How can a community balance the need for outside investment with
the need for local control of its physical and human resources?

4. Should we try to quantify precisely the economic impact of the cultural production of a locality, or would that defeat the whole purpose of
cultural production?

5. There are other ex-coal-mining regions in the world and even within
Canada and the UK. What do you think it is about Cape Breton Island
and County Durham that led them to generate such a prodigious amount
of cultural production?

Notes

1 See Creative City Network of Canada: <http://creativecity.ca>.
2 The following discussion about public policy is based on Power (1996, 2005),
   Power and Barrett (2001), and personal discussions with Power himself.

3 Wages rose for thirty to forty years, until the real earnings of workers in the US and Canada stagnated and then retreated as public policy with regard to unionization and the welfare state regressed.

4 Cape Breton tied with the south island of New Zealand for second place in the *National Geographic Traveler*'s destination scoreboard competition (*National Geographic Traveler* 2004). *Condé Nast* magazine has rated it among the best island destinations in the world (CBC 1998).

5 Groundfish are so called because they are found near the ocean floor. Prominent among these commercially are cod, whose numbers declined drastically in the 1980s and 1990s and precipitated a government moratorium on further commercial fishing.

6 This fact is noted on a plaque in the Miners' Museum, Glace Bay.

7 In June 2005, I was a key organizer of a symposium in Sydney, Cape Breton Island, called "Mining Culture," at which academic and other commentators (including ex-miners) from North America and the UK gathered to compare notes.

8 See <http://www.minersmuseum.com/>.

9 See <http://www.beamish.org.uk/>.

10 'Cotia is short for Nova Scotia. Ironically, it does not refer to the Canadian province containing Cape Breton Island, but rather because many of the original miners were from Scotland. When they moved south to find jobs, they gave their pit the Latin name for "New Scotland."

11 See <http://www.amber-online.com>.

12 I accompanied them to the Gala and to Cape Breton Island in a project comparing cultural regeneration in the two places.

13 The Gala was cancelled for several years during the world wars.

14 In 2005, the Donkin Mine in Cape Breton was sold to a consortium led by mining giant Xstrata, which is exploring the geological and economic possibilities of bringing coal out of the ground once more. Likewise, there is still some coal to be dug in County Durham if conditions become favourable.

References

Barkhouse, J. 1990. *Pit Pony*. Toronto: Gage.

Beynon, H., and T. Austrin. 1994. *Masters and Servants*. London: River Oram Press.

CBC (Canadian Broadcasting Corporation). 1998. "Cape Breton Is Paradise: Poll." 17 November. <http://www.cbc.ca/canada/story/1998/11/16/poll981116.html>.

Currie, S. 1995. *The Glace Bay Miner's Museum*. Wreck Cove, NS: Breton Books.

Dufour, M., and L. Haiven. 2008. "Hard Working Province: Is it Enough? Rising Profit and Falling Labour Shares in Nova Scotia." Ottawa: Canadian Centre for Policy Alternatives. November.

ECBC (Enterprise Cape Breton Corporation). 2003. Annual Report.

Evans, G. 2005. "Measure for Measure: Evaluating the Evidence of Culture's Contribution to Regeneration." *Urban Studies* 42: 959–83.

Florida, R. 2002. *The Rise of the Creative Class: And How It's Transforming Work, Leisure, Community and Everyday Life*. New York: Basic Books.

Frank, D. 1999. *J.B. McLachlan: A Biography: The Story of a Legendary Labour Leader and the Cape Breton Coal Miners*. Toronto: Lorimer.

Glasbeek, H., and E. Tucker. 1999. "Death by Consensus: The Westray Story." In Christopher McCormick (ed.), *The Westray Chronicles*. Halifax: Fernwood. 71–96.

Haiven, L. 2008. "Cultural Production and Social Cohesion amid the Decline of Coal and Steel: The Case of Cape Breton Island." In Robert O'Brien (ed.), *Solidarity First: Canadian Workers and Social Cohesion.* Vancouver: University of British Columbia Press.

Hands, L. 2008. "Washington Colliery Band Will Be Heard Once Again." *The Journal* (Newcastle) 5 July. <http://www.journallive.co.uk/north-east-news/todays-news/2008/07/05/washington-colliery-band-will-be-heard-once-again-61634-21266807/>.

Katz, L. 2006. "New Guide Gives Britain a Rough Ride." June 20. <http://www.guardian.co.uk/travel/2006/jun/20/travelnews.unitedkingdom.uknews.>

Levine, D. 1989. "King Coal's Kingdom: Review." *Journal of Social History* 22 (3): 541–48.

Locke, W., and S.G. Tomblin. 2003. *Good Governance, a Necessary but Not Sufficient Condition for Facilitating Economic Viability in a Peripheral Region: Cape Breton as a Case Study.* Discussion Paper Prepared for The Cape Breton Regional Municipality.

MacLennan, H. 1951. *Each Man's Son.* Boston: Little Brown.

MacLeod, A. 2001. *No Great Mischief.* Toronto: Emblem Editions.

McManners, R., and G. Wales. 2002. *Shafts of Light—Mining Art in the Great Northern Coalfield.* London: Gemini.

Mellor, M., and C. Stephenson. 2005. "The Durham Miners' Gala and the Spirit of Community." *Community Development Journal* 40 (3): 343–51.

Milne, S. 1994. *The Enemy Within: The Secret War Against the Miners.* London: Verso.

Nathan, M. 2005. "The Wrong Stuff: Creative Class Theory, Diversity and City Performance." Centre for Cities discussion paper no. 1. September. <http://www.centreforcities.org/assets/files/pdfs/the_wrong_stuff_discussion_paper_1.pdf>.

National Geographic Traveler. 2004. "Destination Scorecard: 115 Places Rated." 15 March: 60–66.

Northern Echo. 2005. "Researchers Put Region Top of UK's Job Loss List." 1 April. <http://archive.thenorthernecho.co.uk/2005/4/1/18018.html>.

Peach, L. 2008. "Davis Day to be Held in Port Morien This Year." *Cape Breton Post* 8 June. <http://www.capebretonpost.com/index.cfm?sid=141915&sc=150>.

Peck, J. 2005. "Struggling with the Creative Class." *International Journal of Urban and Regional Research* 29 (4): 740–70.

Power, T.M. 1996. *Lost Landscapes and Failed Economies: The Search for a Value of Place.* Washington, DC: Island Press.

——. 2005. "The Resource Model v. the Environmental Model in Peripheral Economies and Geographies." Keynote Lecture. Hewers of Wood and Drawers of Water or Pioneers of the New Economy? Nova Scotia and the World in a Post-Industrial Era. A Symposium at Saint Mary's University. Halifax, Nova Scotia. 8 June. <http://husky1.smu.ca/~lhaiven/powerhalifaxpaper.pdf>.

Power, T.M., and R.N. Barrett. 2001. *Post-Cowboy Economics: Pay and Prosperity in the New American West.* Washington, DC: Island Press.

Pratt, A. 2008. "Creative Cities: The Cultural Industries and the Creative Class." *Geografisker Annaler, Series B, Human Geography* 90 (2): 107–17.

Scott, A.J. 2006. "Creative Cities: Conceptual Issues and Policy Questions." *Journal of Urban Affairs* 28 (1): 1–17.

Stephenson, C., and D. Wray. 2005. "Emotional Regeneration through Community Action in Post-industrial Mining Communities: The New Herrington Miners' Banner Partnership." *Capital and Class* 87: 175–99.

Veugelers, P.J., and S. Hornibrook. 2002. "Small Area Comparisons of Health: Applications for Policy Makers and Challenges for Researchers." *Chronic Diseases in Canada* 23 (3): 100–10.

Waddington, D., C. Critcher, B. Dicks, and D. Parry. 2001. *Out of the Ashes? The Social Impact of Industrial Contraction and Regeneration on Britain's Mining Communities*. Norwich: The Stationery Office.

Part III.   Unions and Forms of Resistance

11. Militancy and Resistance in the New Economy

LINDA BRISKIN

This chapter distinguishes among three types of militancy and examines some of the gender and sectoral shifts in the new economy that have an impact on unions and patterns of militancy. It also explains the conditions under which unionized workers have the legal right to strike, and outlines the available data on strikes and lockouts in Canada. It then turns to some specific trends in the new economy: the decline in strikes, the increase in public-sector militancy, the feminization of militancy, and the increase in government and employer attacks on worker and union rights. A case study of the militancy of Canadian nurses and health-care workers concludes the chapter.

Defining Militancy

This chapter distinguishes among labour, worker, and union militancies. *Labour militancy* speaks to the organized and collective activism of unionized workers. Workers have gone on strike to improve the conditions of and remuneration for their work, and to defend their rights to union protection. They have used the strike weapon to resist not only employer aggression but also government policy. Although in this chapter I focus largely on strikes and lockouts, I do not assume that strikes are the only form of militancy, or of labour militancy in particular. Hebdon (2005) maps other forms of labour militancy. He distinguishes among covert collective actions (such as sick-outs, slow-downs, and work-to-rule), other collective actions such as claims of unfair labour practices, and individual forms of militancy around grievances.

In contrast to labour militancy, *worker militancy* highlights the collective organization and resistance among non-unionized and often marginalized workers, many of whom are women and workers of colour. Among these workers, militancy has taken a variety of innovative and extra-union forms that are of increasing importance in defending workers' rights, given restructured labour markets, attacks by corporate capitalism, coercive state practices, and the difficulties inherent in organizing precarious workers into unions. "Community unionism" is one form of worker militancy. It focuses on attempts by community groups to organize the unemployed and precariously employed, and to build the power of non-unionized workers and the working-class community, often through workers' centres (Cranford et al. 2006). One such Canadian organization is the Workers' Action Centre in Toronto, which is committed to improving the lives and working conditions of people in low-wage and unstable employment. As the *Bad Boss* story in Box 11.1 suggests, it seeks inventive ways to highlight the exploitation of precarious workers and to ensure that their rights are protected.

Box 11.1   Join Santa and Workers' Action Centre on Our Holiday Bad Boss Bus Tour: December 2007, Toronto

---

Join Santa Claus, Workers' Action Centre members and Scarborough residents as we say PAY UP to temp agencies who don't pay public holiday pay. This Holiday BAD BOSS BUS TOUR will be visiting three Scarborough temp agencies on Santa's naughty list. These temp agencies routinely violate the law by refusing to pay holiday pay to temp agency workers, or by making up their own unfair rules on how they want to pay. Because of these unfair practices, thousands of temp workers will receive no pay this Christmas Day, Boxing Day and New Year's Day. Workers are being pushed further into poverty because of this unequal treatment. Workers' Action Centre (www.workersactioncentre.org) believes that temp workers should have the same rights and benefits as regular workers.

SYBIL'S STORY: IT PAYS TO FIGHT BACK!

I worked as a temporary worker doing data entry for the Provincial Government. I worked alongside other workers who were permanent and making more money than I was because the temporary agency took money off my hourly wage to make their profit. This temporary agency also set me up as an "independent contractor", saying that I was self-employed. I knew something was wrong and called the Workers' Action Centre. What I didn't know was that there were more violations of my rights than I had imagined. I was owed unpaid wages, overtime, vacation pay and public holiday pay. I decided to take a stand and fight to make things right. We called the employer and wrote a letter outlining the law and demanding my wages. We also met with ACSESS (the industry body that my agency belonged to) and had them put pressure on the agency to pay up. We did an interview with CBC radio. Finally, the company paid my wages in full.

Source: Workers' Action Centre, <http://www.workersactioncentre.org/Documents/pdfs%20 Newsletters/2007-02%20WAC%20Newsletter.pdf>.

Union militancy focuses on the politics of unions themselves. Inside Canadian unions, the growth is evident in both social unionism, which contests the narrow focus of business unionism on wages, benefits, and job security, and social movement unionism, which builds alliances and coalitions across unions and with social movements. The movement of union women has been instrumental in both these shifts. Women have promoted women's leadership, challenged traditional leaderships to be more accountable, encouraged unions to be more democratic and participatory, organized networks of women's committees to represent their interests, and pressured unions to take up women's concerns as union members and as workers—through policy initiatives and at the negotiating table. Union women also have a long history of building alliances with community-based groups to press for legal and policy reforms (Briskin 2006a, 2006b, 2002, 1999). Drawing out the distinction among labour, union, and worker militancies helps to highlight forms of resistance that are often not very visible to the public. Furthermore, in the new economy, all three forms of militancy will be essential to ensuring social justice.

Militancy and the New Economy

As a result of economic and political restructuring, globalization, and regional integration through trade treaties, Canadian workers face deteriorating conditions of work, competitive wage bargaining across national boundaries, corporate and state attacks on worker and union rights, the dismantling of social programs, decreases in the social wage, and a discursive shift to radical individualism. In particular, the deep restructuring of the labour market from the heavily unionized manufacturing sector toward private and difficult-to-organize services, and the transformation of work from relatively secure full-time employment to part-time, casual, temporary, and precarious employment has permanently altered the realities of work (Vosko 2006). The public sector has sustained particularly aggressive attacks under this neoliberal regime, including wage freezes and rollbacks, downsizing, contracting out and privatization, and government assaults on public-sector bargaining rights (Fudge and Brewin 2005; Panitch and Swartz 2003). As a result of these changes, the struggles of unionized workers have shifted to resisting privatization, contracting out, and employer demands for concessions, on the one hand, and protecting job security, on the other. Undoubtedly the new economy is having an impact on both worker and labour militancies.

Gender is relevant to understanding these economic and social changes. Both the participation rate of women in the labour force and the female share of the labour force have risen dramatically since the 1970s. Women represented 37 per cent of the labour force in 1976, and by 2006 almost half (47 per cent). In 1976, 42 per cent of women were working. By 2006, this figure had risen to 58 per cent, including a sharp increase in labour-force participation by women with young children. Men's labour-force participation declined from about 73 per cent in 1976 to 68 per cent in 2004 (Statistics Canada 2007). The trajectory suggests a significant trend toward feminization that speaks to demographic profiles, that is, the feminization of the workforce (increasing numbers of women workers) coincident with the feminization of work (more part-time, low-paid, and often precarious service jobs, work traditionally understood as women's work).

Economic and political restructuring poses serious challenges to unions in Canada, as in many other Western countries. Resistance to these trajectories will depend on worker mobilization, and the militancy of women workers will be critical. Restructuring has led not only to declining union densities, but also to significant shifts in the sectoral and gender balance in union membership. The somewhat stable density numbers in Canada hide some dramatic changes. In 2004, for the first time, the unionization rate for women was slightly higher than for men (Morissette, Schellenberg and Johnson 2005: 5–7). In 2008, the rate was 30 per cent for women and 28.7 per cent for men. In the public sector where women are clustered, 71 per cent of workers belong to unions, compared to only 16.3 per cent in the private sector (Statistics Canada 2008).

By 2002, women represented half of the more than four million Canadian union members. These shifts have meant the feminization of union density and the concomitant feminization of unions (increasing numbers of women union members), which set the stage for the feminization of militancies; that is, those involved in strikes are more likely than ever before to be women (Briskin 2007a).

The Right to Strike

Many, but not all, unionized workers have the right to strike during the negotiation of a new collective agreement. Disagreement over the content of a new agreement is referred to as an interest or bargaining dispute. As well as some form of compulsory conciliation, a vote (often secret) is required before a strike can take place, In fact, in many jurisdictions, employers can insist on a vote on their final offer. Further, in half the provinces, civil servants (those directly employed by the government) are prohibited from striking (Godard 2005: 296). In other public-sector jurisdictions, some categories of workers are designated as essential and barred from striking (Adell, Grant and Ponak, 2001).

During the term of a collective agreement, strikes and lockouts are prohibited, what is sometimes known as the peace obligation. Disputes, often referred to as rights disputes, are supposed to be settled through grievance procedures but may require binding arbitration. This system for resolving rights disputes emphasizes legal processes and discourages labour militancy. Given their illegality, mid-contract strikes (or wildcats) cannot be openly sanctioned by unions, although they do occur on a regular basis.

The use of replacement workers (often referred to as strikebreakers or scabs) is widespread. However, the province of Quebec "pioneered anti-scab legislation in 1977 following a picket line confrontation that led to loss of life" (Peirce 2003: 240). Since 1993, similar legislation has been in place in British Columbia, and, in both instances, these "provisions are perceived as a significant revision of the balance of power" (Arthurs et al. 1993: 278). In strikes of federal government workers, replacement workers are illegal if their purpose is to break the union. Most jurisdictions also require legally striking workers to be reinstated after a strike. Those involved in unlawful strikes "do not cease to be employees [...] but] may be subject to discipline, up to and including dismissal, in accordance with the terms of a collective agreement" (Commission on Labor Cooperation 2000: 67).

Data on Strikes and Lockouts in Canada

Data on every work stoppage[1] in Canada is currently collected by the Workplace Information Directorate of Human Resources and Social Development Canada (HRSDC). Work stoppages include both strikes and lockouts that last for a minimum of half a day and involve ten or more person-days lost (PDL). PDL is calculated by multiplying the duration of the stoppage in work days by the number of workers involved. (PDL was previously called "mandays." The HRSDC shift in terminology was likely in recognition of the fact that women work and are involved in stoppages.) In the 2005 Work Stoppages manual,[2] a strike is defined as "a concerted work stoppage, by one or more groups of workers, aimed at forcing an employer to acquiesce to the group's demands. Strikes are most commonly the result of a labour dispute between a group of employees and their employer." A lockout "is a work stoppage declared by an employer or group of employers where negotiations concerning wages or working conditions have not been able to bring about an agreement."

The Decline in Strikes

HRSDC recorded 23,944 work stoppages between 1960 and 2004, which suggests that Canadian workers have been quite militant. Generally, industrial relations specialists identify the following trend in Canadian strike activity: moderate until the mid-1960s, when strike activity began to rise. Although 1966 is not the year of the most strikes, it marks the beginning of a dramatic increase in person-days lost to the economy. This statistic is calculated as a percentage of working time, so in 1966 0.34 per cent of working time was lost, compared to 0.17 per cent in 1965 (Peirce and Bentham 2007: 304). From 1970 to 1981, data show extremely high levels of strikes; there were moderate and declining levels throughout the 1980s, and a sharp drop in the 1990s and into the 2000s (Gunderson et al. 2005: 348).

Figure 11.1 demonstrates this decline in the number of strikes, strikers, and work days lost. It shows that the high point for strike frequency was between 1974 and 1981. The 1990s witnessed a relative decline in the number of work days lost, but the number of strikers varied more widely over the whole time period. The highest percentage of worker involvement in strikes was in 1976, when strikes involved 18 per cent of all employees. Since 1999, only about 1 per cent of employees have been on strike, although as Akyeampong (2006) notes, 2004 saw a moderate increase to 1.8 per cent. While this may seem a somewhat insignificant percentage, it amounts to more than 250,000 additional workers on strike. Akyeampong (2006) also notes the increase in work days lost, from 1.7 million in 2003 to 4.1 million in 2005.

Figure 11.1 Labour Militancy in Canada, 1960–2004

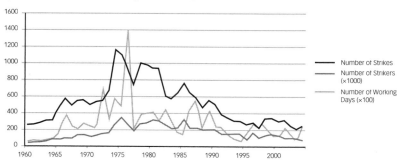

Source: Workplace Information Directorate, Human Resources and Social Development Canada.

The decline in the frequency of strikes beginning in the 1990s is related to a variety of economic, political, and legal factors; however, the disaggregated data and qualitative sources indicate continuing labour militancy, both legal and illegal, in the face of employer aggression and anti-worker government policy.

Public-Sector Militancy

An analysis of the Canadian strike data suggests a shift toward public-sector militancy in the new economy. The roots of this change are complex but certainly include the shift in union membership demographics toward the public sector, as well as the militant response to sustained attacks on that sector. Even though many public-sector workers are deemed essential, denied the right to strike, and possibly legislated back to work, between 1995 and 2004, 27 per cent of all stoppages (787) were in the public sector (the highest percentage since public-sector unionization). These stoppages involved more than 71 per cent of all workers on strike.[3] Furthermore, in this period, almost 20 per cent of work days lost were in the public sector. This suggests the beginning of a reversal in the long-standing dominance of private-sector militancy. (See Table 11.1.)

Table 11.1 Sectoral Strike Activity, 1960–2004

Year	Sector	Number #	Number %	Workers #	Workers %	Work days lost #	Work days lost %
1960–1994	Public	3751	17.8	5,177,586	47.0	77,634	11.8
	Private	17310	82.2	5,831,247	53.0	582,706	88.2
	Total	21061	100.0	11,008,833	100.0	660,340	100.0
1995–2004	Public	787	27.3	1,334,162	71.7	24,392	19.5
	Private	2096	72.7	526,343	28.3	100,376	80.5
	Total	2883	100.0	1,860,505	100.0	124,768	100.0
1960–2004	Public	4538	19.0	6,511,748	50.6	102,026	13.0
	Private	19406	81.0	6,357,590	49.4	683,082	87.0
	Total	23944	100.0	12,869,338	100.0	785,108	100.0

Source: Work Stoppage Data, Workplace Information Directorate, Human Resources and Social Development Canada.

Public-sector strikes have a different profile than private-sector strikes. First, they tend to involve more workers. Between 1960 and 2004, about 20 per cent of public-sector strikes involved 500 or more workers, compared to only about 10 per cent in the private sector. Second, and not surprisingly, given the impact of such strikes on the public, they also tend to be shorter. For example, between 1960 and 2004, almost 30 per cent of public-sector strikes lasted between one and two days, compared to only 19 per cent in the private sector.

Public-sector strikes are clustered in educational services, health care and social assistance, and public administration. In fact, disaggregating the stoppages in education and health care is also revealing. From 1960 to 1994, strikes in these industries represented about 7 per cent of all strikes and 14 per cent of striking workers. However, in the period from 1995 to 2004, the percentages had increased to 17 and 38 per cent, respectively. Many different measures, then, support the argument that public-sector militancy is becoming more significant in the landscape of industrial conflict.

The Feminization of Militancy

In this new public-sector landscape of industrial conflict, gender is increasingly significant. The growth and increasing feminization of the public sector, especially in health and education,[4] the importance of public-sector workers to union density, and the significance of strikes in this sector support the claim for the feminization of labour militancy. Many recent Canadian strikes have involved large numbers of women workers in the public sector: strikes of teachers and school support staff, nurses and other health-care workers, and federal government employees, for example.

Women's involvement in strikes is not a new phenomenon, although this involvement has often not been visible in the public eye, or addressed in research on labour militancy. In fact, women workers and strikers have often been militant, unwavering in the face of great odds. Helen Marot (1910–11) of the Women's Trade Union League in New York City comments on the 1909 strike of 30,000 shirtwaist makers:

> The feature of the strike which was as noteworthy as the response of thirty thousand unorganized workers, was the yielding and uncompromising temper of the strikers. This was due not to the influence of nationality, but to the dominant sex. The same temper displayed in the shirtwaist strike is found in other strikes of women, until we have now a trade-union truism that "women make the best strikers."... The shirt-waist makers' strike was characteristic of all strikes in which women play an active part. It was marked by complete self-surrender to a cause, emotional endurance, fearlessness and willingness to face danger and suffering. (124–28)

There are also many Canadian examples of women's militancy. The 1978 strike at the Fleck Manufacturing Co. Ltd. plant near Centralia, Ontario,

lasted for almost 23 weeks and pitted 140 women seeking a first contract at an automobile-parts plant against management, the police, and
indirectly the state itself (Backhouse 1980; Eaton 1990). The six-month
Eaton's strike from November 1984 to May 1985 involved 1,200 retail
workers also in search of a first contract (McDermott 1993). From
November 1987 to February 1988, a small group of women workers at
a branch of the Canadian Imperial Bank of Commerce went on strike to
obtain a 15-per-cent wage increase and wage parity with tellers at other
Nova Scotia banks (Baker 1993: 74). What has been particularly noticeable in the current period is the involvement of nurses and other health-
care and social-assistance workers, most of whom are women, in both
legal and illegal strikes (Briskin 2007b).

Nurses and Health-Care Workers on Strike
The struggles of Canadian nurses offer a snapshot of work reorganization, especially the move from full-time to part-time and contract work
that is so characteristic of neoliberal economies. Recent research commissioned by the Canadian Nurses Association shows that 20 per cent of
new nurses walk away because of poor working conditions, low wages,
and a shortage of full-time work caused by downsizing and cost-cutting. Only half of the country's nurses work full-time, and two-thirds of
those who work at part-time jobs do so involuntarily and juggle multiple
jobs. Casual nurses are cheaper because they receive no benefits and are
called in only when needed. In Quebec, nurses have worked 1.5 million
hours of forced overtime (the equivalent of 800 full-time jobs), 60 per
cent of jobs are now part-time, and the nurses—mostly women—continue to bear the brunt of health-care cutbacks (*Globe and Mail* 18 June
1999). Furthermore, earnings for nursing graduates are actually declining (*Globe and Mail* 13 July 1999, 10 February 2000).

In *Negotiations '99: Stand Up for Nursing*, the Saskatchewan Union
of Nurses (SUN) stresses that the nursing shortage is "forcing nurses to
work mandatory overtime. Nurses are suffering extreme stress, leading
to many more nurses suffering work-related injuries and chronic illness."
At the same time, "increasing 'casualization' of the nursing workforce"
means that "instead of staffing properly with full-time and regular part-
time nurses, management uses casual nurses to staff for heavy shifts, or
'peak hours', just like fast food outlets. For the remainder of the shift,
that puts patient care at risk."[5]

Recent attacks on health care have translated into militant legal and
illegal action. There were 199 wildcat strikes in the health-care and
social-assistance industry, which represented about 18 per cent of all
strikes in this industry and 4 per cent of all wildcats. However, between

2000 and 2004, a period of declining strike activity but increasing pub-lic-sector militancy, the sixteen wildcat strikes in health care represented 21 per cent of all wildcats.

Furthermore, there were 103 strikes involving nurses between 1960 and 2004. During 1985 and 1986, 22 strikes by Canadian nurses chal-lenged egregious government interventions into wage setting (Palmer 1992: 359–60). In 1998 and 1999, 20 strikes focused mainly on work restructuring and reorganization, and their impact on stress, wages, and working conditions, and importantly, the ability of nurses to deliver quality care. Nurses consistently frame their militant resistance in rela-tion to the public interest and challenge attacks on health care services by neoliberal governments.

In 1988, more than 11,000 staff nurses in Alberta went on illegal strike for 19 days "in the face of extremely punitive retaliatory mea-sures by employers and the state" (Coulter 1993: 44). In reference to this strike, the organization Edmonton Working Women commented, "They defied the law to defend their own democratic rights, and to oppose the erosion of workers' rights on all fronts ... [and to] fight for patients' rights to quality publicly funded health care" (quoted in Coulter 1993: 56). In 1999, Alberta nurses reached a settlement on the brink of what would have been another illegal strike.

In 1999, the first strike in 20 years by nurses in Newfoundland ended after nine days when the provincial government passed back-to-work legislation. Also in 1999, two days of wildcat strikes by 47,500 Quebec nurses, who had previously gone on a week-long strike in 1989, set the stage for a lengthy illegal strike. The nurses faced two draconian pieces of legislation which Michele Biscay, vice-president of the Quebec Federation of Nurses, thought the government was using to try to "kill the union" (*Globe and Mail* 6 July 1999). The nurses resisted the intim-idation of both Bill 160, which levied fines (more than $10 million by the end of the strike), withheld union dues, and docked two days of pay for each day off the job (costing individual nurses around $7,000), and Bill 72, back-to-work legislation that targeted the union leadership. Five days after the passage of Bill 72, 93 per cent of nurses voted to continue the illegal strike. One week later, an agreement in principle was reached, which the membership later turned down by 75 per cent. The nurses con-tinued to use "local guerrilla" tactics, including working to rule, insisting on overtime pay, and filing grievances for all breaches of the collective agreement (*Globe and Mail* 26 July 1999).

Following strikes in 1988 and 1991, Saskatchewan nurses defied back-to-work legislation for ten days in 1999. Saskatchewan nurse Nancy Syles spoke to the convention of the Canadian Labour Congress:

"There were nurses on the picket line who told me, 'I've never even had a speeding ticket.' But you know they never flinched. They were willing to stay on that picket line and maybe even be sent to jail.. All we want to do as nurses is to deliver safe, excellent nursing care. We cannot do this in the working conditions we have now" (*Globe and Mail* 13 July 1999). Laurie Swift, a nurse in Regina, wrote in a letter to the Editor of the *Regina Leader-Post* (7 May 1999), "This issue is really about the nursing shortage which ... has led to horrific and unsafe working conditions and compromised patient care.... We are taking a stand for the people of Saskatchewan: you, me, our families, our communities, as the caregivers and patient advocates that we are."

In June 2001, the issue of the right to strike for Nova Scotia health-care workers and nurses became the centre of a contentious dispute. Health-care workers belonging to the Nova Scotia Government Employees Union were already walking the picket lines when the provincial government passed a new law that took away their right to strike and threatened big fines. In response, the nurses who were due to go on strike within days threatened mass resignations. Fay MacNeil, a cardiac nurse, said, "If it comes to losing my job, I'm not concerned. I didn't sign on to nursing to do slave labour. I didn't sign on to lose my rights" (*Times-Colonist* [Victoria, BC] 29 June 2001).

These nurses' strikes were characterized by strong popular support, and by backing from other unions and the women's movements. The 1999 illegal strike by Quebec nurses garnered massive support from the Quebec public, 72 per cent of whom thought the nurses' wage demands were reasonable (*Globe and Mail* 28 June 1999), and brought out doctors, other unionized workers, and members of the women's rights federation to their picket lines. In reference to the 1999 Saskatchewan nurses' strike, Barb Byers, then president of the Saskatchewan Federation of Labour (SFL) said, "I've never seen a membership so solid and I've never seen this level of support from the public."[6]

Debra McPherson, the secretary-treasurer of the Canadian Federation of Nurses' Unions, interviewed in the Saskatoon *StarPhoenix* (15 April 1999), explained that the resentment stemmed from the fact that governments everywhere have shown no reluctance to cut or freeze the wages of public-sector employees, most of whom are women: "The public sector is constantly bearing the brunt of wage restraint. We have our federal government pushing back pay equity decisions from the courts. But if they think they can keep women working for less, they are going to have to think again. We're past that."

Traditionally, the fact that women did caring work was used to deter women from striking: "Women are trained to feel responsible for the people they care for, whether at home or on the job. Consequently, they can easily be made to feel guilty if they refuse to take care.... And when they do strike, the media may depict them as 'heartless and unfeeling'" (Darcy and Lauzon 1983: 175). Many women who directly serve client groups undoubtedly experience tension between striking and caring. Such conflicts are embodied in the recent wave of nursing militancy. In fact, Brown et al. (2006: 206) point to the fact that all international accounts of strike activity in nursing allude to the conflict between striking and caring: "when nurses offer a defence of strike action they present it as a measure that is in the best interests of patients and the public." In reference to the 1981 illegal strike of hospital workers (housekeepers, lab technicians, dietary workers, nursing assistants, and maintenance workers) in Ontario, over 75 per cent of whom were women, White (1990: 70) makes a similar argument:

> The bond to care-giving work, loyalty to patients, and service orientation created a pressure to strike. The need to protect standards impelled women *to strike*. Women interviewees were asked if they were concerned about the level of care patients would receive during the strike. The most common response involved a defence of the strike *in maintaining health standards*. Typically the hospital worker commented: "It's them that's wrecked it for people, not us. I can't take care of anyone the way it's set up. That's what I want—to get things back." (RNA, General) (emphasis in original)

Furthermore, "labour process changes broke this care-giving bond for many women workers. The desire to re-establish this bond was one consideration in the decision to strike" (125).

The Increase in Employer and Government Aggression

Under a neoliberal regime and in the new economy, increasing corporate and state attacks on worker and union rights are re-shaping patterns of labour and worker militancy. Although major changes to labour law have been relatively minimal, the growing intervention of the state into the management of labour relations, especially in the public sector, is significant. The trend toward the adoption of various statutory income policies began with the implementation of compulsory wage and price controls in 1975. This led to a National Day of Protest involving 830,000 workers, 56 per cent of all workers involved in strikes in that year. Such policies have often been combined with back-to-work legislation in response to legal strikes, and the increased designation of public-sector workers as essential, thereby removing their right to strike. The National Union of Public and General Employees (NUPGE) and United Food and Commercial Workers (UFCW) have recently launched a major campaign to defend free collective bargaining.[7] They point out that since 1982 the federal and provincial governments have passed 170 pieces of legislation that have restricted, suspended, or denied collective-bargaining rights (Fudge and Brewin 2005).

Employer aggression, that is, proactive initiatives against unionized workers on the part of employers to undermine and often prevent the functioning of the union-management relationship, takes a number of forms. They include pursuing profits regardless of the effects on workers, families, communities, and countries; sabotaging the functioning of the union–management relationship; limiting worker input into and control over the labour process; and increasing employment instability by undermining standard and secure jobs in favour of more precariousness (Briskin 2007a).

Lockouts are one form of employer aggression, especially when employers continue to operate with replacement workers. In almost all labour-relations statutes, a lockout "must involve: (1) a closing of a place of employment, the suspension of work, or a refusal to continue to employ, and (2) the purpose of compelling employees to agree to terms and conditions of employment" (Arthurs et al. 1993: 272–73). HRSDC began collecting lockout data in 1976. From 1976 to 2004, 1,839 lockouts—12 per cent of all stoppages—involved more than 7 per cent of all workers who engaged in stoppages, and represented almost 16 per cent of work days lost. The peak period for lockouts was from 1983 to 1986; the 473 lockouts during these years represent 26 per cent of all lockouts in the entire period. Lockouts tend to be longer than strikes: between 1976 and 2004, almost 34 per cent of all strikes were settled in less than one week, compared to only 16 per cent of lockouts. And despite the relatively small number of lockouts overall, more than 30 per cent of all stoppages lasting longer than one year (84 out of 276) were lockouts. Although 88 per cent of lockouts were in the private sector, from 1976 to 2004 there were 220 lockouts in the public sector, 162 of them clustered in three key industry groupings: educational services (50); health care and social assistance (44); and public administration (68). In 1980 alone, 22 public-sector lockouts involved 50 per cent of all workers ever locked out.

The period of lockouts in the 1980s, coincident with a decline in strike frequency, saw intensive employer aggression, sometimes supported by the state. Peirce (2003: 352) notes that "1982 [was] a recessionary year that marked the end of the last significant wave of inflation seen in this country—and the beginning of a second round of wage controls for most public sector workers." It was also a period that saw a shift in employer strategy: employers came into negotiations with confrontational demands that frequently included wage concessions and rollbacks. They often pushed workers toward striking and then resorted to lockouts rather than letting workers set the schedule for the conflict (Heron 1996: 122). Arthurs et al. (1993: 268) argue that "since the severe economic recession of the early 1980s employers have been much more willing to lockout employees as part of their strategy to obtain concessions. This has led to increasingly bitter and lengthy industrial disputes."

Interestingly, the 2006 Industrial Relations Outlook from the Conference Board of Canada reports, "Employers, faced with an onslaught of global competition, are exhibiting new militancy in collective bargaining, including resorting to lockouts, to achieve wage and benefit concessions" (Hallamore 2006: 6). The data tentatively suggest that Canada may be moving into another period of intensified employer aggression, reflected in an increase in lockouts. Lockouts represented 12 per cent of all stoppages between 1976 and 2004; however, between 2002 and 2004, a period of declining strike frequency, lockouts represented 19 per cent of stoppages.

Conclusion

In this chapter I have distinguished among labour, worker, and union militancies and examined some of the gender and sectoral shifts in the new economy that are having an impact on unions and patterns of militancy. I have explained the conditions under which unionized workers have the legal right to strike and outlined the available data on strikes and lockouts in Canada. Finally, I have considered some specific trends in the new economy: the decline in strikes, the increase in public-sector militancy, the feminization of militancy, and the increase in government and employer attacks on worker and union rights.

The widespread increase in the casualization of work, combined with attacks on the wages, rights, and working conditions of unionized workers, suggests that, in the foreseeable future, there will be continuing resistance and unrest. Given changing patterns of union density, public-sector workers will be at the forefront of such struggles as they try to maintain both their rights as workers, and their capacity to deliver quality services. Since unionized workers set standards for all workers, in seeking to preserve their own rights, public-sector workers will also be defending the wages and employment-standard protections for the non-unionized. As women become a greater proportion of those workers who strike, the image of labour militancy in the public imagination, once so connected to working-class men, will be transformed. New research may well find that this gender shift alters the meaning of gender in both public and private spaces, and reconfigures both the social relations of gender and the social positioning of women.

Discussion Questions

1. Describe the images of strikes and workers on strike that are presented in the media. How would you characterize the attitude of the media toward strikes?

2. What is your personal experience with strikes? Have you, a friend, or member of your family ever been on strike? What have you learned about strikes from these experiences?

3. Do you support the right of workers to go on strike? Why or why not? Do you think this right is of any special significance in the new economy? What about the right of nurses and health-care workers to strike?

4. Why do you think that nurses and teachers have been striking more frequently in the new economy?

5. What forms of resistance can non-unionized workers use to defend their rights?

6. Can you identify some instances of the feminization of work and/or workers? For example, do you see men doing paid work you might have traditionally associated with women?

7. To what extent do you think that the feminization of unions will change the politics of unions?

Notes

1   I have negotiated full access to the records of each Canadian stoppage from 1946 to 2004. I wish to thank the Workplace Information Directorate of Human Resources and Social Development Canada for providing the microdata. All HRSDC data quoted in this paper is from the work stoppage data unless otherwise specified. HRSDC was previously Human Resources and Skills Development Canada and previously Human Resources Development Canada (HRDC) and, prior to that, Labour Canada. HRSDC publishes the *Workplace Bulletin*, which includes a list of current settlements, current stoppages, and upcoming negotiations. Available from the main page of the Workplace Information

Directorate <http://www.hrsdc.gc.ca/eng/labour/labour_relations/info_analysis/index.shtml>.

2   This is a working manual that is not publicly available: L. Renaud and M. Lacroix; revised by B. Aldridge, P. Dubuc, M. Hébert, and L. Trépanier. 2005. *Training Manual: Work Stoppages*. Work Stoppage, Labour Organization, and Collective Agreement Analysis Section of the Workplace Information Directorate. Ottawa.

3   Gunderson et al. (2005: 5) suggest that even these rates may be misleadingly low "because the public sector had a substantial proportion of contracts settled through direct legislative intervention (22.4% during the 1990–98 period). In some cases, legislation takes place after a strike occurred; in others, legislation suspended collective bargaining and imposed collective agreements. Furthermore, arbitrated settlements are much more common in the public sector. Combining arbitrated collective agreements with agreements achieved after strike or through legislation would show that between 1990 and 1998, public-sector collective agreements were achieved by the parties themselves (or through the assistance of a mediator or conciliator) only about 70% of the time. By comparison, private sector negotiations successfully produced collective agreements 88% of the time."

4   In the gendered breakdown of the public-sector workforce, women represented 39% of all employees but 45% of public-sector employees in 1976–79, rising to more than 49% of all employees and 60% of public-sector employees in 2000–04. In educational services, women made up 54% of the workforce in 1976 and 64% in 2003; in health care and social assistance, the respective figures were 76% and 82%. Data from Statistics Canada, Labour Force Survey (LFS). Documentation available from <http://www.statcan.ca/english/Dli/Data/Ftp/lfs.htm>.

5   See <http://www.sun-nurses.sk.ca/History/neg_99_pamphlet.pdf>.

6   Quoted by Judy Rebick on CBC online, 16 April 1999.

7   See <http://www.labourrights.ca>.

References

Adell, B., M. Grant, and A. Ponak. 2001. *Strikes in Essential Services*. Kingston: IRC Press.

Akyeampong, E. 2006. "Increased Work Stoppages." *Perspectives on Labour and Income* 7 (8): 5–9.

Arthurs, H.W., D.D. Carter, J. Fudge, H.J. Glasbeek, and G. Trudeau. 1993. *Labour Law and Industrial Relations in Canada*. Kluwer: Deventer-Boaton.

Backhouse, C. 1980. "The Fleck Strike: A Case Study in the Needs for First Contract Arbitration." *Osgoode Hall Law Journal* 18 (4): 495–553.

Baker, P. 1993. "Reflections on Life Stories: Women's Bank Union Activism." In L. Briskin and P. McDermott (eds.), *Women Challenging Unions: Feminism, Democracy and Militancy*. Toronto: University of Toronto Press. 62–86.

Briskin, L. 1999. "Autonomy, Diversity and Integration: Union Women's Separate Organizing in North America and Western Europe in the Context of Restructuring and Globalization." *Women's Studies International Forum* 22 (5): 543–54.

——. 2002. "The Equity Project in Canadian Unions: Confronting the Challenge of Restructuring and Globalization." In F. Colgan and S. Ledwith (eds.), *Gender, Diversity and Trade Unions: International Perspectives*. London: Routledge. 28–47.

——. 2006a. *Equity Bargaining/Bargaining Equity*. Toronto: Centre for Research on Work and Society, York University.

——. 2006b. "Union Leadership and Equity Representation." For the Union Module of the Gender and Work Database. <http://www.genderwork.ca>.

——. 2007a. "Public Sector Militancy, Feminization, and Employer Aggression: Trends in Strikes, Lockouts, and Wildcats in Canada from 1960 to 2004." In H. Dribbusch, D. Lyddon, K. Vandaele, and S. van der Velden (eds.), *Strikes around the World*. Amsterdam: Aksant. 86–113.

——. 2007b. "From Person-days Lost to Labour Militancy: A New Look at the Canadian Work Stoppage Data." *Relations industrielles/Industrial Relations* 62 (1): 31–65.

Brown, G., A. Greaney, M. Kelly-Fitzgibbon, and J. McCarthy. 2006. "The 1999 Irish Nurses' Strike: Nursing Versions of the Strike and Self-identity in a General Hospital." *Journal of Advanced Nursing* 56 (2): 200–08.

Commission on Labor Cooperation. 2000. *Labor Relations Law in North America*. <http://www.naalc.org/english/pdf/study2_canada.pdf>.

Coulter, R. 1993. "Alberta Nurses and the 'Illegal' Strike of 1988." In L. Briskin and P. McDermott (eds.), *Women Challenging Unions: Feminism, Democracy and Militancy*. Toronto: University of Toronto Press. 44–61.

Cranford, C., M. Gellatly, D. Ladd, and L. Vosko. 2006. "Community Unionism and Labour Movement Renewal: Organizing for Fair Employment." In P. Kumar and C. Schenk (eds.), *Paths to Union Renewal: Canadian Experiences*. Peterborough, ON: Broadview Press. 237–51.

Darcy, J., and C. Lauzon. 1983. "Bargaining for Equality." In L. Briskin and L. Yanz (eds.), *Union Sisters*. Toronto: Women's Press. 171–97.

Eaton, J. 1990. *The Fleck Strike: Law on the Line*. Kingston: Queen's University Industrial Relations Centre.

Fudge, D., and J. Brewin. 2005. *Collective Bargaining in Canada: Human Right or Canadian Illusion?* Ottawa: NUPGE and UFCW.

Godard, J. 2005. *Industrial Relations: The Economy and Society*. 3rd ed. Toronto: Captus Press.

Gunderson, M., B. Hebdon, D. Hyatt, and A. Ponak. 2005. "Strikes and Dispute Resolution." In M. Gunderson, A. Ponack, and D. Taras (eds.), *Union-Management Relations in Canada*. 5th ed. Toronto: Pearson Addison Wesley. 332–70.

Hallamore, C. 2006. *Industrial Relations Outlook 2006: Shifting Ground, Shifting Attitudes*. Ottawa: Conference Board of Canada.

Hebdon, R. 2005. "Toward a Theory of Workplace Conflict: The Case of US Municipal Collective Bargaining." In D. Levin and B. Kaufman (eds.), *Advances in Industrial and Labor Relations*. Vol. 14. Amsterdam: Elsevier. 33–65.

Heron, C. 1996. *The Canadian Labour Movement: A Short History*. 2nd ed. Toronto: James Lorimer.

Marot, H. (1910–11). "A Woman's Strike—An Appreciation of the Shirtwaist Makers of New York." In H. Mussey (ed.), *Proceedings of the Academy of Political Science in the City of New York*. N.p. 119–128.

McDermott, P. 1993. "The Eaton's Strike: We Wouldn't Have Missed It for the World!" In L. Briskin and P. McDermott (eds.), *Women Challenging Unions: Feminism, Democracy and Militancy*. Toronto: University of Toronto Press. 23–43.

Morissette, R., G. Schellenberg, and A. Johnson. 2005. "Diverging Trends in Unionization." *Perspectives on Labour and Income* 6 (4): 5–12.

Palmer, B. 1992. *Working Class Experience: Rethinking the History of Canadian Labour, 1800–1991*. 2nd ed. Toronto: McLelland and Stewart.

Panitch, L., and D. Swartz. 2003. *From Consent to Coercion: The Assault on Trade Union Freedoms*. Aurora, ON: Garamond Press.

Peirce, J. 2003. *Canadian Industrial Relations.* 2nd ed. Toronto: Prentice Hall.

Peirce, J., and K. Bentham. 2007. *Canadian Industrial Relations.* 3rd ed. Toronto: Prentice Hall.

Statistics Canada. 2007. *Women in Canada: Work Chapter Updates.* Ottawa: Minister of Industry. <http://www.statcan.gc.ca/pub/89f0133x/89f0133x2006000-eng.pdf>.

———. 2008. "Unionization." *Perspectives on Labour and Income.* August: 1–10.

Vosko, L. (ed.) 2006. *Precarious Employment: Understanding Labour Market Insecurity in Canada.* Montreal and Kingston: McGill-Queen's University Press.

White, J. 1990. *Hospital Strike: Women, Unions and Public Sector Conflict.* Toronto: Thompson Educational Press.

12. Labour Fragmentation and New Forms of Organizing and Bargaining in the Service Sector

DALE CLARK AND ROSEMARY WARSKETT

Organizing workers in the service sector has always been difficult for the Canadian labour movement. Attempts to unionize this sector started in the nineteenth century. At that time, service work, in both the public and private sectors, was very different from today. Like today, there were retail stores, as well as hotels and restaurants, mail was delivered, and banks looked after money; but small businesses predominated and, as a consequence, service workers did not have much bargaining power. But the scale of these operations has changed considerably, and many more Canadians are now service workers. Today, the service sector is dominated by large multi-national corporations and governments. While most public-service workers are unionized, those in the private sector, for the most part, remain unorganized.

There are many reasons for the low rate of union density amongst service workers, but in this chapter we focus on labour fragmentation and the consequent lack of strength by these workers to organize and collectively bargain. We define labour fragmentation by identifying four different ways in which labour's solidarity, organizing strength, and capacity to collectively bargain is undermined: (1) Fragmentation of the labour process. This includes a Taylorized division of labour and a high degree of management control over the tasks to be performed. (2) Fragmentation in terms of non-standard forms of work, with few core workers and many who work part-time, on contract, and on a contingent basis. (3) Fragmentation of the legal certification process. By this, we mean that union organizing and legal certification limit organizing on a multi-employer, multi-establishment basis. (4) Fragmentation of the labour movement in the sense that unions seldom act collectively and co-operatively in organizing service-sector workers. While we have identified and analytically separated these four different kinds of labour fragmentation, we recognize that in practice all these aspects of labour disunity intersect to produce divisions between service workers, making union organizing and collective bargaining extremely challenging. As we examine the organizing of different kinds of service-sector work, we will elaborate on the various forms of labour fragmentation.

We first define the service sector and then provide a brief history of organizing and collective bargaining. This is followed by a focus on four large service sectors: restaurant and hotel, retail, banks, and postal and courier. We then turn to consider new forms of organizing and collective bargaining. We do not focus on the different characteristics of service workers, e.g., as women, youth, new immigrants, or racialized people. While we do recognize that high numbers of workers belonging to such groups are found in the sector, our focus is on structural divisions and the way in which these undermine the capacity to collectively organize and bargain with employers.

The Canadian Service Sector

Defining the service sector in Canada is not straightforward. Statistics Canada identifies industries based on whether they are involved in the production of goods or services. Another way of thinking about this division is to identify specific jobs that provide services, regardless of the industry in which they are found. For our purpose it makes more sense to focus on specific employers who provide services, since when workers organize into unions and apply for legal certification and collective bargaining rights, it is on the basis of who they work for and where. This approach is not without problems, as workers doing identical work may be found in other sectors, such as manufacturing or resource industries. For example, warehouse workers can be classified as being in the service sector, but if they work in a warehouse that is located in a manufacturing plant, they are identified by Statistics Canada as part of the goods-producing sector.

The service sector crosses both the private and the public sectors and in 2004 comprised 75.2 per cent of the Canadian workforce (Human Resources and Social Development Canada 2006). Retail and Health are the largest sub-sectors, at 12.2 per cent and 10.7 per cent respectively. Other sub-sectors include Education, Accommodation and Food Services, and Transportation. From 1987 to 2005, employment in the service sector grew by 1.9 per cent. In the same period, employment in the goods-producing sector grew by only 0.5 per cent. In 2006, the trend continued, with the service sector growing by 2.6 per cent, compared with a growth of only 1.4 per cent in manufacturing (Statistics Canada 2007). Human Resources and Social Development Canada predicts that employment growth in the service sector (1.2 per cent) will continue to be greater than that in the goods producing sector (0.8 per cent) from 2006 to 2015. These projections, however, assume that the economy will continue to grow, something that is not likely to happen in the next few years, given the current economic crisis.

Although the service sector has grown and more jobs have been created in recent years, many of the jobs are part-time, temporary, and often contract jobs that are low-paid, resulting in what has been called precarious forms of work (Vosko, Zukewich and Cranford 2003). In this sense, labour is fragmented because turnover in low-paid service jobs is frequent, making union organizing very difficult. Although Canadian unions have maintained a membership that comprises 30.8 per cent of the total paid workforce (Morissette, Schellenberg and Johnson 2005), there are wide variations in the service sector. For example, in the Accommodation and Food sub-sector only 7.6 per cent of the workforce is unionized, while in Health Care and Social Assistance 54.2 per cent are unionized (Anderson, Beaton and Laxer 2006). While service work in the public sector is generally unionized, there has been an increased use of temporary workers (Harrison 2006). In addition, there has been an increase in the fragmentation of wages, in both the public and private sectors, with new hires receiving lower wages than other employees (Morissette and Johnson 2005).

Another important development is the increased concentration of ownership in the service sector. While in the food industry there are many small independent grocery stores and fast-food outlets, the market is dominated by large corporations such as Loblaws and McDonald's. Loblaws employs over 100,000 people in Canada (Kainer 2002: 111), while McDonald's employs approximately 77,000 workers (McDonald's Canada 2008). Walmart is now the largest retailer in Canada (Fishman 2006: 6), with 305 retail units and over 70,000 workers (Walmart Canada, n.d.). Despite contracting out and downloading to smaller agencies, most workers who provide public services continue to work for large government agencies and are mostly unionized. The postal and courier industry is dominated by Canada Post, a government-owned corporation, employing over 60,000 workers. The large private courier companies employ over 45,000, according to the Canadian Courier and Messenger Association (Courier Research Project 2005).[1] Canada Post and the large courier companies (with the exception of FedEx) are unionized, but the small companies and the same-day courier industry are largely unorganized. The "Big Five"[2] dominate the Canadian chartered banking industry and has done so since the 1960s. In 1998, there was an attempt by the Bank of Montreal to merge with the Royal Bank, and at approximately the same time the CIBC proposed a merger with the Toronto-Dominion Bank. The federal finance minister at the time, Paul Martin, rejected the merger based on recommendations from the Competition Bureau.

Organizing and Collective Bargaining in the Service Sector

There is a long history of Canadian workers organizing unions in hotels, banks, department stores, telephone companies, and other private service enterprises going back to the end of the nineteenth century. This is equally the case in the public-service sector. Organizing and collective bargaining in the first half of the twentieth century, however, was a hazardous activity for trade unions (Fudge and Tucker 2001). There was no requirement in law for employers to recognize and collectively bargain with trade unions. Also in the 1920s, radical changes occurred in the organization of service work. The principles of scientific management, spelled out by Frederick Taylor in 1911, played a leading role in the transformation of work organization. Corporations in their search for greater profits expanded and in the process sought greater control over how work was performed (Heron and Storey 1986: 18). Also, technology was used by employers to change the very nature of clerical and retail service work, resulting in the introduction of the first computerized systems as early as the 1920s (Lowe 1987: 129–30). Work in general became more fragmented through an increased division of labour and mechanization of job tasks. The lack of collective bargaining, together with management's greater control over labour processes, resulted in a pent-up demand by industrial workers for better wages, benefits, and respect on the job, a movement that gained momentum by the end of the 1930s, coming to a head during the years of World War II.

In 1944, the federal government introduced Wartime Labour Relations Regulations through Privy Council (PC) order 1003, compelling employers to recognize and bargain with trade unions. Service-sector employees were watching closely, as there were renewed attempts to organize retail, banking, and the public sector in the postwar period. In September 1948, the *Industrial Relations and Disputes Investigation Act* came into effect, and its provisions were adopted by most provinces. It provided for certification of trade unions based on evidence of majority membership by workers in a single workplace or branch. This remains the dominant way that unions are certified today, resulting in the legal ability to compel employers to come to the collective-bargaining table and negotiate wages, benefits, and other kinds of demands. In general, the union certification process results in a fragmented and weakened col-lective-bargaining structure, since bargaining across different workplaces and firms is permitted only with the agreement of employers. In addi-tion, the use of the strike weapon is restricted until the state conciliation process is completed; this means that any labour disputes during the life of the collective agreement have to be resolved by grievance arbitration. While these provisions limit the use of strikes, employers are legally com-pelled to recognize and bargain with unions.

In the postwar period, jurisdictional fragmentation—both inter- and intra-provincial—grew rapidly. Provinces adopted their own form of labour legislation, and as workers in the public sector demanded the same right to collectively bargain as those in the private sector, the complexity of the labour-relations system grew. Today workers within the same community find themselves under different legal regulations, whether they are in federal, provincial or other kinds of public-service sector work. The fragmentation and complexity of the legal rules oper-ate against building solidarity among service workers, both in spirit and in action.

Restaurants and Hotels

Hotel and tavern workers started organizing in the 1890s, and, while their union history is uneven, there is a renewed attempt today to strengthen their organizations (Tufts 2006). Despite this, the hotel and restaurant sector continues to be difficult to organize and is fragmented along all four lines that we identified at the beginning of this chapter.

The working conditions and work process in the fast-food industry are heavily influenced by Taylorist methods (Reiter 2002: 35). The pro-duction of the fast-food meal is divided into simple tasks that require little thought. There is tight control over how the tasks are performed and the time taken to complete them, and the production process is standardized across all restaurant outlets. The high levels of exploi-tation and corresponding profits create some parallels with industrial goods production; the major difference is that the fast-food industry has been notoriously low paid and unorganized. The archetype is work at McDonald's. Although restaurants are owned by franchisees, the end product and the way it is prepared and served are rigidly controlled by the parent corporation, similar to the case with vehicle manufacturing. The term McJob, which has come to describe low-paid work in the restaurant business (and in the service sector more broadly), is characterized by these factors as well as by the precarious nature of the employment relationship.

There have, however, been some successful examples of organization and unionization. British Columbia and Quebec are where unions have had the most success. BC has a history of master agreements and sectoral bargaining, and in Quebec a system of standards exists in some industries. The Kentucky Fried Chicken (KFC) and White Spot restaurants have long been unionized in BC. Originally, one individual owned these businesses, and when they were sold to General Foods in 1971, the workers continued to work with a master agreement covering all locations. The BC Labour Board ruled that the master agreement had to be maintained even when the locations were franchised (Kainer 2002). Currently, the workers are represented by the Canadian Auto Workers (CAW), which has also been successful in organizing workers at some Starbucks and Robin's Donuts outlets in BC.

In Ontario, Swiss Chalet is partially unionized, but there was competition between the Hotel Employees and Restaurant Employees (HERE) and the United Food and Commercial Workers (UFCW), with the latter accepting voluntary recognition at some outlets but agreeing not to organize at others (Reiter 2002: 40). In the 1990s, the UFCW also organized a Harvey's outlet in Toronto and the Service Employees' International Union (SEIU) was successful in organizing Robin's Donuts outlets in Thunder Bay. In 1999, following lengthy strikes and a Canadian Labour Congress boycott, settlements were finally reached at Robin's Donuts, although shortly afterwards several of the outlets were closed. The Quebec situation is somewhat different from other provinces since there is more than one major union central in that province. Within those centrals, the unions generally do not compete, so the union movement has been successful in organizing some KFC, Harvey's, and Tim Hortons outlets (Huot 1998).

McDonald's is the biggest player in the fast-food industry in Canada, with revenue of $2,400 million in 2000. It has more outlets than any other chain except for Tim Hortons (Kainer 2002). It is a franchised operation, but the full weight of the company's anti-union stance is present during any organizing drive. There have been several attempts at organizing McDonald's. In 1993, the SEIU conducted an organizing drive in Orangeville, Ontario, resulting in 67 of 102 employees signing union cards, but the employer challenged how the cards had been signed and consequently the labour board ordered a vote. The company's aggressive anti-union campaign, and the failure of the union to maintain support, resulted in only 19 votes for the union out of 96 employees (Reiter 2002). In 1997, 80 per cent of the McDonald's workers in St. Hubert, Quebec, signed Teamster union cards. The employer's challenge of the results failed before the labour board, so McDonald's simply took another route to block the union and closed the franchise. The Teamsters, supported by the Québec Federation of Labour (QFL), went on a drive to organize all Montreal McDonald's outlets, but it was unsuccessful and lasted only 16 months (Reiter 2002). The following year, the CAW actually gained a certification in Squamish, BC, which for a year was the only unionized McDonald's in North America. Collective bargaining took place, but the resulting collective agreement was turned down by the workers. Under BC legislation, a decertification vote is allowed if there is no agreement within ten months. This vote was held and the workers voted to decertify (Reiter 2002). McDonald's and other fast-food enterprises have been very difficult to organize due to the fragmentation of ownership through franchises, the high turnover of workers, and the aggressive anti-union strategies coordinated by company headquarters.

Banks and Finance

Bank employees in Canada started to organize as early as 1911, and in 1914 the Associated Bank Clerks of Canada held a founding meeting in Toronto (Lowe 1987: 210). The Bank Employees Association, an affiliate of the American Federation of Labor (AFL), began organizing in 1919, but strong employer opposition quickly ended the drive. Despite these early attempts, the banking industry in Canada remains for the most part non-unionized today.

In the mid-1970s, bank workers renewed their attempt to unionize. A small independent Western union, the Service, Office, and Retail Workers Union of Canada (SORWUC), broke through the "Big Five" banks' defences and organized women bank tellers in British Columbia and Saskatchewan. They managed to sign up over a thousand workers and gained union certification in 26 branches. The certified branches were not concentrated in one region, however, and the banks insisted, given the branch-by-branch certification, that each set of negotiations be conducted separately. This resulted in a fragmented set of negotiations, with negotiators running from one branch to the next and trying, with very little bargaining strength, to compel the banks to negotiate a collective agreement for each bank branch. Added to these difficulties was an ongoing set of unfair labour practices. As the President of the Canadian Labour Relations Board (CLRB) remarked, the actions of the banks brought a "chill to the organizing drive." Given the lack of bargaining strength and the anti-union tactics of the banks, SORWUC gave up its bargaining units (Warskett 1988).

In the meantime, the Canadian Labour Congress (CLC) had launched its own campaign to organize the chartered banking sector, although there was conflict and competition among CLC affiliate unions over who should be able to do the organizing. The CLC met the same difficulties as SORWUC had: fragmented bargaining strength and unfair labour practices by the banks. Because of the CLC's greater financial resources, though, a number of important labour decisions were achieved at the level of the CLRB. These included the possibility of organizing clusters of bank workers. However, even the larger branch clusters organized by the CLC affiliates and the Confederation of National Trade Unions (CNTU) in Quebec proved insufficient to deal with the power of the banks to resist substantial improvements in wages and benefits. Whereas SORWUC rescinded its units, the CLC and the CNTU units slowly decertified over time because the branches lacked the bargaining strength to negotiate (Warskett 1981, 1988).

During the 1990s, increased computerization resulted in the development of bank call centres and greater rationalization and control over bank branches (Nazim 2007). There has been some success by unions in organizing call centres, where the work is highly controlled, and there is a greater concentration of workers there, which increases bargaining strength. Recently the United Steelworkers (USWA) successfully organized two bank-branch clusters of the TD-Canada Trust and CIBC, in Sudbury, Ontario. There have been strikes by both clusters, but both banks continue to resist any substantial improvements to the collective agreements.

Retail

The retail sector has a long history of organizing drives. In 1948, the Retail, Wholesale and Department Store Union (RWDSU) undertook an organizing drive in the Toronto Eaton's store. Organizing was particularly difficult due to the large turnover of staff, and the union narrowly lost the representation vote despite signing up a large majority of the employees over the three-year period (Sufrin 1982). It was not until 1984 that the RWDSU was successful in organizing six Eaton's department stores in southwestern Ontario, and it undertook a strike that lasted almost six months. Finally, the union felt it had no alternative but to reach a disappointing settlement in May 1985 (McDermott 1993). The strike at six unionized stores was not enough to compel the management of Eaton's to raise wages and benefits. The lesson for the union was clear: if a strike is to be successful, it is necessary to shut down the employer's operations completely. In the Eaton's case, the separate store-based certification contributed to the fragmentation of union strength and worked against building a strong organization of workers across several department stores.

While the workers were fragmented, Eaton's was not. As a family-owned business, there was tight control of the company by a few individuals. This concentration of ownership is common in other aspects of the service sector as well. The large supermarket chains in Canada are also largely family owned. The Weston family controls over half of the shares at Loblaws, and the Sobeys family controls two-thirds of its stores through a holding company (Allentuck 2006). Safeway, a multinational, is the exception, but the practice of family ownership is fairly consistent across the industry. Forty per cent of Walmart, the largest retailer in the world, is owned by members of the Walton family, who control the direction of the company (Allentuck 2006), a direction that is notoriously anti-union. When it first entered Canada in the 1980s by buying up and converting existing Woolco stores, it closed those stores that were unionized. The United Food and Commercial Workers (UFCW) approach to organizing Walmart is mostly a traditional model, with inside committees, a paid organizer, and card-signing drives at a single store followed by applications for certification. Currently, there are only two unionized stores in North America; both are in Quebec, at Saint-Hyacinthe and Gatineau.

In addition to anti-union campaigns organized by the corporate headquarters, Walmart strategically uses the courts to challenge and delay union certification applications. In 1996, the UFCW was certified to represent the workers at a Walmart store in Windsor, Ontario, making it the first organized Walmart in Canada. It was granted certification by the Ontario Labour Relations Board (OLRB) due to unfair labour practices by the company. Walmart's appeal of this decision was unsuccessful, but it signalled the pattern that the company would take in using the courts to delay and frustrate future unionization efforts (Adams 2005: 3). The UFCW local in Windsor was ultimately decertified, and the provincial Mike Harris Conservative government changed legislation so that the OLRB could no long grant certification in the face of illegal activity by an employer during an organizing campaign (Tucker 2005). In 2004, although UFCW had enough cards signed to force a vote at seven stores in British Columbia, it ultimately lost the vote. In 2005, it was successful in unionizing the store in Cranbrook, British Columbia, but it soon was decertified.[3] In Weyburn, Saskatchewan, the union applied for certification in 2004, but Walmart delayed the application for three years by challenging the provincial labour board's impartiality and its ability to force the company to provide information about its anti-union campaign.[4] The challenge was ultimately unsuccessful, but the store remains unorganized as a lower court accepted Walmart's appeal of the labour board's decision. The union is appealing that decision.

In addition to using aggressive anti-union campaigns directed toward workers and delaying legal tactics, Walmart holds the ultimate trump card in fighting union organizing on a store-by-store basis: it can close a store. In 2005, Walmart closed its Jonquière store on the day that an arbitrator had been given the authority to impose a collective agreement. Quebec's labour relations board had ruled that the employees were laid off because they had exercised their rights under the Labour Code, but the Quebec Court of Appeal ruled in favour of the company, stating that Walmart did not have to prove why it had closed the store. In October 2008, Walmart also closed down its Lube and Tire Express facility in Gatineau, Quebec, following an arbitration decision imposing a collective agreement. However, the UFCW was successful in organizing and gaining certification for the adjacent retail store and another store in Gatineau. Walmart, in typical fashion, has appealed those certifications to the Quebec Court of Appeal. It is uncertain whether the company will ultimately close the stores in Gatineau, if it fails in the courts, and in Saint-Hyacinthe, where an arbitrator imposed a first collective agreement in April 2009.

Walmart's anti-union policy is conducted with seemingly unlimited resources, resulting in frequent use of litigation and the courts together with a willingness to shut down stores where unionization is successful. This strategy poses serious challenges to any organizing drive on a store-by-store basis. While Walmart is united in its approach, its workers experience division and fragmentation. The UFCW has continued to organize on a store-by-store basis, attempting to combat fragmentation by trying to reach workers across the country through an association based on an approach initiated in the United States. Wal-Mart Workers of America was set up to "empower Wal-Mart workers to force Wal-Mart to change its business practices" (Wal-Mart Workers of America, n.d.) and the union has tried to build a link between the workers and community groups. The Canadian equivalent, Walmart Workers Canada, provides a website with information on legislative rights and a forum for Walmart workers to meet and discuss common issues (Walmart Workers Canada, n.d.). It remains to be seen if these approaches aid in the unionization of

Walmart stores in Canada or the United States or can be sustained without unionization.

Postal and Courier Services

The postal and courier industry is growing rapidly, especially in the area of express deliveries. While there has been some speculation that Canadian postal workers' attainment of the right to strike in 1967 sparked the growth of the industry outside of the post office (Radwanski 1996: 31), it has actually been a worldwide growth phenomenon. In 1998, the World Trade Organization estimated that there had been a growth of 20 per cent worldwide in the express courier part of the sector over the previous two decades (Sinclair 2001: 4). Large companies dominate the courier industry, and most of these, including Canada Post, are unionized. The industry's same-day sector, however, is mainly non-unionized and is characterized by low income, limited legal protections, and very precarious forms of work. While many of the couriers in this sector are deemed self-employed, they are dependent on their "employer" for access to work, since their "employer" controls and directs their delivery schedule. However, because of their self-employed status, they are not covered by employment standards legislation and employment insurance, nor does the "employer" contribute to the Canada Pension Plan on their behalf (Courier Research Project 2005).

Custodial and Janitorial Services

Custodial work is extremely fragmented and precarious for workers who clean large office buildings in metropolitan areas. For the most part, the workers are not employed by the companies occupying the building or even by the large holding companies that own the buildings. Often the large companies sub-contract the work to individual cleaners, making their jobs even more precarious. In Toronto, four companies have the cleaning contracts for approximately 75 per cent of the office buildings and employ approximately 22,000 workers (Daly 2008). These employees have little job security due to the poor successor right legislation, which allows companies to be sold or change contracts to avoid dealing with the union.

In most of the sectors described above, several unions compete for members among unorganized workers. In the restaurant and hotel sector, HERE-UNITE, the UFCW, the CAW, the Teamsters, and others all try to organize. While the UFCW dominates the unionized retail sector, the CAW and the USWA have made some inroads. The postal and courier sector has a variety of unions involved including CUPW, PSAC, the

Teamsters, the UFCW, and others. SEIU has a major campaign to organize custodial services in the large cities, but other unions like PSAC, the
USWA, the Laborers' International Union of North America (LIUNA),
and the Canadian Construction Workers Union (CCWU) also organize
in this sector, the latter currently being in direct competition with SEIU
in Toronto.

New Forms of Organizing and Collective Bargaining
in the Service Sector

Despite continuing efforts to unionize the private service sector, union
density in this sector remains low and labour fragmentation in all its
forms adds to the difficulties of union organizing. The problems of fragmentation, however, increased during the 1990s when employers, in
search of greater profits, moved toward more contract and temporary
forms of work. By 2002 only 62 per cent of Canadian workers held full-
time permanent jobs (Vosko, Zukewich and Cranford, 2003). Work in
hotels, restaurants, retail stores, and even in banks is often precarious, as
is the case with the custodial and same-day courier industries. Workers in
the private service sector are particularly vulnerable, which adds to the
difficulty of organizing. In this sector, there have been some new attempts
to overcome the challenges and find new ways of organizing and collective bargaining. Below we examine four recent examples.

Justice for Janitors
The Service Employees International Union (SEIU) has been successful
in organizing cleaners on a city- and industry-wide basis by adopting a
model that was developed in downtown Los Angeles in organizing the
largely Hispanic cleaners: the Justice for Janitors (J4J) campaign. Instead
of trying to organize cleaners building by building and focusing on the
cleaning companies, the union pushed for city-wide industry standards
and contracts by putting pressure on the building owners through community and worker action (Bronfenbrenner and Juravich 1998).

   This approach has been adopted with some success in Montreal and
Toronto. In Toronto, the SEIU has made alliances with the Canadian
Hispanic Congress and the Portuguese Canadian National Congress
due to the large numbers of recent immigrants working in the industry.
Recently it has been able to achieve city-wide collective agreements with
two of the large companies, Unico and Hurley. In addition, the Laborers'
International Union of North America (LIUNA), which is a partner in
Justice for Janitors (SEIU n.d.), has a collective agreement with a third
company, OMNI. The remaining large company, Hallmark, has resisted

SEIU's organizing efforts, and the union and its community partners have called on the Ontario Minister of Labour to investigate the company's employment practices, which allegedly include deducting a 10-percent fee from wages for miscellaneous expenses (SEIU n.d.). In January 2008, Hallmark signed an agreement with another union, the Canadian Construction Workers Union, which SEIU has accused of being a company union. This type of accusation is often common when unions are in competition, and a deeper investigation is needed to determine its validity.

Rural-Route Mail Carriers

In 2003, the Canadian Union of Postal Workers (CUPW) used collective bargaining to force Canada Post to contract in rural-route mail carriers who had been working as subcontractors without the legal right to collective bargaining. This in effect broke through the restrictions that limit unions to negotiating only for the group of workers that they legally represent. It also sidestepped legislation that had taken away the rights of the rural carriers to collective bargaining. When the government of Canada changed the national postal service from a government department to a Crown Corporation in 1981, the *Canada Post Corporation Act* denied rural mail couriers rights under the Canada Labour Code, including the rights to organize and to bargain collectively, on the basis that the Post Office was in a financial crisis. The struggle to organize and gain collective bargaining rights and employee status for rural-route mail couriers combined collective bargaining, political action, and organizing (Warskett 2007; Bourque and Bickerton 2004; Pollack 2004).[5]

In the late 1990s, CUPW decided it would work more actively with the rural-route couriers to help them gain rights to collective bargaining. The mail contractors had been successful in front of the CLRB in ruling that they were employees and had the right to collective bargaining, but Canada Post had that ruling overturned by the courts. There was an appeal to the Supreme Court, but it was unsuccessful. The CUPW campaign cost millions of dollars and represented an innovative strategy that went beyond a traditional organizing campaign. It required intensive capacity building by the workers themselves and the ongoing and active support of the union's traditional membership. It also required strong links with the union's political allies in Parliament and the community in lobbying efforts to change the law (Bourque and Bickerton 2004).

The main feature of the strategy was for the union to assist the rural-route contractors in forming their own association, the Organization of Rural Route Mail Couriers (ORRMC), which almost two-thirds of the rural couriers joined (Bourque and Bickerton 2004). The ORRMC and

CUPW's approach was to act as if the ORRMC already had the right to represent the contractors regardless of the law. In practice, it acted like a union. In 2000, the ORRMC executive drew up a set of bargaining demands, had them ratified at a national meeting, and presented them to Canada Post. This set the stage for the upcoming 2002 negotiations between CUPW and Canada Post for the already legally unionized workers at the Post Office. By 2002, the ORRMC decided that the time was right to formally join CUPW, and a majority of couriers signed up with the union (Bourque and Bickerton 2004).

CUPW put the issue on the bargaining table in 2002. It demanded that Canada Post make the couriers employees and no longer subject to the law excluding them from collective bargaining. At first, Canada Post refused to discuss the issue, but in January 2003, the work was contracted in and the couriers became employees with a graduated increase in wages and benefits. They also became members of the CUPW bargaining unit and union. While the initial focus had been on changing the law, ultimately collective bargaining and contracting won the day. The law was never changed. The union had to work to convince its traditional members that increased unionization of Canada Post, especially if the workers were represented by CUPW, would ultimately strengthen the union's bargaining position. Despite this argument for greater strength and solidarity, and support for the campaign in principle among union activists, there was serious opposition within CUPW due to changes made to the severance-pay package for postal workers retiring in the future. The traditional members ratified their collective agreement by just under two thirds. The rural-route carriers, however, ratified their agreement by nearly 87 per cent (Bourque and Bickerton 2004).

Delivery Drivers Association of Manitoba

CUPW has also tried a similar approach to organizing by helping set up a separate organization for same-day couriers in Winnipeg. Many of these couriers are not legally entitled to collective bargaining rights, as they are deemed to be independent contractors and therefore are self-employed. Beyond the legal impediments to unionizing, the workforce is transient and working in isolation from each other, making building solidarity a difficult task.

The CUPW was successful in organizing couriers at Dynamex in Winnipeg, where some workers were direct employees while others were under individual contracts. In the case of these latter workers, the union used a model that involved acting as if there were already a union in place. CUPW published a newsletter, used small-claims courts to challenge certain aspects of the employment relationship, and brought in government inspectors to investigate health-and-safety code violations. The union also challenged the status of the same-day couriers at this Dynamex branch and was successful in having them deemed employees. There are still, however, many couriers in the city and across the country who do not have a union or the current right to collective bargaining.

In 1997, however, the Delivery Drivers Association of Manitoba was formed to advocate for couriers. While not a union, it has negotiated with Manitoba Public Insurance for greater flexibility when couriers park vehicles, and has lobbied, in conjunction with the Workers Organizing and Research Centre (WORC), the Manitoba Employment Standards Board to ensure that couriers are covered and provided with employment standards protection.

Workers' Centres

Recently, workers' centres have developed in a number of Canadian cities. They seem to be a response to the exploitation and poor working conditions that certain non-unionized workers are experiencing in a number of sectors, whether they are low-paid contingent workers in the private service sector, migrant workers doing agricultural work, or home workers in the garment trade. All of these are vulnerable, low-paid workers who lack union representation. Workers' centres are a way of organizing workers who are not part of a union and who are finding themselves unprotected by employment standards and other types of labour legislation. Some centres also put pressure on governments to reform employment law and target employers who fail to adhere to employment standards (Cranford et al. 2006: 237). In some cases, it was unions that helped to initiate the centres; in others, they were developed by community activists, and in some cases it was a combination of both. Below we briefly focus on two examples: one centre in Winnipeg that is closely associated with CUPW, and another in Toronto that was founded by community activists.

The Winnipeg Workers Organizing Resource Centre (WORC) was started in 1998. It is run as a collective composed mainly of community volunteers and CUPW activists and receives financial support from CUPW. It has three major objectives: "to work with and strengthen local progressive coalitions, to do advocacy work for individuals and groups, and to assist in the unionization of workers" (Bickerton and Stearns 2002: 51). The WORC has enabled activists, who use the centre for their own organizations, to come together with others to work on political issues that affect workers in general. Advocacy work takes considerable time and resources and at the WORC is not limited to the employed; welfare recipients also receive help and representation. Injured workers are assisted with workers' compensation claims, and others with labour standards issues. Assisting with union organizing can take the form of simply referring workers to the appropriate union. In the case of the Dynamex couriers referred to above, the Centre became their organizing centre (Bickerton and Stearns 2002).

In Toronto, the Workers' Action Centre was formed in 2005 through the merger of two community groups: Toronto Organizing for Fair Employment (TOFFE) and the Workers' Information Centre. It aims to organize and mobilize low-paid workers with the goal of improving their working conditions. It has pressured the Ontario government to change employment laws and is very active in the current "raise the minimum wage" campaign. Providing advice and support to individuals through a phone line is a large part of its work. Workers who are in contact this way are invited to workshops to learn about their rights, and the centre produces fact sheets in many languages with the aim of helping workers know their rights (Workers' Action Centre 2006). The centre also does research and publishes reports. In 2007, it produced *Working on the Edge*, a report that focuses on precarious forms of work and recommendations for better employment standards and better enforcement (Workers' Action Centre 2007).

As can be seen from these two examples, workers' centres play an important role in building the capacity of workers to act individually and collectively, whether it is in education, advocacy, pressure to change legislation, pressure on employers to conform to employment standards, or through assisting with union organizing.

The Effectiveness of New Forms of Organizing

Have the new forms of organizing been able to overcome the limitations of the four kinds of fragmentation that we identified, and build the capacity of workers to act individually and collectively through education, advocacy, bargaining with employers, and politically? Through the above examination of new types of organizing, we can identify some of the opportunities they present for building workers' capacity, as well as some of their limitations.

The Justice for Janitors campaign, for example, seeks to overcome the legal fragmentation created by bargaining groups based on an establishment, by stepping outside the legal framework and organizing janitors on a city-wide basis. This has resulted in building solidarity and organizing capacity among these workers. The limitation of the legislation, however, still remains to a great extent, and union certification can only occur on an employer basis. Yet capacity has been building and could be directed toward a political challenge of the legislation itself.

The success of the rural-route mail carriers and CUPW was in large part based on ignoring the labour legislation and using the bargaining strength of unionized postal workers to gain collective bargaining rights for non-unionized postal workers, in effect breaking down the separation and fragmentation of the two groups of workers. There were dangers in the strategy in that some of the unionized group opposed giving up some rights in order to gain rights for others. Nevertheless, the overall success raises questions about how the bargaining strength of organized workers might be harnessed to organize the unorganized and increase the economic and political power of all workers.

Workers' centres have developed in major cities in Canada and the United States and have had some success in advocating for low-waged, unorganized workers. The limitations that they face, however, are many. Because they have no formal status or recognition from employers in the workplace, they are unable to engage in collective bargaining and come to a collective agreement with the employer. This also means that subsequently they are unable to represent workers based on that agreement. They also face the difficulty that their members or constituents are spread out over many different workplaces and neighbourhoods. In this sense, they challenge the fragmentation of the working class, but forming a common identity and hence solidarity presents a greater challenge than for a traditional union whose members all work for a single large company or corporation. Responding to the demands of individual problems—for example, employers' non-compliance with employment standards, occupational health and safety, or employment insurance—means that workers' centres are continually pulled toward servicing their constituents rather than building the capacity of those constituents to act and organize themselves economically and politically. This is the greatest challenge they face.

Conclusion

Compared to other countries, Canadian unions have maintained their overall numbers and continued to be a strong force, particularly in the public sector. In the private service sector, they face many obstacles in organizing workers due to fragmentation and other factors. In this chapter we have discussed four types of fragmentation while examining organizing and collective bargaining in the service sector. In large companies such as McDonald's and Walmart, workers experience a fragmented labour process with routine, low-paid tasks that require little training and are rigidly controlled by management. Although it would seem that such work is ripe for unionization, high worker turnover makes organizing difficult. In such companies, there is also fragmentation of non-standard forms of work, with few core workers and many who work part-time, on contract, and on a contingent basis. This is currently the case in the fast-food industry and the same-day courier industry, and used to be the case for the rural-route mail carriers.

We have also examined the fragmentation of the legal certification process. We have seen that the failure to organize Walmart and McDonald's and to retain organized branches of the chartered banks is in large part related to how legal certification limits organizing on a multi-employer, multi-establishment basis, which in turn limits the power of workers, especially in small franchises and bank branches. Finally, we have considered the fragmentation of the labour movement itself, and the competition and divisions between unions in organizing custodial services, the fast-food industry, and the banks. Such divisions only lead to a weakened labour movement.

There have been partial successes in organizing the private service sector, and they have taken place either when unions and workers have used strategies that challenged the fragmentation directly, as in the case of the rural-route mail carriers, or when unions have worked around the problems of fragmentation and forced employers to agree to city- or industry-wide bargaining, as was the case in the Justice for Janitors campaign. The example of the rural-route mail carriers also raises the issue of using the strength of workers engaged in collective bargaining to assist others to become organized and achieve negotiation rights. This case opens the possibility for other unions to examine how this might be done.

We have also discussed attempts to overcome fragmentation through the recent development of workers' centres. These organizations are important in helping workers build capacity through the role they play in advocacy, representation, organization, and education. While they are not legally recognized as unions, they do engage in some union-type activities. Their main limitation, however, is that they are not able to act within the workplace either to negotiate collective agreements, or represent their members on complaints and grievances.

All of these innovative strategies—and, for that matter, traditional organizing and bargaining approaches in the sector—require commitment from unions in both financial and organizational terms. One of the challenges that unions will face is ensuring that their existing membership is willing to support these new strategies and increase resources into organizing unorganized workers.

Discussion Questions

1. What are the reasons for such a low rate of unionization in the service sector?

2. What legislative changes are needed to make it easier for workers to unionize in the service sector?

3. What strategies can unions develop to face the challenges of fragmentation?

4. How can the new forms of organizing, discussed in this chapter, lead to collective bargaining?

5. How do unions work with their existing membership to build support for organizing in the service sector? What else could they do?

Notes

1   It is only the very large companies that the Association is referring to. There are thousands of small companies that have one or two employees, and these companies come and go, so the total number of employees in the sector is impossible to determine.

2   The Big Five banks are the Royal Bank, Canadian Imperial Bank of Commerce (CIBC), Bank of Montreal, Toronto Dominion-Canada Trust (TD), and Bank of Nova Scotia (BNS).

3   *United Food & Commercial Workers Union Local v. Wal-Mart 1518 & Wal-Mart Canada Corp.* (2005) SCBC.

4   *Wal-Mart Canada Corp. v. Saskatchewan Labour Relations Board, et al.* (2007) SCC.

5   One of the authors, Dale Clark, is a former president of CUPW and was on the union's executive board during the organizing campaign.

References

Adams, R.J. 2005. "Organizing Wal-Mart: The Canadian Campaign." *Just Labour* 6 & 7: 1–11.

Allentuck, A. 2006. "The Eve of Battle." *Canadian Grocer* 120 (8): 38–41.

Anderson, J., J. Beaton, and K. Laxer. 2006. "The Union Dimension: Mitigating Precarious Employment." In L.F. Vosko (ed.), *Precarious Employment: Understanding Labour Market Insecurity in Canada.* Montreal and Kingston: McGill-Queen's University Press. 301–17.

Bickerton, G., and C. Stearns. 2002. "The Struggle Continues in Winnipeg: The Workers Organizing and Resource Centre." *Just Labour* 1: 50–57.

Bourque, D., and G. Bickerton. 2004. *Stepping Out of the Legal Framework: Organizing Rural Route Couriers.* Paper prepared for the International Colloquium on Union Renewal, Interuniversity Research Centre on Globalization and Work, University of Montreal. November.

Bronfenbrenner, K., and T. Juravich. 1998. "It Takes More than Housecalls: Organizing to Win with a Comprehensive Union Building Strategy." In K. Bronfenbrenner, T. Juravich, S. Friedman, R. Hurd, R. Oswald, and R. Seeber (eds.), *Organizing to Win: New Research on Union Strategies*. Ithaca, NY: ILR Press. 19–36.

Courier Research Project. (2005). *Straddling the World of Traditional and Precarious Employment: A Case Study of the Courier Industry in Winnipeg*. Winnipeg: Canadian Centre for Policy Alternatives.

Cranford, C.J., M. Gellatly, D. Ladd, and L.F. Vosko. 2006. "Community Unionism and Labour Movement Renewal: Organizing for Fair Employment." In P. Kumar and C. Schenk (eds.), *Paths to Union Renewal: Canadian Experiences*. Peterborough, ON: Broadview Press. 237–50.

Daly, R. (2008). "Status of 'Subcontractors' and Wages Form Core of Drive to Unionize." *Toronto Star* 28 January. <http://www.thestar.com>.

Fishman, C. 2006. *The Walmart Effect*. New York: Penguin.

Fudge, J., and E. Tucker. 2001. *Labour before the Law: The Regulation of Workers' Collective Action, 1900–1948*. Don Mills, ON: Oxford University Press.

Harrison, J. 2006. *Casualization of Public Sector Labour*. Toronto: Centre for Research on Work and Society, York University.

Heron, C., and R. Storey (eds.) 1988. *On the Job: Confronting the Labour Process in Canada*. Montreal and Kingston: McGill-Queen's University Press.

Human Resources and Social Development Canada. 2006. *Looking Ahead: A 10-year Outlook for the Canadian Labour Market (2006–2015)*. Ottawa: Human Resources and Social Development Canada.

Huot, C. 1998. "Unionizing the Impossible: A Strong National Campaign Could Open the Door to Unionization in the Infamously Anti-union McDonald's." *Canadian Dimension* 32 (5): 24.

Kainer, J. 2002. *Cashing In on Pay Equity: Supermarket Restructuring and Gender Equality*. Toronto: Sumach Press.

Lowe, G. 1987. *Women in the Administrative Revolution*. Toronto: University of Toronto Press.

McDermott, P. 1993. "The Eaton's Strike: We Wouldn't Have Missed It for the World!" In L. Briskin and P. McDermott (eds.), *Women Challenging Unions: Feminism, Democracy and Militancy*. Toronto: University of Toronto Press. 23–43.

McDonald's Canada. n.d. <http://working.canada.com/profiles/mcdonalds/index.html>.

Morissette, R., and A. Johnson. 2005. *Are Good Jobs Disappearing in Canada?* Ottawa: Business and Labour Market Analysis, Statistics Canada.

Morissette, R., G. Schellenberg, and A. Johnson. 2005. "Diverging Trends in Unionization." *Perspectives on Labour and Income* 6 (4): 1–8.

Nazim, Z. 2007. *Interrogating Restructuring: A Critical Ethnography of Ethno-racial Women Bank Workers in Canadian Retail Banking*. Unpublished doctoral dissertation, OISE, University of Toronto.

Pollack, M. 2004. "Stamping Out Contingent Workers at Canada Post." *Canadian Woman Studies/Les cahiers de la femme* 25 (3 & 4): 105–7.

Radwanski, G. 1996. *The Future of Canada Post Corporation: Report of the Canada Post Mandate Review*. Ottawa: Queen's Printer.

Reiter, E. 2002. "Fast Food in Canada: Working Conditions, Labour Law and Unionization." In T. Royle and B. Towers (eds.), *Labour Relations in the Global Fast-Food Industry*. London and New York: Routledge. 30–47.

SEIU (Service Employees' International Union). n.d. <http://www.seiu.ca/>.

Sinclair, S. 2001. *The GATS and Canadian Postal Services*. Ottawa: Canadian Centre for Policy Alternatives.

Statistics Canada. 2007. *Labour Force Survey August 2007*. Ottawa: Statistics Canada.

Sufrin, E.T. 1982. *The Eaton's Drive: The Campaign to Organize Canada's Largest Department Store 1948 to 1952*. Toronto: Fitzhenry and Whiteside.

Tucker, E. 2005. "Wal-Mart and the remaking of Ontario Labour Law." *International Union Rights* 12 (2): 10–11.

Tufts, S. 2006. "Renewal from Different Directions: The Case of UNITE-HERE Local 75." In P. Kumar and C. Schenk (eds.), *Paths to Union Renewal: Canadian Experiences*. Peterborough, ON: Broadview Press. 201–21.

Vosko, L., N. Zukewich, and C. Cranford. 2003. "Precarious Jobs: A New Typology of Employment." *Perspectives on Labour and Income* 4 (10): 16–26.

White, J. 1983. "Patterns of Unionization." In L. Briskin and L. Yanz (eds.), *Union Sisters: Women in the Labour Movement*. Toronto: The Women's Press.

Walmart Canada. n.d. <http://working.canada.com/profiles/walmart/profile.html>.

Walmart Workers Canada. n.d. <http://www.walmartworkerscanada.ca/>.

Wal-Mart Workers of America. n.d. <http://wakeupwalmart.com/wwa>.

Warskett, R. 1981. *Trade Unions and the Canadian State: A Case Study of Bank Worker Unionization 1976–1980*. Unpublished master's thesis, Carleton University, Ottawa.

——. 1988. "Bank Workers and the Law." *Studies in Political Economy* 25: 41–74.

——. 2007. "Remaking the Canadian Labour Movement: Transformed Work and Transformed Labour Strategies." In V. Shalla and W. Clement (eds.), *Work in Tumultuous Times: Critical Perspectives*. Montreal and Kingston: McGill-Queen's University Press. 382–400.

Workers' Action Centre. 2006. *Annual Report*. Toronto: Workers' Action Centre.

——. 2007. *Working on the Edge*. Toronto: Workers' Action Centre.

Glossary of Terms

alter-globalization movement: a movement promoting a shift in the current ideology and practices of neoliberalism, a reform of the welfare state, practices of reduced consumerism, and the non-commodification of labour.

alternatives (to neoliberalism): alternatives to neoliberalism might be defined by two key principles: first, the principle that democratic citizenship begins from rights to work, leisure, and a living income; second, political compromises at the international level must be built around the principle of maximizing the capacity of different national and local collectivities to democratically choose alternative development paths.

branding: the process of attaching a brand (e.g., a logo) to a product, service, or person in order to attach certain meanings and values to it.

capitalism: a system of generalized commodity production. It is dominated by the pursuit of profits, with money mediating all social interactions through the dominance of markets. Labour takes the form of free wage-labour.

casualization: the erosion of a standard employment relationship where full-time, full-year, long-term, or permanent jobs are reduced and work that is part-time, temporary, and/or self-employed is created, providing precarious, uncertain employment rather than stable, ongoing, full-time waged work.

civil service: the body of any level of government employees who are usually hired and promoted on the basis of job competitions. Civil servants are not political appointees, and the terms of their employment may be similar to those of the private sector.

class consciousness: a sense of fellow-feeling and identification with others who share some of the same features, which can in turn form the basis for developing forms of organization through which the common interests of the group can be represented.

class polarization: the gap between the (upper and lower) classes.

collective agreement: an agreement concerning the wages and working conditions of a group of workers negotiated between the employer and the union.

collective bargaining: a formal process in Canada where a trade union and employer (singly or in a group) meet to negotiate the terms of a collective agreement that spells out workplace rights, conditions of employment, wages, and benefits. The process is governed by specific labour legislation for that group of workers.

commodification: the process of treating everything as having been produced for sale on the market and as subject to the supply-and-demand mechanisms interacting with price.

commodities: goods or services that are both use-values and exchange-values sold in a market to meet needs.

concrete and abstract labour: as use-values, commodities are produced by concrete labour: the labour, for example, that goes into making a television or providing a haircut. As exchange-values, different commodities exchange with one another: they have in common the general (or abstract) labour that has gone into each of them. Abstract labour is the socially necessary labour-time that goes into producing commodities, and money serves to represent abstract labour in commodity exchanges.

contracting out: the decision by a government or organization to contract with an individual or company to provide services previously done in-house, or which could be done in-house.

core and periphery: this concept describes geographical, economic, and political entities. The core is the central part, where much of the most important activity takes place. The periphery describes the more remote parts, where less important activity takes place. However, there is a dialectical relationship between the two: sometimes the activity in the periphery nourishes what is in the core, sometimes the opposite occurs, and sometimes it works both ways at the same time.

cultural capital: an individual's knowledge, experience, and understanding, and how they use it over their lifetime.

culture economy: the idea that increasingly "culture" and "economy" are inextricably tied in the new economy of contemporary capitalism, and that one cannot understand one concept without including the other.

decommodification: an attempt to minimize the impact of market calculation and market forces upon the production and exchange of goods and services.

deregulation: the process by which governments remove certain restrictions from the operation of business in general and corporations in particular. Deregulation consists of policies that are intended to promote "free-market" economies. Most commonly, deregulation involves minimizing state governance of financial and labour markets, privatizing public industries and services, weakening environmental protection, and reducing spending on social programs.

dialectic: this can be a very complicated philosophical concept, but, simply put, it describes the situation where two things that appear to be opposites sometimes work together and sometimes work against each other.

discourse: the way we understand the world around us. A discourse is socially constructed knowledge. It is how we think and talk about the world. The concept was coined by sociologist Michel Foucault (1926–84), who argued that our perception of reality is influenced by the way we think and talk. A discourse shapes and regulates human behaviour as we internalize and act upon its assumptions.

economic clusters: groupings of businesses that are centred on specific industries. For example, in the wine industry the "wine cluster" may include grape growers, barrel makers, suppliers of tanks and bottling equipment, maintenance companies for wineries, cork, bottle and label suppliers, as well as advertising and public-relations companies.

emotional labour: work characterized by the requirement for workers to elicit positive feelings in clients, to contain their own emotions, and to maintain a smile and a positive outlook regardless of the circumstances and tasks at hand.

emotional proletariat: most service workers whose job includes eliciting good feelings in clients in the workplace.

exchange-value: workers produce commodities with new value (the new goods and services, or use-values, continually being produced). These then become the commodity capital of capitalist firms to be sold as exchange-values in the market to consumers. Exchange-value has the appearance of day-to-day prices of goods for sale in the wholesale or retail markets of capitalist societies.

family wage: a worker's earned wage sufficient enough to sustain an entire family.

feminization: feminization speaks to changing demographic profiles, specifically the increase in female participation in the labour force and in the female proportion of union membership. It also refers to the increase in the proportion of jobs traditionally understood as "women's work" (the feminization of work).

financialization: refers to an economy dominated by finance capital and financial markets as opposed to a more traditional economy dominated primarily by industrial pursuits.

flexibilization: occurs when employers increase the number of part-time and/or short-term, limited-term, or casual employees relative to their full-time permanent or core work force.

folk economics: "folk" refers to something that is popular and taken as "common sense," though not necessarily wrong and not necessarily right. For example, a folk remedy is one that has been passed down through the generations as a treatment for some illness. Folk economics refers to commonly held ideas about how the economy works.

Fordism: the concept of Fordism has several dimensions. In terms of the labour process, it refers to the combination of fragmentation of skills and tasks with flow-line assembly of production, utilizing semi-skilled and unskilled workers. In the labour market, Fordism refers to the linking of the wage growth of workers in line with the productivity growth of firms to allow workers annual increases in their purchasing power and thus effective demand for mass-produced products. In the postwar period, these market structures were coupled with Keynesian economic policies and an expansionary welfare state to provide conditions of high growth and employment. The term Fordism is also used as a shorthand to describe this historical period.

gender: the sociological significance attached to someone being female or male, defined around dominant ideas of female and male traits and behaviours.

gender stratification: the unequal distribution of jobs, wealth, and power between sexes in a society.

guestworker programs: these facilitate the entry of workers into a host country's labour market, generally for a specified period of time, often with restrictions on their economic and social rights. They may be regulated through regional agreements such as NAFTA, national immigration policies, or industry-specific arrangements. Guestworker programs are increasingly viewed as a key policy measure for managing both labour forces and migration patterns in the new economy.

habitus: a concept coined by Pierre Bourdieu (1930–2007) that refers to the completed internalization, or habituation, of social norms and values. They become guiding principles of people's way of thinking and interacting. After internalization, they become second nature, or habit.

heritage: one's official immigrant and citizenship status in a country, along with socially constructed notions of race and ethnicity, language, religion, and regional identities.

indigenous: belonging to oneself or one's family or community, originating inside a particular geographic location.

information and communications technologies (ICTs): computer-based systems and applications designed to store, retrieve, manage, convert, and transmit, disseminate, or communicate information.

internalization: occurs when a person adopts social values and norms, making them their own in the sense that these principles guide and influence their interactions.

knowledge economy/society: the contemporary economy is marked by a focus on training, learning, and education because knowledge-based skills are deemed crucial for successful careers. There are three main points regarding the valuation of knowledge and the emphasis on learning and training in the new economy. First, learning is increasingly taken as an individual issue. Second, the valuation of knowledge and skills does not always correspond with the job market, especially when job creation is at the discretion of private firms. Third, not all social groups have equal access to training, and work is becoming more segmented within and across sectors.

Live-in Caregiver Program: a foreign-worker program in Canada that employs migrant women workers (primarily from the Philippines) in child and elder care, as well as domestic work. Unlike workers in the SAWP (see below), these workers may apply for permanent residence in Canada, but not before completing 24 months of employment over a period of three years.

Labour Force Survey (LFS): a long-running Statistics Canada survey that provides the most comprehensive information available monthly and annually on employment trends in Canada.

labour-market segmentation theory: a theoretical framework developed to analyze the structural divisions that exist within labour markets and to identify the sources of these divisions.

localism: the view that in the context of globalization, local elites and boosters argue that the "local" requires a renewed image with emphasis on its unique qualities.

migrant labour: workers who have moved from their primary place of residence in search of work. Labour migration may take place both within and between countries. Foreign migrant workers often do not have permanent residency rights in the "host" country where they are employed.

modularization: involves a fragmentation of labour processes. It contributes to a further division of existing divisions of labour and hence increases the possibility of replacing workers. Once processes have been successfully modularized, they can be reconfigured rapidly in different ways, by centralizing a range of different functions on a single site or decentralizing them to many different sites around the globe. As it is based on further dividing labour processes, modularization contributes to a lengthening of value chains.

neoliberalism: the set of policies that seeks to reinforce free-market, private-property, and capitalist social relations through privatization, deregulation, flexibilization, free trade, de-unionization, and financialization. Neoliberalism has become the social form of rule in this phase of capitalism.

new economy: this central term refers to the continual development of new goods, technologies, and social relations in capitalism. Some of the features of the new economy today are flexible production systems, flexibilization of labour markets, international production networks, internationalization, and neoliberal policies.

new economy ideology: neoliberal ideas and policies, which involve promoting privatization and deregulation of the economy. This ideology has been used to shift the role of the state away from promoting social welfare, where social assistance is being replaced by "workfare" to increase economic productivity. In this respect, the modern welfare state in Canada is being redesigned to accommodate employers' needs for economic restructuring in the new economy.

new technologies: the diffusion of hardware and software into work processes: a process that has implications for the execution, autonomy, and supervision of work. New technologies involving computerization and digitization—often referred to as, but not limited to, Information and Communications Technologies—are altering the structure of work not only within but also between firms. They require new tasks from employees and place new burdens on them as well.

organized labour: refers both to workers who are members of unions and, more generally, to the labour movement and its goal to represent union members' interests in the social and political arena.

out-migration: the migration of people out of an economic region. Out-migration often occurs as a result of economic decline, as workers seek employment in more prosperous locations, for example migration from rural to urban areas.

permanent full-time work: the standard employment relationship, where employees work at least 30 hours a week (or 1,560 hours in a 12-month period) and are not seasonal, cyclical, agency, or contract workers; there is no set term to their period of employment.

permanent part-time work: employees regularly work less than 30 hours a week, and there is no set term to their period of employment.

political economy of migration: a theoretical approach developed to explain why and how migrations happen. It focuses on the economic, political, and cultural factors that produce inequality related to patterns of migration. Key to this perspective is the recognition that the migration decisions and actions of individuals and families are rooted in contemporary manifestations of histories of economic and political inequalities between sending and receiving countries. This approach places primary emphasis on the importance of structural factors in explaining both the determinants of migration and the nature in which migrants are incorporated into a destination society.

policy prescription: "policy" refers to the plans that governments make to deal with social, political, and economic issues. A policy prescription is a possible government answer to a problem.

post-Fordism: the period when the Fordist economy has been restructured and the new emphasis is on just-in-time production and other measures that keep production costs as low as possible. Companies become more global and relocate wherever labour is the cheapest. The economic shift means that fewer workers are needed in manufacturing, and subsequently there is a shift in labour to the service sector. The term also refers to a society where insecurities and anxieties are permanent states of being.

precarious employment: a form of employment involving one or a combination of the following: (1) atypical employment, in the form of temporary, casual, seasonal, short-term work or work with a limited duration and/or a low degree of job security; (2) persistently low earnings that may result in poverty; (3) a limited number of key fringe benefits such as paid vacation leave, paid sick leave, unemployment insurance, and a pension plan; (4) a working environment where employees are not in a position to defend their interests in working conditions and practices, wages and discrimination. The intersection of race, gender, and class relations accentuates the segregation of certain social groups such as women of colour into precarious employment.

precarity: this term indicates that precariousness in the labour market has now become a fact of life for many working class members in the capitalist North.

privatization: any initiative designed to transfer public-sector work in whole or in part from any level of government to the private sector. Privatization initiatives include public–private partnerships, contracting out, and shifting regulatory responsibility to the private sector.

post-industrialism: refers broadly to the growth of the service economy. Related to this change in the nature of work is a change in the social composition of workers. Educational levels are considerably higher in the service sector compared to the goods sector, although there is variation among sub-sectors. In addition, the increase in the service sector has been accompanied by a shift from a predominantly male to a more gender-mixed labour force, although women are often segregated in sub-sectors of the service economy.

public sector: the definition used here is derived from Statistics Canada. It includes all publicly funded entities controlled by government and is composed of four major elements: federal government; provincial and territorial governments, including universities, colleges, health and social-service institutions; local government; and government business enterprises.

Seasonal Agricultural Workers Program (SAWP): a foreign-worker program in Canada that employs migrant workers from the Caribbean and Mexico in seasonal agricultural production. The workers must return to their home country once their seasonal contract is complete and they may not look for other employment while in Canada.

social policy: in a capitalist system, social policy is more accurately referred to as capitalist social policy or welfare capitalism. Social policies are the activities and principles enacted by government that determine the distribution of social resources (i.e., wealth) and the level of well-being of citizens.

social rights: social rights cover a whole range of rights, from economic security to the right to share in the heritage and living standards of a civilized society. Social rights are comprised of *civil rights*, i.e., those rights concerned with individual liberty and including freedom of speech and thought, the right to own private property, and the right to justice; and *political rights*, i.e., rights of participation in the political process of government, either as an elector or as an elected member of an assembly.

social welfare: services, usually provided by the state, designed to address social-policy needs, for example, social- and income-security policies.

standard employment relationship: full-time, full-year, long-term employment, considered the standard, at least for middle- and working-class white men, in the postwar period.

(the) state: the state is not a single entity; rather it is a set of institutions, the interaction of which constitutes the state system. The institutions include the legislative and executive functions of government, including taxation, the police and military forces, the judiciary, and educational and welfare services. A central purpose of these institutions is to facilitate the direction of economic and social affairs through the regulation of employment, private property rights, investment, trade, and commodity markets.

surplus value: workers sell their labour power as a commodity to capitalists. The use-value of labour power is the capacity to produce new value (or things). Actually expended labour-time is the concrete use that capitalists seek to deploy in the labour process: they want to extract as much labour out of labour power within the time purchased. The harder the worker works in a given time, the more the value that is produced over and above the wage that has been paid for labour power, and the more surplus-value the capitalist is able to appropriate.

telework/telemediated work: a work arrangement in which the worker is connected to customers, clients, the office, and/or his or her employer via telecommunications links, including computers, telephones, or satellite devices. This process enables a worker to work from home or from a location that is distant from the parties with whom the worker is required to interact.

temporary foreign-worker programs: these facilitate the entry of workers into a host country's labour market for a specified period of time, often with restrictions on the economic and social rights of the migrant workers. These programs are increasingly viewed as a key policy measure for managing both labour forces and migration patterns in the new economy. Workers in temporary-labour programs are often not permitted to settle permanently in the country in which they are working.

temporary full-time work: employees work at least 30 hours a week for a specified period of time. This includes jobs that are term, contract, seasonal, casual, temporary agency, and all other jobs with a specific end date.

temporary part-time work: employees work less than 30 hours a week and there is a set term to their period of employment.

Third Way: the Third Way refers to the search for a political road somewhere between capitalism and socialism. The Third Way accepts the reality of globalization and the supremacy of the market system, however a market system that is informed by values of social democracy.

unfree wage labour: refers to the capacity of wage labourers (those who sell their labour power in exchange for a wage) to circulate (look for jobs) in a labour market. Those in guestworker programs are often incorporated into a "host" economy as unfree wage labour, as their labour-market mobility is limited by the migrant-labour contract.

union density: the proportion of paid employees covered by collective agreements, expressed as the union membership as a percentage of non-agricultural paid employment.

unions: collective organizations of workers to establish a capacity to struggle effectively against the concentrated economic and political power of capitalists. The combination of market-dependence and antagonistic interests makes the relationship between workers and employers quite contradictory. This means that the organizational capacity, form, and ideological orientation of unions and workers will vary quite substantially across places and different phases of capitalism.

value chains: a chain of production or service provision based on the spatial dispersion of work. Value chains include a growing number of steps in creating a final product, and an increasing role for intermediaries in smoothing over these steps. While based on decentralized processes, they are also characterized by an increasing centralization of control over those processes.

wage-labour: in capitalism, workers are free to sell their labour power where they wish, but they are also dependent upon the sale of their labour power to earn the means of subsistence.

welfare state: legislatively sanctioned and publicly or quasi-publicly administered spending on welfare benefits such as health, education, social assistance, unemployment, and pensions. Because the modern welfare state developed within a structure of industrialized capitalism and organized labour, it would be more accurate to refer to welfare states as "welfare capitalism."

winner-take-all market: a market in which the cost of most products is very low while the cost for a few is very high. Cultural production is usually like this. The vast majority of cultural producers make very little for their product while a few "superstars" make exorbitant amounts of money.

work stoppage: a general term used by Human Resources and Social Development Canada that includes both strikes and lockouts.

Notes on Contributors

Luis L.M. Aguiar is an associate professor of sociology at the University of British Columbia—Okanagan. He researches racialization in the Okanagan Valley, as well as new economy sectors such as tourism and play. He also studies neoliberalism as it applies to marginalized workers and is currently developing a project to study the emergence of global unionism.

Gregory Albo teaches political economy at York University, Toronto. He also is on the editorial boards of *Studies in Political Economy*, *Socialist Register*, *Relay*, *Canadian Dimension*, *The Bullet*, and *Historical Materialism*. His research interests are the political economy of contemporary capitalism, labour-market policies in Canada, and democratization. He teaches courses on the foundations of political economy, Canadian political economy, alternatives to capitalism, and democratic administration.

Linda Briskin is a professor in the Social Science Division and the School of Women's Studies at York University, Toronto. In addition to numerous articles, she has authored *Equity Bargaining/Bargaining Equity* (2006); co-edited *Women's Organizing and Public Policy in Canada and Sweden* (1999), *Women Challenging Unions: Feminism, Democracy and Militancy* (1993), and *Union Sisters: Women in the Labour Movement* (1983); and co-authored *Feminist Organizing For Change: The Contemporary Women's Movement in Canada* (1988), and *The Day the Fairies Went on Strike* (for children) (1981). She is currently researching worker militancies, union leadership, and strategies for ensuring equity representation inside unions.

Dave Broad is a professor of social policy in the Faculty of Social Work at the University of Regina, Saskatchewan. His research focuses on issues of international development and underdevelopment, work, the labour market, and social welfare. His publications include *Hollow Work, Hollow Society? Globalization and the Casual Labour Problem* (2000) and *Capitalism Rebooted? Work, Welfare and the New Economy* (2006).

Dale Clark is a former national president of the Canadian Union of Postal Workers and holds a life-time membership in that union. He has an MA in political economy and is currently a PhD student at the School of Canadian Studies at Carleton University in Ottawa.

Wallace Clement was educated at McMaster University (Hons. BA) and Carleton University (MA and PhD). He was elected to the Royal Society of Canada in 1991 and appointed as a Chancellor's Professor at Carleton in 2002. His books *The Canadian Corporate Elite* (1975) built on his Master's thesis and *Continental Corporate Power* (1977) on his doctoral thesis. He has published two studies of resource labour processes: *Hardrock Mining* (1981) and *The Struggle to Organize* (1986), as well as two collections of his essays: *Class, Power and Property* (1983) and *The Challenge of Class Analysis* (1988). *Relations of Ruling* (with John Myles, 1994) won the 1995 Harold Adams Innis Book Prize awarded by the Social Science Federation of Canada for the best English-language academic book. He has also edited *The New Practical Guide to Canadian Political Economy* (with Daniel Drache, 1985), *The New Canadian Political Economy* (with Glen Williams, 1989), *Swedish Social Democracy* (with Rianne Mahon, 1994), *Understanding Canada* (1996), *Changing Canada: Political Economy as Transformation* (with Leah Vosko, 2003), and *Studies in Political Economy: Developments in Feminism* (with Caroline Andrew, Pat Armstrong, Hugh Armstrong, and Leah Vosko, 2003).

Simone Dahlmann is the senior research officer at Analytica Social and Economic Research, where she has been involved in a range of European and international research projects on the restructuring of work in organizations, global outsourcing, and issues of equality and diversity in the workplace. She also teaches social research and evaluation methods at London Metropolitan University. Recently, she was a research fellow at the Working Lives Research Institute at London Metropolitan University, working on a European research project investigating changes in work organizations and the impact of restructuring processes on organizations and workers.

Larry Haiven is an associate professor in the Faculty of Management at Saint Mary's University in Halifax, Nova Scotia. His research interests are in the working lives and labour markets of cultural workers, and industrial relations in health care.

John Holmes is a professor of geography at Queen's University in Kingston, Ontario. His broader research program focuses on the political economy of economic and social change with a particular emphasis on the contemporary reorganization of production and work in North America. Current research projects include the impact of economic integration on workplace governance in Canada–US cross-border regions and the adaptation of employment and work in Canada to the challenge of climate change.

Ursula Huws is a professor of international labour studies at London Metropolitan University and the director of Analytica Social and Economic Research. She is also the editor of *Work Organisation, Labour and Globalisation*. For 25 years she has been carrying out pioneering research on the economic and social impacts of technological change, the telemediated relocation of employment, and the changing international division of labour in services. The author of *The Making of a Cybertariat: Real Work in a Virtual World* (2003) she has directed a large number of international research projects in Europe, Asia, North America, Latin America, and Australia and carried out consultancy for government bodies across the world. An internationally recognized expert on offshore outsourcing, she has authored many research reports for international and national government bodies as well as writing and editing books and articles aimed at more popular audiences. Her work has appeared in translation in over a dozen languages.

Garson Hunter is the past director of the Social Policy Research Unit and an associate professor in the Faculty of Social Work, University of Regina, Saskatchewan. His research focuses on the topics of income inequality, employment, unemployment, poverty, and vulnerable groups of poor such as intravenous drug users and the homeless.

Tina Marten is an interdisciplinary MA candidate (sociology and geography) in the Interdisciplinary Graduate Studies department at the University of British Columbia—Okanagan. She studies neoliberalism and its transformational processes, focusing especially on Kelowna and the Okanagan Valley, British Columbia.

Sophie Mathieu is a PhD student in the Department of Sociology and Anthropology at Carleton University, Ottawa. Her areas of interest are social policy, gender inequalities, and welfare-state regimes. Her PhD research is a comparative analysis of the Quebec and Canadian fertility regimes since the 1960s.

Andrea Noack is an assistant professor in the Department of Sociology at Ryerson University, Toronto. She specializes in research methods and social statistics. She is currently involved in research projects studying the working conditions in federal government call centres, the effect of "contracting in" on Canadian postal workers, and the experiences of same-day couriers in Toronto.

Steven Prus is an associate professor in the Department of Sociology and Anthropology at Carleton University, Ottawa. His current research interests lie in the areas of medical sociology, social inequality, and social statistics.

Norene Pupo is an associate professor in the Department of Sociology and Director of the Centre for Research on Work and Society (CRWS) at York University, Toronto. She was Principal Investigator of the Research Alliance, *Restructuring Work and Labour in the New Economy*, funded by SSHRC under the Initiatives on the New Economy program. She is editor of *Just Labour*, an electronic journal published through the CRWS. In addition to co-authoring an introductory sociology textbook with Daniel Glenday and Ann Duffy, entitled *Sociology: A Down-to-Earth Approach*, she has written on the restructuring of public-service work, call centres, and part-time work. She is currently conducting research on changes in labour process in the mail and messenger industries.

Jane Stinson has worked for change in and through the union movement for over 30 years. For most of that time she worked at the national office of the Canadian Union of Public Employees (CUPE) in Ottawa. While with CUPE she has been a researcher, director of the Research and Job Evaluation Department, and managing director of the National Services and Union Development departments. She has written extensively on raising women's wages, ending discrimination, and promoting equality. Her research interests have focused on the causes, extent, and consequences of privatizing public services in Canada, especially for women and other equity-seeking groups. She has also been a member of the federal Health Sectoral Advisory Group on International Trade (SAGIT), a member of the federal Information Highway Advisory Council's subcommittee on Social Impacts and Workplace Issues, and on the Board of Directors of the Canadian Centre for Policy Alternatives.

Mark Thomas is an associate professor in the Department of Sociology at York University, Toronto. His research interests are in the areas of political economy and economic sociology, with a primary research focus on the regulation of labour standards at local, national, and transnational scales. He is the author of *Regulating Flexibility: The Political Economy of Employment Standards* (2009). His research on labour standards in Canada has also been published in *Labour/Le Travail* and *Studies in Political Economy*. His most recent project, titled "Emerging Approaches to Labour Standards in the Global Economy," examines practices and processes that shape the regulation of transnational labour standards, with a focus on the role of transnational labour-rights networks.

Steven Tufts is an assistant professor in the Department of Geography at York University, Toronto. His current research focuses on the use of strategic corporate research by labour unions in their renewal efforts. Other research interests include labour-market adjustment in the hospitality sector, the impacts of climate change on labour institutions, and the role of young workers in economic development. His work has been published in *Antipode*, *Geoforum*, and *Environment and Planning*.

Emre Uckardesler is a PhD candidate in the Department of Sociology and Anthropology at Carleton University, Ottawa. His areas of interest are social policy, state theory, and the disciplinary boundaries between sociology, economics, and political economy. His PhD research is a comparative analysis of the post-crisis transformation of social policy in Turkey and South Korea.

Rosemary Warskett is chair and teaches in the Department of Law at Carleton University, Ottawa. Her current research concerns the working poor in Canada and the way in which relations of class, gender, and ethnicity produce socially unjust outcomes. In particular she is researching how legal regulation fails to address the exploitation of low-paid workers in the service sector, and migrant workers in the agricultural sector.

Index

increased corporate power, xv
insecurity, xiv, 15
internationalization of value flows,
    13
learning and training in, 56
militancy and the, 219–20
more highly skilled and more low-
    skilled workers, 11
new and exciting employment
    opportunities, 23
normalization of precarious work,
    xiii
promoted by business and
    government, 25
proponents of, 23
recommodification of labour, 21, 24
role of state, 22–24, 37
same old capitalism, xvix, xvii, 24,
    34, 37
self-employment, 46
transformation in workplace
    relations, xi
weakening workers and unions, xiii,
    xiv, xvi, xix, 13, 16, 25
new economy (in the capitalism of
    today), 3–19
new economy public policy. *See*
    neoliberal governments; state
A New Framework for Economic Policy
    (Government of Canada), 31
new social order, 19
new social risks (NSR), 48–49, 58
new technologies, xi, xii, xviii, 7, 10–11,
    23, 43, 49–53
business strategy and, 51
cross-national comparisons, 50–52
economic optimists on, 49
economic skeptics on, 49
human resources strategy and, 51
intersection with social stratification,
    47
national labour-market policies and,
    51
productivity impact, 50
silicon chip, 69
sociological optimists on, 49–50
sociological pessimists on, 50
unemployment and, 50
"A New Way of Doing Business"
    (Government of Saskatchewan),
    34
New York media workers, 85

New Zealand, 32
Newcastle upon Tyne, 201, 204, 207
Niagara wine region, 188
Nk'mip (Aboriginal-owned winery), 182
"No. 26 Mine Disaster" (MacGillivray),
    203
No Great Mischief (Macleod), 204
Noack, Andrea, xviii, 272
non-standard jobs, 56–57, 98–100,
    116, 236. *See also* precarious
    employment
    diversity within, 57
    growth in public sector, 98
    immigrants in, 56
    men in, 100
    women in, 98
Nordic countries, 49, 56
North American Agreement on Labour
    Cooperation (NAALC), 166–67
North American Free Trade Agreement
    (NAFTA), 14, 35
    Chapter 16, 150, 159, 165
North East of England Mining Archives
    and Resource Centre (NEEMARC),
    205
North-South divide, 151, 155
Nova Scotia Government Employees
    Union, 227
"Now That the Work is Done"
    (Cormier), 203
nurses and health-care workers
    move from full-time to part-time and
    contract work, 225
nurses and health-care workers on
    strike, 225–28
    Alberta (1988), 226
    back-to-work legislation, 226
    illegal strike (Ontario 1981), 228
    Newfoundland (1999), 226
    popular support, 227
    Quebec (1999) wildcat, 226
    right to strike issue (Nova Scotia),
        227
    Saskatchewan (1991), 226–27

occupational identities, xiv, xvi, xviii,
    66–67, 79
    challenges to, 67
    changes (*See* changing occupational
        identity)
    class identities and, 66–67, 82

socialization of tourists, 183
in tandem with golf, 177
winemakers, 187
wine-production workers, 186–87. *See
also* Seasonal Agricultural Workers
Program (SAWP)
wine-shop workers, 185, 187
Winnipeg Workers Organizing Resource
Centre (WORC), 249
women, 85. *See also* feminization;
gender
class position and identity, 66
in knowledge economy or society,
55–56
new social risks, 49
non-standard jobs, 56
precarious employment, 58
public sector jobs, 95, 98, 137
retail and personal services, 48
social-protection deficit, 58
use of computer and Internet at
work, 70
worker militancy, 218, 220
women bank tellers, 241
women's labour-force participation, 43,
47, 58, 220
Women's Trade Union League, 224
work and family life balance. *See* work-
life balance issues
work intensification, xiii, xiv, 13, 15,
24, 177
work restructuring, xv
effect on worker commitment, 84–85
work restructuring in federal public
service
impact on union rights, 115–16
risks and benefits to the general
public, 115
Work Stoppage manual (HRSDC), 221
work stoppages. *See* lockouts; strikes
work transformation in the public
service

call-centre jobs (*See* Service Canada
call-centre workers)
worker autonomy, 16
worker-controlled labour processes, 18
Workers' Action Centre (Toronto), 218
"raise the minimum wage" campaign,
250
workers and employers
inherent conflicts, 6
workers' centres, 218, 249–52
Workers' Information Centre, 250
Workers Organizing and Research
Centre (WORC), 249
workfare, 25, 28–29, 34. *See also* active
welfare programming
forcing work under new conditions,
28, 36–37
language of social inclusion, 32
working class, 26, 79, 185
blue-collar workers, 12, 70
male working class, 174
post-industrial, 188
working hours. *See* hours of work
"Working Man" (MacNeil), 203
Working on the Edge, 250
work-life balance issues, xii, 48–49,
83–84, 86
Workplace Information Directorate
(HRSDC), 221
WORKS project, 81
World Social Forum, 19
"Another World is Possible," 38
World Trade Organization, 14
Wray, David, 207

York University's Centre for Research
on Work and Safety, x, 112,
117–18
young workers, xvi, 49, 56, 59. *See also*
student labour